W9-BMU-967

Mere Discipleship

Compliments!

**Burning
Bush**
MINISTRIES
PO Box 7233 Salem OR 97303
bbm@open.org •503-585-0627

Mere Discipleship

RADICAL CHRISTIANITY

IN A REBELLIOUS WORLD

Lee C. Camp

Brazos Press
A Division of Baker Book House Co
Grand Rapids, Michigan 49516

Copyright © 2003 by Lee C. Camp

Published by Brazos Press
a division of Baker Book House Company
P.O. Box 6287, Grand Rapids, MI 49516-6287
www.brazospress.com

Second printing, June 2004

Printed in the United States of America

All rights reserved. No part of this publication may be reproduced, stored in a retrieval system, or transmitted in any form or by any means—for example, electronic, photocopy, recording—without the prior written permission of the publisher. The only exception is brief quotations in printed reviews.

Library of Congress Cataloging-in-Publication Data

Camp, Lee C.
    Mere discipleship : radical Christianity in a rebellious world / Lee C. Camp.
        p.   cm.
    Includes bibliographical references. (p.   ).
    ISBN 1-58743-049-5 (pbk.)
    1. Free churches. 2. Dissenters, Religious. I. Title
BX4817.C36 2003
230′.97—dc22   2003015443

Unless otherwise noted, Scripture is taken from the New Revised Standard Version of the Bible, copyright 1989 by the Division of Christian Education of the National Council of the Churches of Christ in the USA. Used by permission.

To Laura

Jesus was not just a moralist whose teachings had some political implications; he was not primarily a teacher of spirituality whose public ministry unfortunately was seen in a political light; he was not just a sacrificial lamb preparing for his immolation, or a God-Man whose divine status calls us to disregard his humanity. Jesus was, in his divinely mandated prophethood, priesthood, and kingship, the bearer of a new possibility of human, social, and therefore political relationships. His baptism is the inauguration and his cross is the culmination of that new regime in which his disciples are called to share. Hearers or readers may choose to consider that kingdom as not real, or not relevant, or not possible, or not inviting; but . . . no such slicing can avoid his call to an ethic marked by the cross, a cross identified as the punishment of a man who threatens society by creating a new kind of community leading a radically new kind of life.

John Howard Yoder, *The Politics of Jesus*

Contents

Acknowledgments

*C*onventional wisdom has it that books are not written alone, but in community. My experience bears witness to this truth. I have been blessed by innumerable good teachers, but two have deeply shaped the contents of this book: Leonard Allen, my thesis director while at Abilene Christian University, and John Howard Yoder, my initial dissertation director while at the University of Notre Dame. The idea for this book actually began shortly after John's death, while I was still a graduate student at Notre Dame. When some of my colleagues and I were eating a meal together following John's memorial service, Laurel Jordan mentioned that she and John had discussed Laurel writing something like a Yoderian *Mere Christianity*. There was a perceived need for a more popularly accessible work presenting Yoder's Anabaptist reading of the New Testament and his understanding of the basic Christian message. I was intrigued with the idea and found quickly in my subsequent teaching and preaching that such a work was greatly needed. Laurel graciously consented to my request that I try my hand at such a task. So I thank her.

Readers familiar with Yoder's work will notice his influence. Part 1 is particularly indebted to an unpublished course outline simply entitled "Constantine,"[1] the first chapter of *The Politics of Jesus*,[2] and "The Constantinian Sources of Western Social Ethics."[3] Part 2 is partially indebted to the remaining portions of *The Politics of Jesus*. Part 3 is at least conceptually indebted to *Body Politics*.[4] Were John still alive, I could hope only to get a long memo from him telling me all the ways I could have done this better; that was a sign, as a student, that he took you seriously! In any case, I hope it is a work that opens more readers up to John's work, which I take to be a very biblically grounded understanding of the gospel of God's kingdom. I hope, too, given my current institutional setting, that this work serves as an impetus to recover some of the currently unappreciated and overlooked theological trajectories not only of David Lipscomb (the namesake of the Christian university where I am pleased to teach), but other nineteenth-century "American Restorationists" as well. I am, in many ways, saying here some of the things Lipscomb said a century ago, just in updated garb.

Rodney Clapp at Brazos Press graciously encouraged me, and I am truly indebted for his patient guidance and careful critique with a novice author like me. I thank the provost and the administration of Lipscomb University, who afforded me a summer grant with which to begin the project; the Center for International Peace and Justice at Lipscomb, which has provided intellectual "space" in which to constructively argue over some of these issues; and the Donelson Church of Christ for affording me partial summer breaks from preaching responsibilities in which to pursue writing. I thank the number of good friends, fellow travelers, and patient guides who continue to help me make sense of my own soul-sickness, and the indispensable way in which they have ministered the grace of God to me—they know, I trust, who they are. I thank my colleagues in the College of Bible and Ministry at Lipscomb for our shared vision of calling our students to service in the kingdom of God. We sometimes vigorously disagree about what such a vision concretely entails, and I celebrate that we continue to practice a ministry of reconciliation with one another—clearly evidenced, I think, in the laughter and prayer we share daily in spite of our disagreements. Finally, I especially thank the following individuals, who provided very helpful feedback after reading portions of the manuscript or helped me in various other ways with the work: Gary Holloway, Tom Olbricht, Andrew Gallwitz, Richard Goode (Richard once said he was going to stop sharing quotes and illustrations with me, so he would have something to write about himself), George Goldman, and Phillip Camp.

I am blessed with a wonderfully supportive family, both immediate and extended. I am deeply appreciative for the ongoing support of my parents, Jim and Gayle Camp, as well as the support of my parents-in-law, Sue and Steve Brumfield. I am profoundly grateful for the love my wife Laura and I share, and I thank her for her support, patience, and encouragement while I was working on this project. For her and for our three sons Chandler, David, and Benjamin, I give great thanks; it is my deep joy to share with them all the adventure of being on the Way with Lord Jesus.

This being a first book, I have found it a humbling experience. Too often I find I cannot even articulate my thoughts or feelings to my wife!—and in writing one tries to articulate some particular passion to an audience one does not even know. And then there is the humility that comes from realizing how little one knows, and how finite one's understanding. I am sure that there are many deficiencies in this work, and all that remain after following many excellent suggestions of reviewers are of course my own responsibility. But the task has been humbling not only because of the immense nature of the task of communication or because of the ever-present sense of my own finitude. The task has been humbling because my own words—which I pray bear some measure of faithful witness to the gospel—have echoed in my own heart and rattled my own cage. I find the gospel story always disconcerting; that I continue to be troubled is, I take it, good news in itself. To never be rattled, to not be open to ongoing repentance, would be bad news indeed. That the God revealed in Jesus Christ always affords the opportunity for repentance, to receive abundance of life in God's kingdom, I take as a passion worth sharing, and I offer this work in that spirit.

Ash Wednesday, 2003
Nashville, Tennessee

PART 1

Reenvisioning Discipleship

"Radical" Discipleship

Today, as in days past, there is no way to tell from a person's life,
from his deeds, whether or not he is a believer.

Leo Tolstoy[1]

Christianity without discipleship is always Christianity without
Christ.

Dietrich Bonhoeffer[2]

"The Most Christian Country"

On an April morning in 1994 I heard the radio transmission of the BBC's report—my wife Laura and I were far from our home, working with a Christian school
in Nairobi, Kenya, and not more than several hundred miles from the location of
the strife. The airplane carrying the president of Rwanda had crashed. Foul play
was suspected, and the terror had begun. But at that point, no one appeared to
have any premonition of the extent of the slaughter soon to occur. Over the next
several months, Rwanda—"the most Christian country in Africa," with as much
as 90 percent of the population claiming some Christian church affiliation—became the site of genocide unlike any in recent history, with as many as 800,000
men, women, and children slaughtered within a one-hundred-day period. Ethnic

15

tensions between the two dominant tribes, the Tutsis and the Hutus, erupted into widespread slaughter, with neighbor killing neighbor. The national army, vigilante groups, and average citizens hunted those of different ethnic identity, often using machetes to hack their enemies to death.[3]

Much of the subsequent international attention focused on the breakdown of U.N. "peacekeeping forces" to restrain violence effectively or to protect the weak.[4] But the breakdown of Rwandan Christianity, unable to stem the tide of mass murder, is all the more puzzling. Rwanda had often been cited as a case study for the success of "Christian missions," after the so-called *Tornade* in the 1930s swept the Tutsi aristocracy into the folds of the Catholic church. Following the conversions of the leaders of Rwanda, the country was dubbed a "Christian Kingdom." But the genocide demonstrated—in a graphic and horrific way—that the Western Christianity imported into the heart of Africa apparently failed to create communities of *disciples*. In actuality, the "triumph of Christian missions" preceded the triumph of ethnic hatred. When push came to shove, the Jesus who taught his disciples to "love your neighbor" was missing when young men were hacking old men, women, and children to death, simply because these neighbors were of a different ethnic background. Numerous Christian martyrs of both Hutu and Tutsi ethnic identity died because of their resistance to the massacres. But that these faithful martyrs were a minority among the fold of Christians has led critics to suggest that the "gospel" imported into Rwanda failed to ever challenge the ethnic identities of its "converts"—they "became Christian," but many remained first and foremost either Hutu or Tutsi.[5]

In fact, the Rwandan genocide highlights a recurrent failure of much historic Christianity. The proclamation of the "gospel" has often failed to emphasize a fundamental element of the teaching of Jesus, and indeed, of orthodox Christian doctrine: "Jesus is Lord" is a radical claim, one that is ultimately rooted in questions of allegiance, of ultimate authority, of the ultimate norm and standard for human life. Instead, Christianity has often sought to ally itself comfortably with allegiance to other authorities, be they political, economic, cultural, or ethnic. Could it be that "Jesus is Lord" has become one of the most widespread Christian lies? Have Christians claimed the lordship of Jesus, but systematically set aside the call to obedience to this Lord? At least in Rwanda, with "Christian Hutus" slaughtering "Christian Tutsis" (and vice versa), "Christian" apparently served as a faith brand name—a "spirituality," or a "religion"—but not a commitment to a common Lord.

A Rwandan couple, who barely escaped the slaughter themselves, shared their story at our university campus. Faculty and students listened in disbelief. Their report of the carnage was simply mind-boggling. But as I listened, a frightening question occurred to me: We American Christians, are we any different? Do we have all the same cultural assumptions about Christianity that would allow us to shelve our discipleship, to compartmentalize our faith, so that we too could fall prey to such demonic forces? Do we have on the same blinders? We good American Christians, *could we do that same thing?*

The Most Christian City

Raised in the "Bible Belt," my upbringing in Alabama provided personal experience with "cultural Christianity." Particularly in the South there is a Christianity thoroughly sanctioned and supported by the prevailing cultural forces, a Christianity I sometimes suspect to be not too different from the failed Rwandan Christianity. My wife, three sons, and I now live in Nashville, Tennessee, which has been dubbed by some to be the "Protestant Vatican." It is, in addition, the "Jerusalem" for my own Christian heritage, with over one hundred congregations of Churches of Christ in the greater metropolitan Nashville area. According to some reports, as many as one thousand houses of Christian worship find Davidson County alone as their home. Add to that mix the multitude of denominational boards and institutions, Christian book publishers, the contemporary Christian music industry, and even the largest Christian diet marketer in the country, and you get a culture in which "church" is inextricably intertwined with every facet of life. Nashville is as "Christian" as it gets.

Ryman Auditorium aptly symbolizes the relationship between Christianity and southern culture. In the heart of Nashville, the Ryman Auditorium was built in the late 1800s as a home for revivals. Were one to be plopped, unknowingly, in the midst of the Ryman, one could only presume to be in a church building, given the trademark pews and churchy architecture. Southern gospel has long been tied to southern sectionalism and patriotism, and so the balcony of the Ryman aptly represents this facet of the larger culture—the "Confederate Gallery," it's called, built to hold the Confederate veterans for one of the last reunions of those who fought in the "Lost Cause." And then the real claim to fame of the Ryman—the site of early Spirit-led revivals in time became the locale of the internationally renowned Grand Ole Opry, whose roots are inseparable from gospel music. Beer-drinking, wife-cheating, flag-waving, and "Amazing Grace" appear almost as one, so subtly are country-and-western culture and Jesus woven into the same fabric of both the Ryman and Nashville.

The two largest Christian traditions in Nashville have a long tradition of mutual enmity: the Southern Baptists and the Churches of Christ. Baptists—often unaware of their own tradition of exclusivity—have often chided members of Churches of

Christ: "You think you're the only ones going to heaven, don't you?!" There was a basis, though, for the accusation of sectarianism. Particularly in north-central Alabama, we in the Churches of Christ embodied Luke's account of Jesus' proclamation, "Whoever is not with me is against me" (11:23). My adolescence was inundated with preaching that drew lines in no uncertain terms between the ("New Testament") church and the world; and often, those lines were drawn through a number of boiled-down points, among which the most important were the proper acts of worship (like *a cappella* singing and weekly communion), adult baptism by immersion (for "remission of sins"), and upright personal moral conduct (no drinking, dancing, or cussing).

Whatever one makes of such a list, that preaching taught me a particular habit that, depending upon one's perspective, could be taken as either a virtue or a vice: the habit of questioning professions of Christian faith sanctioned by a larger unrepentant culture. Perhaps in our well-intentioned efforts to bring all things under the lordship of Christ, American Christian culture has been guilty of baptizing unrepentant social systems and structures. Is it sufficient to "sprinkle" the culture of a city or nation-state and dub it "Christian"? Which brings us back to the question of whether Rwandan Christianity is all that different from Nashville Christianity, or American Christianity. Has American Christianity too often shelved its discipleship, compartmentalized its faith, and thus been blinded by unredeemed cultural forces that leave us prey to the principalities and powers of this world?

The namesake of the Christian university where I teach, David Lipscomb, shared the sentiment of many nineteenth-century Christians in his great optimism about the United States, and its experiment in democracy. But the U.S. Civil War dashed Lipscomb's optimism. Lipscomb witnessed the Battle of Nashville, in December 1864, in which 1,500 Confederates and 3,000 Union soldiers died in a two-day period, the battle lines of which passed just a few blocks north and, a day later, just to the south of his farm—which is now the campus of Lipscomb University. How, Lipscomb wanted to know, could southern Christians slaughter their northern Christian brothers? How could northern disciples make widows out of their southern sisters in Christ? Over the course of the war, six hundred thousand men were slaughtered—most of whom claimed Jesus as Lord. Brothers in Christ, on opposite sides of the battle lines, seeking to kill one another, their battles bathed not only in blood but in prayer—and witnessing this, Lipscomb knew that there was some agenda other than the kingdom of God at work. So he began to insist that disciples prioritize *God's* kingdom, rather than the self-seeking agendas of the kingdoms of this world.

Lipscomb's prioritization of God's kingdom over all other kingdoms led him to profound commitments. First, Lipscomb refused to be cowed by either the Confederate or Union forces and admonished disciples to refuse to kill on behalf of either. During the war, the famed Confederate commander Nathan Bedford Forest (subsequently a cofounder of the Ku Klux Klan and now heralded in Nashville in a privately funded memorial prominently placed alongside Interstate 65) sent a soldier to hear Lipscomb preach so that he might judge whether Lipscomb was advocating treason. After the sermon, the soldier remarked, "I have not reached a conclusion as to whether or not the doctrine of the sermon is loyal to the Southern Confederacy, but I am profoundly convinced that he is loyal to the Christian religion."[6] Neither the piety of a Robert E. Lee nor the religion of the Yankees would suffice in Lipscomb's eyes. Lipscomb refused to separate the gospel from the real world, believing the Good News to proclaim a kingdom that held to Jesus as its head: the kingdom of heaven is a real kingdom in the midst of time and history. It is in the world but not of the world, and thus would refuse either to submit to sectional war-making and southern racism, or to turn a blind eye to the needs of the poor.

In addition to this countercultural commitment, Lipscomb's allegiance to the kingdom of God led him to other practices profoundly opposed to the norms of southern Christian culture of the late nineteenth century. Not only should allegiance to the kingdom dissolve commitments to sectional and war-making factions. It should also undercut racist distinctions. Racial barriers grew only more entrenched in the decades following the war, fostered not only by the Christians who populated Nathan Bedford Forest's KKK but perhaps more perniciously by the moderate Christians who silently supported and perpetuated segregation. But Lipscomb refused to be silent. The kingdom of God, Lipscomb insisted, knew no such distinctions. So, for example, when a church in McKinney, Texas, objected in 1878 to an African-American man placing membership in their ranks, Lipscomb denounced such as "sinful" and "blasphemous." "The individual who assumes such a position shows a total unfitness for membership in the church of God. A church that will tolerate the persistent exhibition of such a spirit certainly forfeits its claims to be a church of God."[7]

No realm of culture was exempt from the church's calling to bear witness to the way of Christ and the kingdom of God. Thus Lipscomb founded a school in 1891 whose aim was to provide a liberal arts education;[8] but that education was never intended for the service of upward social mobility in the New South, but for service in Jesus' kingdom. In the same way, Lipscomb had earlier insisted that money could not be hoarded but stewarded for the good of the poor. Thus Lipscomb had admonished those Christians in the poverty-stricken Reconstruction south to share their goods. "The man that can spend money in extending his already broad acres, while his brother and his brother's children cry for bread—the woman that can spend money in purchasing a stylish bonnet, an expensive cloak, or a fine dress, merely to appear fashionable, while her sister and her sister's children are shivering with cold and scarce able to cover their nakedness, are no Christians . . . they are on the broad road that leads to death."[9] Thus position and power could properly be used only in authentic service for those in need. So when a cholera epidemic struck Nashville in 1873, Lipscomb refused to flee the city along with the wealthy who made their way to safer environs, but himself worked in the homes of the destitute and diseased, helping to clean and care for them. [10] Allegiance to God's kingdom, for Lipscomb, was an all-or-nothing proposition.

The Hamlet of Rose-Colored Cataracts

Imagine a remote hamlet, removed from the rest of the world, in which all the inhabitants were afflicted with a strange eye disease. Suppose that this genetically inherited disease manifested itself with only one symptom—a strange cataract, which did not blur the victim's vision. Instead, the cataract simply cast a rose-colored tint to the afflicted's vision. In such a scenario, it's quite likely that all the inhabitants of that small, provincial village would simply assume that the world is rose-tinted. So strong, in fact, would be this presupposition—that the world is rose-colored—that the inhabitants of that little hamlet would likely never even discuss it, and certainly never question it! And anyone who might question such an empirical assumption would certainly be considered a bit strange—if not simply irrational. What more do you need—you can see it with your own eyes?!

But just *what if*—what if the Christian church looks at the world with some long-inherited presuppositions, assumptions so long held that for anyone to question them leaves us looking for a way to get out of the conversation? What if what has so long been presumed to be "common sense" and "reality" and "truth" is neither true nor real?

Logically, of course, one cannot deny that this may be a possibility. Thus, each generation of followers of Jesus must reassess our faithfulness to our calling; we must grapple with how our viewpoint and understanding has been shaped by tradition and history. James Cone, for example, is a classic example of a theologian who asks questions about historical identity and assumptions. Cone designates himself a "Black theologian," and argues that the (white) Western tradition of theology has forgotten that our history, our "social location," our position of wealth and prestige shapes the questions we ask of Scripture. Consider Athanasius, Cone suggests, a fourth-century theologian involved in the debates regarding the nature of the relationship between the Father and the Son who pushed for the use of the Greek philosophical term *homoousion*, asserting that the Son is one substance with the Father. There is indeed, notes Cone, a place for philosophical concerns like these. But had Athanasius been a black slave in America, "he might have asked about the status of the Son in relation to slaveholders." Similarly, Protestant Reformer Martin Luther concerned himself with the "ubiquitous presence of Jesus Christ at the Lord's table." Had Martin Luther been an African, kidnapped and sold on the slave market in the United States in the nineteenth century, "his first question would not have been whether Jesus was at the Lord's table, but whether he was really present at the slave's cabin." Luther might have asked "whether slaves could expect Jesus to be with them as they tried to survive the cotton field, the whip, and the pistol."[11]

What Cone wants us to see might be put this way: someone reading the story of God's chosen people will tend to ask different questions depending upon one's own history, one's own social location, one's own position of relative power or powerlessness. One asks different questions of the meaning of "God," depending upon whether one finds oneself in the "ivory tower" or in the slave cabin, in Pharaoh's throne room or Pharaoh's mud-pits, in the boardroom or the sweatshop. Where we are and where we have been deeply affects who we think God is and what we think God wants us to be.

The "Constantinian Cataract"

If one's social location impacts or affects one's understanding of who God is and what God is concerned with, it would appear that the *church's* social location may affect its understanding of Jesus. For this reason, many have suggested that the meaning of "Jesus" depends upon whether one finds oneself on this side of Emperor Constantine or the other. But what possible difference could an early-fourth-century Roman emperor make to our understanding of Jesus?

Before attempting to answer that question, a brief bit of storytelling may be in order for those unfamiliar with the rise of Constantine. For the first three centuries of the church, the Roman Empire, at best, ignored Christians; at worst, it killed them. Periods of persecution were sporadic, and though persecution was never a constant feature of early Christian history, the uncertain social position of Christianity persisted. But the minority, persecuted status of Christianity suddenly changed, symbolized by Emperor Constantine's battle of the Milvian Bridge, just outside Rome, in October 312. There, according to one legendary account, a vision called Constantine to draw the Chi Rho—the first two letters of the Greek word for "Christ"—on the shields of his soldiers. "By this sign you shall conquer," the vision is said to have revealed.

Constantine's opponent, meanwhile, was busy preparing for battle, offering sacrifices to the Roman gods. In short order, Constantine triumphed in battle, his foe withdrawing in defeat across the Milvian Bridge, his dead body discovered the next day in the Tiber River. The Romans hailed the triumphant Constantine as their new ruler, and Constantine hailed the victory as a gift from the God of the Christians: the power of Christ had triumphed over Constantine's enemy. How, then, should he respond?

Constantine and his fellow ruler in the East issued an empire-wide edict of general religious toleration: good news for the Christian church indeed! More, Constantine restored previously confiscated property to the church. Soon the Christian church served a new, very visible social and political role within the empire. Moreover, the emperor appeared to care even for the unity and purity of doctrine in the church. Calling the Council of Nicea, the emperor desired that debated matters of the nature of the relation between the Father and the Son be settled, so that nothing would disrupt the unity of the church.

By the end of the century, the emperor Theodosius finalized the conquest of Christianity, making the faith of the Christians the only legal religion in the empire. Within one century, the Christian church had moved from the status of a minority, persecuted sect to that of the only legally sanctioned religion in the Roman Empire. Indeed, as some historians tell the story, Christianity had "triumphed" over its enemies.[12] There arose, from there, "Christendom"—an alliance between church and empire. The Christian church had arrived, or so it appeared.

On the other hand, other historians and theologians recount these events as the "fall of the church." This type of storytelling is perhaps too naïve, simplistic, or sweepingly judgmental—surely there is much to be learned from post-Constantine Christians. Nonetheless, one finds in "Christendom" particular ways of thinking about Jesus that obscure (if not set aside) his teaching. In other words, some serious consequences came in the wake of the "triumph of Christianity." Painting in too-broad strokes, one might characterize some of these consequences this way: "Christianity" increasingly loses the biblical emphasis upon discipleship, and replaces it with an emphasis upon religious ritual. "Church," rather than connoting the New Testament concept as a community of disciples living as the "body of Christ," begins to connote a hierarchy that protects "orthodoxy." "Salvation," instead of being construed as the gift of a transformed, abundant life in the now-present kingdom of God, begins to be equated with an otherworldly reward. More crassly put, "salvation" is increasingly viewed as a fire-insurance policy—rather than the gift of new life in the here and now that stands confident even in the face of death, "salvation" becomes a "Get Out of Hell Free Card," guaranteeing an escape from the fires of torment and ensuring the receipt of treasures in heaven. In Christendom, the "whole world" may be dubbed "Christian," and yet it is un-Christlike.[13]

In such a way, Christianity becomes its own worst enemy: the "triumph" of Christianity actually inhibits discipleship, for the masses already too easily believe themselves to be Christian. Any call to be "truly Christian" is seen through a Constantinian cataract: "What do you mean, become 'truly Christian'? We already are!" Leo Tolstoy described his experience of nineteenth-century Christendom this way: "Today, as in days past, there is no way to tell from a person's life, from his deeds, whether or not he is a believer."

We in the Western world are long removed from those days of governmental establishment of Christianity, living in the day of "separation of church and state." Nonetheless, such habits of thought remain, Christendom assumptions remain pervasive, and "Christianity" gets sold short, removing any commitment to giving all to Christ, seeking first and only the kingdom of God and its righteousness. "Christianity without discipleship," nonetheless, "is always Christianity without Christ," said Dietrich Bonhoeffer. "Whosoever boasts that he is a Christian, the same must walk as Christ walked," asserted the sixteenth-century radical reformer Menno Simons, just as John asserted that "whoever says, 'I abide in him,' ought to walk just as he walked" (1 John 2:6). Jesus of Nazareth, the Gospel accounts relate, always comes asking disciples to follow him, not merely "accept him," not merely "believe in him," not merely "worship him," but to follow him: one either follows Christ, or one does not. It is all or nothing. There is no compartmentalization of the faith, no realm, no sphere, no business, no politic in which the lordship of Christ will be excluded. We either make him Lord of all lords, or we deny him as Lord of any.

"Radical" Christianity

The call of the gospel is, in other words, "radical." The word "radical" can be taken in at least two senses. For many, the word "radical" connotes "far-out," or "overly zealous," or "extreme," or "fanatical." Something "radical" is thus something to be discounted, not to be taken seriously in a mature world of responsible adults. "Radical" is akin to an adolescent stage of rebellion against the establishment order, a phase some pass through on their way to maturity. It seems precisely this sense of "radical" that Christendom affords us: following a Jesus who commands love of enemies, or sharing of one's provisions, or ongoing practices of forgiveness, is looked upon as "far-out," as an extreme viewpoint with little to offer the "real world." Such "radical" claims are looked upon as idealistic, unrelated to the pragmatic concerns of those who are trying to "make a difference" in the world. Thus we fashion a religion that suits this model—we "go to church," are offered pious sentiment to warm our hearts, theological warm-fuzzies intended to assure us of our eternal reward or a life filled with "meaning," with little word of the kingdom of God.

But taken etymologically, the word "radical" simply means "to the root." And it is in *this* sense that the Christian faith *is* radical: it demands thoroughgoing transformation, thoroughgoing conversion, of every realm of human endeavor, in personal relations, economics, and politics, in homes, culture, and social order. The gospel demands radical discipleship.

There is, I must confess, a deep part of me that is embarrassed to advocate a "radical Christianity." For I find, especially in these recent days of my pilgrimage, that the more I seek to surrender to Christ, the more I discover those idols to which my "old self," as the apostle Paul calls it, has been desperately clinging. It turns out, of course, that my sins are not all that interesting, but the same as the lot of all humankind: pride, ambition, lust, greed, self-seeking. The more I pursue the light of Christ, the more he illumines the diseases of my heart, the dysfunction of my soul. I have long desired quick fixes for my thorns in the flesh, my defects, my failings—but Christ has granted me none. But he does, as I walk behind him, alongside him, and alongside others on the Way, grant me daily bread, daily sustenance, his grace being always sufficient for the day.

I also fear speaking of "radical discipleship" because I continue to encounter innumerable souls deeply wounded by moralistic perversions of discipleship, by legalistic religion, good souls burdened with shame, knowing neither the joy nor peace that are born from the Spirit of Christ. I have walked that long, lonely road, too, and have found in it not life, but shame, and anger, and resentment. But this is not following the Master, in spite of its weighty religious veneer, for the true religion, the true life is found in the One who first loved us, even while we were yet self-centeredly rebelling; in the One who forgives us seventy times seven, even before calling us to do so; in the One who was tempted in all ways, like as we are, in order to share our suffering, to know our weaknesses, so that he might love us even there in our weaknesses.

The call to "radical discipleship" is thus not a call to a burdensome moral perfectionism, but a call to leave the old ways of death and darkness, and walk in the new way of abundant life and glorious light, with the Christ who is Light and Life. There, on the path with Christ, we are loved even when we do not deserve to be loved. And there, on the path with Christ, we too are called to love those about us who do not deserve to be loved. On pilgrimage with Christ, we are forgiven with an extravagant love—he washes our feet, even when we would betray him. And there, on pilgrimage with Christ, we too are called to forgive with such extravagance. On the way with Christ, God's abundance, provisions, and goods are shared with us, joyfully consumed and used, for we eat in the kingdom of God! And on the way with Christ, the provisions and goods in our hands are shared with those around us, for we do not live according to the rebellious kingdoms of the world, which hoard and hold, but according to the kingdom of God, in which God clothes the birds of the air, the flowers of the field, and us, too, so that we live with a lightness and ease that befits sons and daughters of God.

And so I write not so much to instruct as to understand, to make more sense myself out of Christ's call to follow him. I write to share my deep suspicion that our Western culture continues to pervert the word of Christ. I write with a sense of burden, suspecting that even the religious rhetoric that appears to take Jesus so seriously has domesticated him, cleaned him up, made him respectable so as not to embarrass us good church-going folk with our agendas of upward social mobility and social "responsibility," and in so doing has limited the answers believed to be possible or sensible or respectable to that commonly asked question, "What would Jesus do?" And I write hoping to find more fellow travelers who share this suspicion, so that we might help one another on the way.

The ongoing Bible Belt experience notwithstanding, we are nearing the end of the cultural establishment of Christianity in the United States. Nonetheless, it appears that the reflexes of "Christendom," that the cataract of the "establishment of the church," continue in their own updated guises even today. Consequently, it may be that if we desire to follow Jesus, we will have to diagnose the cataract that wrongly colors, and thus distorts, our vision. The significance of these assumptions for our understanding of discipleship might not be readily apparent; nonetheless, if not questioned and challenged, they subtly and steadfastly compartmentalize, reduce, and trivialize a call to "follow Christ." The shape and nature of this cataract is discussed in chapters two and three.

Then, in chapters four, five, and six, I suggest a reading of the New Testament that should help us configure our understanding of discipleship in a more biblical way, in a manner that does not continue to hold up the false assumptions that subtly corrode our understanding of discipleship. In brief, the basic narrative might be summarized this way: God's good creation has rebelled against the good purposes of its Creator. This rebellion brought death, anguish, violence, lust, greed. And God, in Christ, has announced and acted to redeem the rebellious creation, restoring it to God's good, original intentions—the kingdom of God is at hand! But surprise of all surprises, the redemption comes not through power and might, but by his sharing in our suffering, taking the very brunt and blow of our rebellion; the Son was crucified, refusing to be cowed by the rebellious principalities and powers, and in his crucifixion, triumphed over them; and in his resurrection, was vindicated by the Father. The church, then, a community called to follow in the way of Christ, a community that is "the body of Christ," exists not to show the world how to be "religious," but to show the world how to be the world God created it to be. We are to be salt and light—and as he was in the world, so are we to be.

But it is not sufficient for us simply to "tell the story right" or "hold to right doctrine." A sufficient account must provide something concrete, and it is this more concrete task that I take up in the remaining chapters. There I discuss some of the "practices of the church" that help us sustain the life to which we have been called. Rather than understanding things like worship, baptism, and prayer as things we "must do" in order to be pleasing to God, we should understand that these are God's gifts to us, and to the world. Rather than seeing these practices as mere religious ritual, we should understand these practices as the very type of good life for which we were created, and at the same time as practices that help sustain us in the good life to which we have been called.

God's Way of Working

He willed to save man by persuasion, not by compulsion, for
compulsion is not God's way of working.

Letter to Diognetus, ca. second century A.D.[1]

If there is anyone of the Saxon people lurking among them
unbaptized, and if he scorns to come to baptism and wishes to
absent himself and stay a pagan, let him die.

Charlemagne, ca. A.D. 785,
while Christian King of the Franks[2]

The Ends Justify the Means

The contrast between the *Letter to Diognetus* and Charlemagne's dictate regarding the conversion of the Saxons speaks volumes about the change between the early church and that of Christendom. According to the anonymous author of the *Letter to Diognetus*, Jesus Christ reveals a God who saves by "persuasion, not by compulsion, for compulsion is not God's way of working." Moreover, disciples in the early church, he asserted, "love all men, and by all men are persecuted. They are unknown, and still they are condemned; they are put to death, and yet they are brought to life. They are poor, and yet they make many rich; they are completely destitute, and yet they enjoy complete abundance. They are dishonored, and in their very dishonor are glorified; . . . they are reviled, and yet they bless; when they are affronted, they still pay due respect. When they do good, they are punished as evildoers; undergoing punishment, they rejoice because they are brought to life."[3]

Though the early church may not have esteemed compulsion to be "God's way of working," Christendom found compulsion to be a very satisfactory mode of operation. "The earlier time . . . represented the former age of emperors who did not believe in Christ, at whose hands the Christians suffered because of the wicked; but the later time represented the age of the successors to the imperial throne, now believing in Christ, at whose hands the wicked suffer because of the Christians," summarized Augustine, not too long after the rise of Constantine.[4] In time, this change found ultimate expression in a method thought to be more effective than that modeled by Jesus: you can either be baptized, or we will kill you, said the Christian Charlemagne. One of the perennial assumptions that undergirds the Christendom cataract thus begins to cloud the vision of discipleship as the logic of "the end justifies the means" develops. Some worthy goal set forward, some lofty end advocated, and the "necessary" means are then sought to attain the goal. So Charlemagne, Charles the Great, crowned emperor of the Holy Roman Empire by Pope Leo III on Christmas Day, A.D. 800, stands as perhaps the climax of such logic. While king of the Franks, Charlemagne set forward the above-mentioned policy of forced conversion of the newly conquered Saxon peoples in 785: "If there is anyone of the Saxon people lurking among them unbaptized, and if he scorns to come to baptism and wishes to absent himself and stay a pagan, let him die." This policy apparently flows from a decision made ten years earlier by Charlemagne in his expedition against the Saxons; according to the *Royal Frankish Annals*, the king decided in 775 "to attack the treacherous and treaty-breaking tribe of the Saxons and to persist in this war until they were either defeated and forced to accept the Christian religion or entirely exterminated."[5] The Saxons were defeated, and they submitted to mass baptisms over the next two years. In time, Charlemagne helped restore church discipline, unity of practice in worship, and the proper adherence to church doctrine. So Charlemagne's grandson described the emperor in this way: "Emperor Charles, deservedly called the Great by all peoples, converted the Saxons by much effort, as is known to everyone in Europe. He won them over from the vain adoration of idols to the true Christian religion of God."[6]

Though Charlemagne's grandson believed that the "true Christian religion" had converted Saxon culture, it rather appears that the war-making Roman culture had, instead, converted Christianity. At least for the early church, ends and means were not easily separable — if one's goal is to bear witness to the lordship of Christ, then the way of the Lord must necessarily be employed. If one's desire is to participate in the inbreaking of God's kingdom of true justice and peace, then the methods of warfare will not do. "The means may be likened to a seed, the end to a tree: and there is just the same inviolable connection between the means and the end as there is between the seed and the tree."[7] So accepting the legitimacy of compulsion transforms the end itself, too: baptism of the masses through coercion becomes a realizable goal, but bearing witness to the way of Christ, by definition, is not. Religion wins, and discipleship loses. Many more "adherents," but few followers; many more admirers, but few disciples.

Charlemagne is by no means an exception, but appears rather to be a natural outgrowth of medieval Christianity. When King Ethelbert of Kent (560–616) received the Christian party led by the missionary Augustine (not the better known, and earlier, Augustine of Hippo), he ultimately received the Christian message and was baptized. The king reportedly did not force anyone in his dominion to accept Christianity, but in time was admonished by Pope Gregory to pursue zealously conversion of his people:

> [H]asten to extend the Christian faith among the people who are subject to you. Increase your righteous zeal for their conversion; suppress the worship of idols; overthrow their buildings and shrines; strengthen the morals of your subjects by outstanding purity of life, by exhorting them, terrifying, enticing, and correcting them, and by showing them an example of good works; so that you may be rewarded in heaven by the One whose name and knowledge you have spread on earth.[8]

After all, suggests Gregory, "it was thus that Constantine, the most religious emperor, converted the Roman State from the false worship of idols and subjected it . . . to Almighty God."[9]

Though Gregory admonished Ethelbert to encourage the "morals" of his subjects by "outstanding purity of life," missing is any charge to take the way of Jesus as the way to rule Ethelbert's kingdom: no mention of the way of the humble Jesus, no suggestion that the way of suffering servanthood should become the way of the king, no calling to "take up his cross and follow." There is, instead, a desire to spread the "knowledge of the one God, Father, Son and Holy Spirit," so that Ethelbert may "cause . . . your subjects to be cleansed from their sins."[10]

There is, in other words, a sharp contrast between Gregory's commission to Ethelbert and Matthew's recounting of Jesus' "great commission" to the apostles. Jesus charged the apostles to make *disciples*, while Gregory charged Ethelbert to "terrify" the masses into accepting the "morals" of the church. By the time of Ethelbert's conversion, then, it appears that "gospel" has become an abstract set of doctrines to be "instilled" in the people under Ethelbert's charge, so that they might receive "forgiveness of sins." Ethelbert is not admonished to employ the means of Jesus in spreading the gospel; he is, instead, admonished to use those very means Jesus had renounced, the way of "lording authority" over those in one's charge.[11] "Orthodoxy" may have won over the Roman Empire, but "orthodoxy" lost Jesus, and Christianity had lost the Christ. Doctrine and ethics had been ripped apart. And the end now justified the means. One could be a Christian without being a disciple.[12]

Constantinian American Christianity

In our day of "separation of church and state," we suppose that we do not fall prey to such faulty medieval church logic. But perhaps the same logic remains alive and well in the church today, only updated for a change of context. After the April 1999 massacre at Columbine High School in Colorado, an angry letter to the editor appeared in one of the Nashville papers:

> To the Editor:
> Once again we experience the tragedy of a mass shooting at one of our schools—[this] time in Colorado. The news anchors and President Clinton wring their hands and say, "What shall we do? What shall we do?"
> The standard knee-jerk reaction is to try to pass more laws restricting gun ownership, but that is not the answer. The answer is simple: Execute the little bastards.
> Texas has the highest per-capita rate of executions in the country, and you don't hear about school shootings there. Maybe when we start punishing criminals, we will see a reduction in the crime rate. It's time we realize that turning the other cheek doesn't work.[13]

In spite of the writer's confidence about the efficacy of the Texas death penalty, within a number of months a gunman entered Wedgwood Baptist Church in Fort Worth, and killed seven of the Christians gathered for a youth prayer service.

In any case, the letter-writer's logic merely updates the logic and faith employed by Charlemagne centuries earlier: certain things work, and certain things don't. "Turning the other cheek," it is claimed, "doesn't work." And in our concern to accomplish certain noble ends, we must make sure to be "effective." How shall we "convert" the masses? Or how shall we accomplish a "reduction in the crime rate"? "The answer is simple: Execute the little bastards."

Instead of grappling seriously with what Jesus could have possibly meant by "turning the other cheek,"[14] the letter-writer's crass reflex provides yet an updated example of the old Constantinian reflex to be "effective," to "get the job done," and do "whatever it takes." Such a reflex appears deeply indoctrinated with a faithlike trust in the radical *impracticality* of Jesus' teaching: if one wants to maintain culture, maintain civilization, maintain any good within the community, the assumption goes, one must utilize means that "everybody understands." In this way, "discipleship" gets castrated, or at least sharply curtailed in its assumed rightful place. "Following Jesus" becomes something one does on Sundays and in one's quiet time in order to "go to heaven," but the way of Christ has no place in the real world of violence, injustice, and greed. "Church" becomes an institution necessary to instill "moral values" in the citizenry of a democracy, but the fundamental teachings of its Messiah are taken to be irrelevant to the way the world "really works."

"If we have struggled to bring about a kingdom of heaven on earth, we have been willing to borrow our tools from the kingdom of hell." Or so a contemporary philosopher described the dropping of the atomic bomb on Hiroshima and Nagasaki.[15] But might his words aptly describe not only the U.S. atomic bombing of Japan, but significant components of Christian history?—that in the name of the kingdom of God, we have made use of the tools of hell?

In his autobiographical account *Brother to a Dragonfly*, Will Campbell recounts, after working as a "liberal" for issues of racial justice in the United States in the 1950s and 1960s, how he attempted to understand the forces, convictions, and societal wounds undergirding the white racism of those in the Ku Klux Klan. One elderly white man told Campbell at one point that the KKK stands for "peace, harmony, and freedom." When Campbell asked the man who defined those noble words, the Klansman responded, "I define the words." Campbell pressed him:

"What means are you willing to use to accomplish those glorious ends?"

"Oh I see what you're getting at. The means we are willing to use are as follows: murder, torture, threats, blackmail, intimidation, burning, guerrilla warfare. Whatever it takes."

And then he stopped. And I stopped. I knew that I had set a little trap for him and had cleverly let him snap the trigger.

But then he started again. "Now, Preacher. Let me ask you a question. You tell me what we stand for in Vietnam."

Suddenly I knew a lot of things I had not known before. I knew that I had been caught in my own trap. Suddenly I knew that we are a nation of Klansmen. I knew that as a nation we stood for peace, harmony and freedom in that war, that we defined the words, and that the means we were employing to accomplish those ends were identical with the ones he had listed.[16]

Whether it be the "preservation of civilization," "making the world safe for democracy," "reducing the crime rate," "peace, harmony, and freedom," or even "the spread of the gospel," carrying a big stick can now be done with a "spiritual" focus, and thus for "good." The coercive power of empire, the power of wealth, or just simply *power* becomes envisioned as the most "effective" means of spreading the gospel, of furthering the influence of Christianity, of fostering the growth of the church, or of spreading "Christian morality." Innumerable businesses, schools, and churches, all run by Christians, begin to assume that the final measurement of success is "effectiveness" and "efficiency." And yet "effectiveness," as if a quantitative "bottom line" is the only and sole measure of "success," completely ignores the question of faithfulness: to what are we called, and to whom are we accountable?

The assumed rightness of the criterion of "effectiveness" is further buttressed by the language of "responsibility." Questioning the legitimacy of bottom-line calculations and mere concern for "efficiency" appears paramount to adolescent irresponsibility: now having the mantle of power at their disposal, Christians should act "responsibly." Once the emperor allows the church to influence policy, Christians would be forsaking their "responsibility" if they did not seek to use the power of empire for "good ends."

At the Christian university where I teach, an operative of the National Security Agency recently presented a lecture on the gains and losses resulting from intelligence operations during the Korean War. Accounts of Cold War espionage and counterespionage, covert operations and betrayal abounded. Given that the "integration of faith and learning" serves as one of the purpose statements of our university, I hoped someone (namely, one of my students!) might raise an obvious question: How can a Christian community justify the intentional use of deceit, when our commitments as a people of faith require the virtue of truthfulness? How does the Jesus who taught us to let our "yes be yes, and no be no" fit into the systematic use of duplicity? That such questions are seldom raised might betray the extent to which Charlemagne's logic is ours: as long as the end is acceptable, the means need not be questioned.

In our case, the logic more particularly works this way: the nation affords us "freedom of religion." One necessary method in protecting "freedom of religion," so the logic continues, is deceit. To question the logic, or to question the methods employed, appears simply as forthright disloyalty—a betrayal of both the nation (which affords you the "freedom to practice your religion"), *and* Christianity (as if one cannot be a Christian unless the government allows you to do so). In this subtle way, "Christianity" is again employed to set aside discipleship. "Christianity" has become a vaccination, inoculating us, protecting us from discipleship.

Modern war-making provides numerous examples: at the height of the Persian Gulf War, the elder President Bush addressed the forty-eighth convention of the National Religious Broadcasters, a conference of evangelical-related Christians. Bush defended U.S. involvement in the war, asserting that the war was "just" and the cause was "moral." Bush noted that Saddam Hussein had characterized the conflict as a religious war—a charge Bush rejected, and indeed had to reject given our constitutional commitment to the separation of church and state.[17] But his defense provides a stereotypical example of the ends justifying the means: even though the war has "nothing to do with religion per se, it has on the other hand, everything to do with what religion embodies: good versus evil, right versus wrong, human dignity and freedom versus tyranny and oppression." Religion, in other words, provides a set of abstract ends or goals for which we must strive; then we seek the means that will get us there, and in this case, the means is war.[18]

Perhaps the climactic statement illustrating the "the ends justify the means" came in May of 1996, during the Clinton administration's ongoing struggle with Saddam Hussein, in which they continued to wage war against Iraq through means of harsh economic sanctions. As a consequence of the Western world's insistence upon ongoing economic sanctions in the face of Saddam Hussein's incorrigibility, the children and poor of Iraq suffered, with hundreds of thousands of children dying as a result. Leslie Stahl of CBS's *60 Minutes* interviewed then–U.S. Ambassador to the United Nations, and soon-to-be-appointed Secretary of State Madeleine Albright. Stahl asked Albright: "We have heard that a half million children have died. I mean, that's more children than died in Hiroshima. And—and you know, is the price worth it?" Albright responded: "I think this is a very hard choice, but the price—we think the price is worth it."[19]

Such logic differs little from that of the Cold War–era senator Edwin Johnson, who shortly after World War II suggested that "God almighty in his infinite wisdom [has] dropped the atomic bomb in our lap. . . . [W]ith vision and guts and plenty of atomic bombs, . . . [the United States] can compel mankind to adopt a policy of lasting peace . . . or be burned to a crisp."[20] Johnson is unlike many Cold War Christians only in his crassness: in the name of "peace," the majority of Christian policy-makers endorsed the legitimacy of nuclear counterstrikes.

The current "war on terror" is no exception: With the apparently righteous goal of "defense of civilization" in place, there are no limits to the means legitimately employed by those who are the embodiment of "good" in their attempt to "destroy evil." The Crusades of the Middle Ages are typically looked upon as a relic of the un-Enlightened past; but the convictions that gave rise and legitimacy to the Crusades find themselves resurrected in very different times and places, even in the age of "separation of church and state." Employing apocalyptic language, presidents and prime ministers convince Christians and non-Christians alike that the very existence of civilization depends upon our loyalty to the war-making nation-state: "We wage a war to save civilization itself," asserts George W. Bush. And yet when the stakes are thought to be so high, the way of Christ will not suffice. Instead of loving our enemies, the president would have us "hunt down our enemies."[21]

But in the midst of such crusades, so confident that God is on our side and so full of entreaties that God will bless America in its righteous cause, is it sufficient for Christians to set aside the way of Christ? At worst, self-centered nationalism seeks the sanction of God: "USA Kick Ass and Take Names! God Bless America!" recently proclaimed a large sign in Key West, Florida. At best, Jesus' teaching is still thought to be nominally authoritative in wartime, but only at the level of Christians' *attitudes*, not at the level of what Christians actually *do*. Even so, does this sufficiently witness to a biblical Christianity that in numerous and various ways proclaims that the disciple is to follow the way of the Master?

What Would Happen If Everybody Did (Not Do) That?

If "the end justifies the means" serves as one of the assumptions underneath the "Constantinian cataract," a very similar assumption gives that cataract even more substance. For underneath the "end justifies the means" logic lies the assumption that the way of Christ is simply not a relevant social ethic, lest injustice reign and the violent vanquish the righteous. Christians cannot take the way of Christ seriously, or society will fall apart, will sink into a spiral of unmitigated violence. Justice is at stake. Civilization itself is at stake. Jesus could not have meant that we take him seriously in the realm of social and political realities—after all, *what would happen if everybody did that?!* Consequently, "Jesus," "Christianity," and even "discipleship" are reduced to mere "spirituality," a realm that has little if anything to do with the concrete realities of culture, civilization, and politics.

"An eye for an eye, a tooth for a tooth. A .38 for a .38?" Or so queried a 1998 Associated Press account that reported on the amendment to Kentucky state law that extended the legal right to ministers and church officers to carry a concealed weapon in church buildings, even during church services. Reports cited a preacher in Somerset, Kentucky, as having a pivotal role in the new legislation. Interviewed by Maria Shriver on NBC's July 16, 1998, *Today* show, the preacher reported that individuals looking for money often visit churches and further intimated that having a gun would provide protection from those who might desire to steal church contributions. Bewildered Maria Shriver—representing the media, which Christians often portray as having little comprehension of the Good News of Jesus Christ—asked the preacher if he did not understand that his reliance upon a handgun stood at odds with the Christian proclamation of peace and reconciliation.

Imagine having the wife of Arnold Schwarzeneggar—Hollywood's poster boy for violent entertainment—remind the church that the gospel bids believers to resolve conflict with methods markedly different from those that rely upon physical force. The preacher simply responded that he was merely interested in having the right to carry a licensed weapon, a right granted to all other citizens. An on-air critic remarked that had Jesus heard of this, it would have made him want to "puke." The critic reminded the preacher that churches are supposed to be an enclave of values markedly different from the world around: Christians are supposed to be protected in the armor of light, the breastplate of truth. Of much importance, the preacher stated his disinterest in that argument as having any significance to the current debate; such concepts, he replied, are about a *spiritual* battle.

The gun-toting preacher stands in stark contrast to the account of Joan Black, a nurse at the University of Southern California Medical Center in Los Angeles. Tom Tripp recounts that in August of 1993, a young woman, Sopehia Mardress White, brandishing a .38, came looking for a nurse named Elizabeth Staten, who had allegedly stolen away White's husband. Firing six shots, White hit Staten both in the stomach and in the wrist. When Staten ran into the emergency room, White followed her, firing again.

> There, with blood on her clothes and a hot pistol in her hand, the attacker was met by another nurse, Joan Black, who did the unthinkable. Black walked calmly to the gun-toting woman—and hugged her. Black spoke comforting words. The assailant said she didn't have anything to live for, that Staten had stolen her family. "You're in pain," Black said. "I'm sorry, but everybody has pain in their life. . . . I understand, and we can work it out." As they talked, the hospital invader kept her finger on the trigger. Once she began to lift the gun as though she would shoot herself. Nurse Black just pushed her arm down and continued to hold her. At last Sopehia White gave the gun to the nurse. She was disarmed by a hug, by understanding, by compassion. Black later told an AP reporter, "I saw a sick person and had to take care of her."[22]

The contrast between these two accounts aptly illustrates two different ways of construing "Christianity": the Christendom reflex, in which Christianity is a "religion" (even if it was given the presumably honorable place of the official religion), or an emphasis upon discipleship, in which Christianity is "the Way," to be taken with deadly seriousness. With the rise of Christendom, the content of the "Christian ethic" was transformed: the empire began to call upon the church to guide and approve the deeds of the emperor, deeds that the early church rejected. But since Christianity was now legally mandatory, one's inner nature, one's "heart," now served as the central focal point of discipleship. An outwardly disciplined life became reserved for a special class of "religious," but was certainly not expected of the Christian masses. Whereas the early church did not, for example, spend a great deal of time asking whether "Jesus really meant" what Matthew records in the Sermon on the Mount, later Christianity began to "spiritualize," to interiorize, Christian discipleship—discipleship becomes more a matter of one's "heart" than *all* of one's life. The "hard sayings" of Jesus become reserved for those who are not involved in the "real world," but cloistered away in a monastery.

To use different language, the Christendom project separated "doctrine" and "ethics" into two separable categories, rather than seeing them as two sides of the same coin. Numerous times, the book of Acts describes the Christian faith as "the Way" (9:2; 18:25–26; 19:9, 23; 24:14, 22), a designation that strikes one as remarkably different than our word "religion." "Religion" often connotes a set of beliefs and practices separable from everyday life; as such, "religion" is a sphere distinct and separate from things like politics and society and culture. But if the claim that Jesus is Lord is a "Way"—or "*the* Way"—then we will not so easily separate his lordship from every facet of life. To understand that Jesus is the Messiah entails a particular lifestyle or a particular *way*, namely the way of the Messiah.

But the move to "interiorize" or "spiritualize" the gospel obscures this concern: Christ's teachings are meant to inform our *attitudes*, but not our actions, it is claimed. We, for example, "love our enemies" in our hearts, while our role as emperor or hangman or soldier requires that we kill our enemies. With regard to Matthew 5:39—"But I say to you, Do not resist an evildoer. But if anyone strikes you on the right cheek, turn the other also"—Augustine, for example, commented that "what is here required is not a bodily action, but an inward disposition."[23]

Or consider Jesus' commandment regarding wealth: "Do not store up for yourselves treasures on earth" (Matthew 6:19a). Increasingly it was suggested, to use contemporary language, "It's the heart that matters"; one can accumulate immense wealth so long as one's "heart is not greedy." "We don't lay up treasures in our *hearts*," and so that makes it quite acceptable to amass treasures in our stock portfolios. This is, however, a notion foreign to the early church. Very early on, for example, Hermas saw the holding of wealth itself as an obstacle to Christian discipleship, and the early church fathers unanimously agreed that the charging of interest was sinful. In a short time, though, the distinction arose between accumulation and greed, between the act of acquiring and the heart of grasping. Nonetheless, this distinction did not become an easy out for the wealthy—instead, the most commonly held view was that avarice always accompanied accumulation. Furthermore, early church fathers commonly asserted that those who accumulate wealth and withhold their possessions from the poor are guilty of theft.

With Augustine, however, this development went a step further: though Augustine still emphasized the earlier teaching of sharing with the poor (and emphasized that a tithe, ten percent of one's income, should be the *minimum* given away), the emphasis of his teaching began to fall upon the attitude of the heart. Augustine emphasized an attitude of *detachment* from material things—too great a concern with material things, which are simply to be *used* to enjoy God, can occasion sin. Thus the wealthy have a burden of conscience lifted—they need not be concerned that they live in comfort while others live in oppressive poverty. Simultaneously, a burden of conscience is placed upon the poor—in spite of pressing material need, they must not be overly concerned with those needs.[24]

So Augustine's development simultaneously heralded and furthered a significant shift in Christian faith: "spirituality" begins to replace lifestyle, and "religion" begins to replace discipleship. In time, then, a new source of ethics is needed. The way of Christ, now that we must run the world, must be laid aside. Since "Everyone is a Christian," Christian thinkers begin to believe they must accept a new set of questions with regard to the teaching of Christ: "What would happen if everyone did that?" and "How can you ask that of everyone?"

Not far under the surface of these questions is the assertion that ethics must begin with "realistic" expectations. After all, we are not all saints, we are not all moral superheroes, and you'd be a fool to think that we are; it's simply naïve to ask too much of people. "I'm not Jesus, after all," the objection continues. So Jesus' expectations cannot be taken seriously as an ethic we would ask of everyone. Imagine the consequences if everyone were to "love their enemies" or "give to those that ask of them"—there could be no civilization, no order, no justice. The supposed need to run the world sets aside the way of Christ, and a new way begins to inform the ethic of the "Christian in the world," as well as the "Christian in the church." So, early in the fifth century, Metropolitan Synesios of Cyrene was imposed upon to deal with a dispute that had arisen in his diocese. An elderly bishop, prior to his death, had been removed from office and replaced with a younger bishop by the two small towns served by the bishop. The reason? Those supporting the new bishop saw him as capable of exacting "harm to his enemies and [able to] serve his friends."[25]

One of the most ardent pagan critics of the early church posed the "what would happen if" question to the early Christians' refusal either to employ violence or to venerate the empire as the primary means through which they might contribute to society. Castigating the second-century disciples, the pagan Celsus angrily maintained that "if all were to do the same as you, there would be nothing to prevent [the emperor] being left in utter solitude and desertion, and the affairs of the earth would fall into the hands of the wildest and most lawless barbarians; and then there would no longer remain among men any of the glory of your religion or of the true wisdom."[26] What would happen if everybody did that, asked Celsus? The empire would fall apart, we would be overcome by our enemies, and, on top of that, you wouldn't get to practice your religion!

But the response of the early Christian theologian Origen demonstrates that the "commonsensical" nature of Celsus's attack was not always seen as a trump card. First off, Origen realized that the one who asks the "what would happen if everybody did that" question does not, of course, mean for us to take the question literally. If *everyone* loved their enemies, then Jesus' teachings would not be seen as problematic. If *everyone* shared their wealth, then Jesus' commands would not be a stumbling block. If *everyone* forgave offenses "seventy times seven," then Jesus' insistence would fail to disturb us. So Origen responded to Celsus, if in following Christ "'they do as I do,' then it is evident that even the barbarians, when they yield obedience to the word of God, will become most obedient to the law, and most humane."[27]

But the reality, of course, is that "everybody" does not "do that." And thus when faced with the "reality" of a world in which people appear to always "look out for number one," when our world claims that "if you don't take care of yourself, then no one else will," when our culture surrounds us with a message that we should "go for the gusto" and make sure that we are happy—then the call to discipleship sounds quite threatening. The "reality" of sin, the "reality" of injustice and oppression, the "reality" of "market expectations," the "reality" of "how things work" are thought to trump the calling to follow Jesus: "Many people will not love you in return," and "some people'd just as soon kill you as look at you," and "some people are always looking to take advantage of you." Jesus' way works in an "ideal" world, but not in the "real world" where you must "get your hands dirty" if you're going to "make a relevant contribution to society."

But Origen questioned whether the logic of Celsus was very realistic, after all. To the unbeliever, Origen maintained that it is not the warring and self-seeking peoples of the earth who preserve society—instead, it is the people of God who are "assuredly the salt of the earth: they preserve the order of the world; and society is held together as long as the salt is uncorrupted."[28] Similarly, when a particular Quaker had been publicly proclaiming his pursuit of pacifism, someone remarked: "Well, stranger, if all the world was of your mind I would turn and follow after." The Quaker responded, "So then thou hast a mind to be the last man to be good. I have a mind to be one of the first and set the rest an example."[29] In other words, the question ought not be "What would happen if everybody did that?" but "What would happen if disciples acted like Jesus?" Or, more ominously, "What will happen if disciples refuse to act like Jesus?" For Origen, if disciples refuse to act like disciples, there will be no salt, there will be no light, and then indeed there will be no "order," "justice," or "civilization." And if the salt has lost its saltiness, so Jesus said, it is foolish, insipid, good-for-nothing, but to be thrown out in the mud and be walked upon.

Nonetheless, the pagan logic of Celsus ultimately won over a large number of adherents among the Christian tradition. The perceived need to run the world, or the empire, or the market economy, or the nation-state gives rise to the apparent commonsensical basis of the pagan's logic: if you take Jesus seriously, things will just fall apart. And so in varied, nuanced, and subtle ways, the way of Christ has been set aside in favor of other authorities, which would show us what we should do and how we should do it, when we're out in the "real world."

But this move, at a very profound level, overlooks the basic Christian claim that Jesus, both fully human and fully God, revealed to us what the Creator intends humankind to be and to do. Can those who claim Jesus to be divine grant so little authority to this One who showed us what it means to live a human life in accordance with the will of God? "Hey, be realistic, none of us are Jesus!" it is objected. But do such objections not overlook the New Testament claim that the people of God, the "body of Christ," continue the ministry and work of Christ right in the midst of real human history, right in the midst of oppression, injustice, violence, and greed?

On that cross at Golgotha was nailed the One who was unjustly abused, tried, and murdered—and in his dying words he prayed that the Father would forgive those who killed him. But instead, imagine the result if Jesus had lived in Kentucky, and just before they nailed him to a cross, he claimed his rights as a citizen and pulled out a .38.

Pledging Allegiance to the Kingdom of God

Let no one have gods of his own, neither new ones nor strange ones, but only those instituted by the State.

Law from the Twelve Tables, 450 B.C.[1]

Gott mit uns.

"God with us," the inscription on the belt buckles of German soldiers during World War I[2]

*T*he Constantinian cataract, I suggested in the previous chapter, comprises at least two assumptions. First, "the ends justify the means." Second, it is assumed that the way of Christ cannot be relevant to matters of this-worldly concern, and thus Jesus' way gets cast aside when we (not too seriously) ask, "What would happen if everybody did that?" Undergirding these assumptions is yet a more basic assumption: the Christendom cataract makes us believe that it is our task to be in control, to run the world, to make things turn out right. And this false belief, in turn, gives rise to yet another assumption in the cataract: that it is the power brokers who are the only major players in human history. Given all these assumptions, we begin to be quite comfortable (if not very Christian) pledging our allegiance and unquestioning obedience to an empire or a nation-state wielding inordinate power, in hopes that we can, after all, make things turn out right. Consequently, the God whom we are supposedly serving by whatever means necessary turns out to be a god who serves the power-wielding empire rather than the God revealed in the Suffering Servant Jesus.

This not-so subtle use of "God" to sanction the interests of the power brokers may be illustrated by innumerable historical events, but one such event struck fairly close to home for me. While in seminary at Abilene Christian University in west Texas, I had several occasions to visit Dyess Air Force base, just outside the city limits. I was particularly struck by one of the very large hangars situated alongside the midpoint of the main runway — not because anything about the building itself was impressive, but because of the very large block letters, inordinately larger than any other sign on the base, words in all caps, which apparently articulated the evangelical mission of the base: GLOBAL POWER FOR AMERICA.

Just a few months prior to moving to Abilene, something of a scandal had occurred there at Dyess. Lieutenant Colonel Garland Robertson, at the time a chaplain for the United States Air Force, had spent years in the military, winning a Distinguished Flying Cross for a rescue operation in Vietnam, and he subsequently commanded a nuclear missile site. After leaving the military, he went to seminary to study theology, and in time returned to the military as a chaplain. While at Dyess, Robertson had received very positive assessments of his pastoral work. But that soon began to change.

When the 1991 Persian Gulf War began, soldiers began to ask Robertson whether the war was a "just war." When Vice President Dan Quayle publicly made a speech in which he suggested that everyone in the United States supported the use of the military in the Persian Gulf, Robertson wrote a letter to the editor of the *Abilene Reporter News*, expressing reservations about the legitimacy of military force being used against Iraq. He questioned whether the war was actually "just."

Though Robertson reports he expected some negative consequences, they proved overwhelmingly more punitive than anticipated. The military powers slowly stripped Robertson of all his pastoral duties, strangely charged him with "fraud," and accused him of "flouting" the authority of the president of the United States. After two examinations found no evidence of psychological disorders — and after apparent pressure on the psychologist who first examined Robertson — he was judged (without another exam) to have a "personality disorder so severe as to interfere with the normal and customary completion of his duties." Ultimately, Robertson was forced to retire from military service.

During the fiasco, Robertson was counseled by an officer from the Washington, D.C., Chief of Chaplains office, who told Robertson, "compromise [is] essential for becoming a successful military chaplain." "I suggested," Robertson reports, "that 'cooperation' was the more suitable word, but he quickly confirmed his intentional use of 'compromise.' 'If Jesus had been an Air Force chaplain,' he told me, 'he would have been court-martialed.'" Compromise, the officer told Robertson, is necessary "in order to maintain a presence."

As a result of his own experience, Robertson concluded that chaplains are not on military bases to bear witness to theological convictions, but to serve the military establishment: what was desired was a "morale officer." Or, as Robertson put it, "the chaplain only succeeds in encouraging soldiers to accept the preferences of the state without question." Robertson must not have been too far off the mark, given that the senior chaplain at Dyess *reworded* the official statement of the mission of chaplains at Dyess. To the duty of "providing free exercise of religion," the senior chaplain added the qualifier "consonant with 96th Wing Commander directives."[3]

Robertson experienced a very old move of the principalities and powers. The powers find it useful to fashion a god in their own image, a god that supports their own agenda, that rallies around their own imperialistic purposes. This god is then set forward as "God," and the citizenry told to bow the knee. As the Law from the Twelve Tables proclaimed in the fifth century B.C., "Let no one have gods of his own, neither new ones nor strange ones, but only those instituted by the State."

This appropriation of "the gods" underlies the Christendom cataract. Having accepted the falsehood that we must run the world, we seek to get hold of the mantle of power. Consequently, "discipleship" gets transformed: "following Jesus," rather than denoting a walking in the way of the humble Suffering Servant, denotes being "spiritual" as we seek to wield power over our fellows. "Christianity" becomes a chaplain to the empire's agenda. "Christianity" provides "morale" while the agents of the empire pursue the empire's agenda. Or, perhaps even more insidious, Christians become convinced that they are pursuing the purposes of God by pursuing the purposes of the empire.

What Should We Do about . . . ?

We might put the problem this way: the Constantinian cataract results from a very basic case of false identity. The cataract not only clouds our vision, but psychologically and culturally shapes our understanding of our most basic identity. While biblically informed discipleship requires us to give ourselves in absolute allegiance to the kingdom of God, the Constantinian cataract threatens the purity of that allegiance by mixing it with an allegiance to the empire or nation-state. Or, perhaps more accurately, we begin to believe that a pursuit of the agenda of the empire or nation-state may be placed comfortably alongside our pursuit of the kingdom of God, even though the ends and goals of the kingdom of God and the kingdoms of this world are clearly different, and clearly at odds with one another.

Consider a thought experiment in order to get at the difficulty. Using contemporary garb, a key question might be put this way: do we American Christians see ourselves as *American* Christians, or as American *Christians*? Do we fundamentally envision ourselves as U.S. citizens who espouse the "Christian religion," or as disciples of Jesus who happen to live in the United States? *What is our fundamental identity?* Citizens of our nation-state, or citizens of the kingdom of God?

Most Christians, one might conjecture, would immediately respond that our first allegiance is undoubtedly to the kingdom of God. But our debates often appear to assume that the fundamental identity, the primary lens through which we must make decisions about how to act in our world, is that of the nation-state. One might find ample evidence that we do envision our primary identity in terms of the nation-state by simply examining the questions we often ask: "What should we do about terrorism?" The *we* in that question is most often, one may safely assume, the United States. "What should we do about Saddam Hussein?" "What should we do about inner-city poverty?" "What should we do about homelessness?" "What should we do about the threat of nuclear war?" "What should we do about peace in the Middle East?" "What should we do about welfare?" "What should we do about abortion?" And so the questions go, always assuming that the all-important *we* is the nation-state.[4]

Consequently, *discipleship*—defined as taking seriously the way of Christ in *all* our affairs and concerns—gets shelved as irrelevant to the real concerns of the world. But what might happen if we took such questions seriously from a biblical viewpoint? For instance, what should we, as disciples of Jesus, do about homelessness? What should we, as the body of Christ, do about the threat of nuclear war? What should the church do about Saddam Hussein? What should we believers do about peace in the Middle East? What should we who bear the name of Jesus do about inner-city poverty and the plight of single mothers? What should we followers of the Way do about abortion?

Does the word of God incarnate in Jesus Christ not have something to say to the injustices and oppression of our world?—or are the people of God simply to accept the claim that the only appropriate response to injustice is the ethic of nations, the ethic of power checking power? Christians appear often to assume that to make significant cultural change we must approach change from the "top down"—that until we can get those who hold the mantle of power to use that power to bring about change, there can be no real change. But Jesus taught and practiced something quite different: "You know that among the Gentiles those whom they recognize as their rulers lord it over them, and their great ones are tyrants over them. But it is not so among you; but whoever wishes to become great among you must be your servant, and whoever wishes to be first among you must be slave of all" (Mark 10:42–44). That is, Jesus called his disciples not to get hold of empire power—this is precisely what some of his disciples wanted, to get hold of the rein of command, and use it on behalf of the people of God, on behalf of the good guys, on behalf of righteousness, justice, and God's purposes. Instead, he called them to an altogether different route of bringing about the radical change of the kingdom of God—that of servanthood.

But since the time of the Reformation, it has been assumed that "religion" is "private," and that matters of the "state" are "public." Or, to put it differently, it begins to be assumed that the church worries about souls, and the state worries about bodies. This "privatization of religion," this move to make religion a "private" matter, results in a profound change of thought: when we ask the "What are we going to do about . . ." question, we of course assume that the *we* is the nation or government, because we have long been trained to think of the church as having no social or political significance. To ask, "What are we Christians going to do about terrorism?" sounds ludicrous!—Nothing! That's the government's job.

Bill Tibert, minister for Covenant Presbyterian Church in Colorado Springs, suggested one such response to the "what should we do" question, which takes the church and the way of Christ seriously:

> During the 1960s and 70s there was an antiwar slogan that asked, "What if they gave a war and nobody came?" The point was what if there was a declaration of war and all the people just refused to participate? What if there were abortion clinics but nobody went in? What if abortion was a legal choice, but it was a choice nobody took? Changes in the law, blocking abortion clinics, demeaning name-calling will not stop abortions. The history of the church through the ages has been the history of changes brought about in society through the church demonstrating and living an alternative vision of life. We need to stop telling our nonbelieving neighbors how wrong their way of life is, and we need to start showing the power of the gospel in the way we live. . . . Let me ask you: Which has greater power? Ten thousand people who fill the streets in front of abortion clinics and shame those seeking abortions, or ten thousand people in California who take to the state capital a petition they have signed stating they will take any unwanted child of any age, any color, any physical condition so that they can love that child in the name of Jesus Christ?[5]

So "What are we going to do?" Respond with the way of Christ. The world may think that way irrelevant, even foolish. But what the world takes as foolish is actually the wisdom of God and the only hope for our world. We do not need more "effective" kingdoms of men; we do not need more "responsible" kingdoms of this world; we do not need more "realism" among the kingdoms of a fallen order. We need the kingdom of God.

The Eusebian School of History

The "what should we do" question thus wrongly assumes that the really important actors in the scheme of human history are the power brokers, those who supposedly can "get things done." This is yet another question that flows from the Christendom cataract, an apparently commonsensical question that clouds our vision, distorts the faith by making Christian discipleship ultimately irrelevant to how we think the world "really works." That we think it is the power brokers who are the truly important ones is nowhere more apparent than in our understanding of "history." The manner in which we relate the events of "human history" often bears witness to the fact that we do not take seriously the way of Christ as having social and cultural significance.

The wisdom of that old maxim — "a little child shall lead them" — has struck me numerous times in my few years of parenting young sons. So it occurred recently during a conversation with my oldest son, who had just turned seven years old, and had accompanied my wife Laura and myself on a study-abroad trip to London. At breakfast one morning, he began,

> "Is Big Ben the baddest place in London?"
> "What do you mean?"
> "The place where kings killed all those many people."
> "Oh, no, you're talking about the Tower of London."
> "Oh."
> A pause, and then, "Why is it so important—the Tower?" he asked.
> "Oh, lots of things happened there that became history—and kings killed lots of people there—so its become a very historically important place," I replied.
> Another pause, and then . . .
> "Well why do we make it history when all those bad things happened there?"

I was delighted with the question, and many contemporary historians would also like the question because it points to the manner in which "history" is no mere value-free repetition of "historical fact." Instead, "history" always carries with it certain value commitments that lead us, for example, to select certain "facts," and omit others, in our storytelling. So it has become conventional wisdom that the victors write the history books. Those defeated in battle—the last thing they worry about is writing a history of their own demise. The conquerors write the accounts of victory. And most often, it turns out that in these histories of the victors, there is a common element: it is the bearers of economic, military, and cultural power who are the primary characters in the story.

So to read history books, or listen to presidential addresses, one would think that it is the emperors, the czars, the kings and queens, the prime ministers, the presidents who are the primary movers and shakers of world history.[6] Those with their hands on the mantle of power, it is assumed, are the ones who move history. So the history of the world is written in the history of empires and kingdoms, nation-states and republics. The important characters are the powerful ones, and their kingdoms; the crucial players are the strong ones, and their dominion; the significant performer on the stage of world history is the one who wins and controls. A chronicle of defeat, on the other hand, is a tale of the insignificant.

But such history writing often includes another crucial element: history needs to do more than merely chronicle the events of victory. The history must do something more—it must cloak victory and the use of power with the approval of God. In fact, it is typically assumed that God must have provided the victory—it must have been his strength that destroyed our enemies, that preserves our self-interest. Our conquest, our rule, our governing over others must have been the will of God. We are a mighty people, a powerful people, because God is on our side; we are on the side of God, and so we conquer our enemies. To rule this land, to lord authority over that people—this is our manifest destiny, sanctioned by God, guaranteed by God's power.

It is precisely here that we see the manner in which Christendom-like faith makes Jesus irrelevant: for he came not, as already mentioned, as those among the Gentiles, who lord authority over others, who dominate and coerce (Mark 10:41–45). In such history-telling, religious talk may abound, "spirituality" may overflow, but the way of the One who came to serve rather than be served, the way of the One who came to give his life rather than take life, gets laid aside as irrelevant to the way history "really works."

One might call this kind of storytelling "Eusebian," for shortly after Emperor Constantine's death, Eusebius, the bishop of Caesarea, authored a book praising the work of Constantine. *The Life of Constantine* declared in no uncertain terms that God was at work in the life and conquests of Constantine. The church must honor the martyrdom and suffering of saints in centuries past; but now, Eusebius confidently declared, God is at work in the midst of history by destroying the enemies of the faith. The new age has come, and Christianity has triumphed over its enemies through the power of empire.

Eusebius chronicled how Constantine's armies, protected by the sign of the cross, had conquered its enemies. The enemies of Constantine, because they were pagan, became the enemies of God. And as the pagan enemies of God became the enemies of the newly Christian empire, so the military triumphs of the Roman Empire were interpreted as the triumphs of God over the forces of evil.[7] In the early church, the faithful martyr served as the paradigm for faithfulness to the ways of God; but in the new age, professed Eusebius, the emperor now provided a "lesson in the pattern of godliness to the human race." There was abundant evidence, continued the bishop, that Constantine was favored by God—besides long life, God "appointed him victor over the whole race of tyrants and destroyer of the God-battling giants." Through Constantine God "cleansed humanity of the godless multitude, and set him up as a teacher of true devotion to himself for all nations."[8]

"Eusebian" history thus takes the power and exploits of the heads of empires and nation-states and "baptizes" those exploits with the approval of God—in spite of the fact that when God was revealed in human form, he did not take the form of conqueror or power broker, but of servant. Thus to reenvision discipleship without the distortion of a Christendom cataract requires that we renew our pledge of allegiance to the kingdom of God, revealed most fully in the way of Jesus, the way of suffering servanthood. As a consequence, the way we narrate the events of human history will likely take a profoundly different tack.

The Neo-Eusebian School of History: American Christian Storytelling

President Woodrow Wilson epitomized "Eusebian storytelling" in a speech to the Senate in 1919:

> Our participation in [World War I] established our position among the nations. . . . The whole world saw at last . . . a Nation they had deemed material and now found to be compact of the spiritual forces that must free men of every nation of every unworthy bondage. . . . The stage is set, the destiny is disclosed. It has come about by no plan of our conceiving, but by the hand of God who led us into this way. We cannot turn back. We can only go forward . . . to follow the vision. It was of this that we dreamed at our birth. America shall in truth show the way.[9]

Wilson's deification of the United States is only one of many examples of Eusebian history-telling in our country. Such history was especially prominent in the early years of the young republic. Shortly after the conclusion of the American Revolutionary War, the president of Yale University, Ezra Stiles, was invited to preach an "election sermon" to sanctify the election of the new governor of Connecticut. A deeply respected scholar and churchman, Stiles mounted the pulpit to declare the glories of what he believed God had been doing in their midst. So convinced was he that God was at work in the young American republic, Stiles repeatedly alluded to the young nation as "Israel." Moreover, he professed America would be the site of the literal fulfillment of some of the prophecies of Moses. The United States can expect no less than what Moses predicted for Israel. God, Stiles prophesied, will "'bring them into the land which their fathers possessed; and multiply them above their fathers, and rejoice over them for good, as he rejoiced over their fathers.' Then the words of Moses . . . will be literally fulfilled, when this branch of the posterity of Abraham shall be nationally collected, and become a very distinguished and glorious people, under the great messiah, the Prince of Peace. He will then 'make them high above all nations which he hath made, in praise, and in name, and in honor, and they shall become a holy people unto the Lord their God.'"[10] In fact, Stiles further conjectured, the native American Indians are quite likely the literal descendants of the original Canaanites, driven out by the conquest of Joshua—leaving his listeners to assume that the American Israel has the warrant to drive them out, to conquer them yet again. Giving lip service to the "Prince of Peace," this Eusebian storytelling could easily be read as a warrant for genocide.[11]

As evidence of God's favor, Stiles pointed to what he deemed to be the miraculous triumphs of the young republic in the Revolutionary War under the leadership of George Washington. Stiles (along with many Christian hagiographical accounts of American history) conveniently overlooked the text of Romans 13, in which the apostle Paul prohibits the revolutionary overthrow of one's government. Instead, the "glorious act of Independence" was "heaven inspired." And the rapid pace with which men quickly took up arms was evidence enough for the hand of God leading them: "the ardor and spirit of military discipline was by Heaven, and without concert, sent through the continent like lightning." This decision to overthrow the yoke of British authority "was sealed and confirmed by God Almighty in the victory of General Washington. . . ." In fact, "time would fail me to recount the wonder-working providence of God in the events of this war."[12]

Thus throughout American history, just as in the Holy Roman Empire, Christianity often became a "religion" suffused with the assumption that God has given to "us" the manifest destiny to conquer. Conservative Christians are thus not wrong to note that Christianity played a major role in the founding of the United States, a role that revisionist historians allegedly want to overlook in their storytelling because of their anti-Christian bias. Nonetheless, this Christianity—which too often justified genocide of Native Americans and the enslavement of Africans—was often a religion not worthy of the name of Christ. The early U.S. republic did indeed more publicly profess and assume a Christian veneer; abundant proof texts and quotes from founding fathers suggest that the early republic was more explicitly "Christian" than is our public square today. But this fails to raise the more important question: was that widespread Christianity of the early republic merely a variation on Eusebian Christianity? Does this kind of "God and country" faith bear witness to a Good News that seeks to break down barriers, reconcile peoples, and proclaim peace? How does being discipled by the Suffering Servant fit into a storytelling that assumes, because we are conquering, because we are growing wealthy, because we have amassed power and wealth, that God must be on our side?

Eusebian Christianity apparently remains alive and well in the United States two centuries later. The same claims are yet made: to many Protestant evangelicals and fundamentalists, the history of America, as sociologist James Davison Hunter summarized it in the 1990s, is the "embodiment of Providential wisdom." As evangelical journalist Rus Walton claimed, "the American system is the political expression of Christian ideas," just as a different evangelical author wrote that "God's hand was in the founding of this country and the fiber of Christ is in the very fabric of America." For another, "America was founded upon Christian principles." Indeed, concluded yet another evangelical, the United States is "the greatest Christian nation the world has ever known."[13]

Since Eusebian storytelling portrays particular nations or empires as the agents of God's kingdom, those nations or empires are thus particularly tempted to depict all conflict as a battle between the agents of light and the agents of darkness. Imperial conquest and foreign policy are interpreted as the work of God's chosen ones arrayed against the forces of evil. Demonizing the foe, portraying the other side as Satan and ourselves as agents of righteousness, the subjects of the light-bearing empire are forced to choose: you are either for us in our war-making, or against us. Conquering one's enemies becomes a holy crusade, in which the destruction of evil justifies whatever means are thought necessary. Thus the Germans, in World War I, were convinced God was on their side: *Gott mit uns*—"God with us," or so proclaimed the inscription on the belt buckles of German soldiers. Given God's approval and sanction of one's endeavors, one's enemies become, even, less than human, less than deserving of full moral recognition. So Christian President Truman described the strategy against the Japanese near the end of World War II: "When you deal with a beast, you have to treat him as a beast."[14] Near the end of the Cold War, President Reagan dubbed the Soviet Union the "evil empire" while commonly alluding to the United States as the "city set on a hill." And shortly after the beginning of the war on terror, President George W. Bush identified Iraq, Iran, and Korea as an "axis of evil," while depicting the United States as the bearer of God's light. Along with such crusade language, the president co-opted language reminiscent of Jesus' claim to ultimate allegiance: "Around the world, the nations must choose. They are with us, or they're with the terrorists."[15]

Such an only slightly veiled allusion to Jesus' demand—"whoever is not with me is against me"—would have us co-opt Jesus into the agenda of empire rather than the agenda of the kingdom of God. The kingdom of God belongs to those, declared Jesus, who are poor in spirit, who are deeply aware of their own inadequacies, failings, and rebellion; the kingdom belongs to those who are merciful in response to injustice; the kingdom belongs to those who love even enemies. The way of the kingdom of God stands in stark contrast to the way of the kingdoms of this world, though the kingdoms of this world desperately seek to sanction their interests in the name of God.

"The gods are on the side of the stronger," declared Tacitus.[16] This pagan assumption apparently undergirds a great deal of Eusebian storytelling. But such an assumption appears to undo the appropriate task of Christian ethics. For whom are Christians to do moral reasoning? The empire, or the church? To whom are we disciples accountable? The emperor, or the Lord?

If we assume that our basic moral commitments must be easily accessible to the emperor, or the prime minister, or the president—say as a "spirituality," or a "religion," or a "piety"—will we not in turn construct a moral logic that refuses to take Jesus seriously? As a student said to my colleague Richard Goode at the time of the most recent presidential election, "I don't want a president whose conscience is too sensitive. He might need to do some mean things to get the job done." With such careless discounting of the way of Christ in mind, Russian novelist Leo Tolstoy satirically recounted the tale of the "triumph" of Christianity, in which he believed the church sanctioned the "robber-chief" Constantine:

> No one said to him: "The kings exercise authority among the nations, but among you it shall not be so. Do not murder, do not commit adultery, do not lay up riches, judge not, condemn not, resist not him that is evil."
>
> But they said to him: "You wish to be called a Christian and to continue to be the chieftain of the robbers—to kill, burn, fight, lust, execute, and live in luxury? That can all be arranged."
>
> And they arranged a Christianity for him, and arranged it very smoothly, better even than could have been expected. They foresaw that, reading the Gospels, it might occur to him that all this (*i.e.*, a Christian life) is demanded. . . . This they foresaw, and they carefully devised such a Christianity for him as would let him continue to live his old heathen life unembarrassed. On the one hand Christ, God's Son, only

came to bring salvation to him and to everybody. Christ having died, Constantine can live as he likes. More even than that—one may repent and swallow a little bit of bread and some wine, and that will bring salvation, and all will be forgiven.

But more even than that: they sanctify his robber-chieftainship, and say that it proceeds from God, and they anoint him with holy oil. And he, on his side, arranges for them the congress of priests that they wish for, and order them to say what each man's relation to God should be, and orders every one to repeat what they say. . . .

And as soon as one of the anointed robber-chiefs wishes his own and another folk to begin slaying each other, the priest[s] immediately prepare some holy water, sprinkle a cross (which Christ bore and on which he died because he repudiated such robbers), take the cross and bless the robber-chief in his work of slaughtering, hanging, and destroying.[17]

The Offense of the Gospel

Against the Eusebian reflex to see the power brokers as the primary movers and shakers in world history, biblical proclamation can appear little less than offensive. After all, the Old Testament prophets proclaimed that it is not the powermongers and prideful militarists who control history. It is *God* who is over all the nations. There is not merely "one nation under God," but *all* nations and peoples are under God, whether they accept his rightful reign or not. Furthermore, God intends to bring about his purposes for human history—to provide a light to all the nations—through the paltry little federation of tribal groups called Israel.

Similarly, the gospel proclaims that the kingdom of God—the ultimate purpose and end of human history—is revealed most fully in a suffering, crucified One. The "city set on a hill" is not a Western liberal democracy madly protecting its self-interest through the headlong pursuit of the "security" that comes from weapons of mass destruction or a market economy that allows us to glut our self-centered whims. The shining city, instead, is a people marked by the Beatitudes, forsaking all lusts, giving up pursuit of security, refusing to amass wealth, and insisting upon the love of enemies. The "light to all the nations" shined not through the mighty and wealthy, but through the One who, "though he was rich, yet for your sakes he became poor," through the One "who, though he was in the form of God, did not regard equality with God as something to be exploited, but emptied himself" (Philippians 2:6–7). And linked with that offensive-enough claim is the demand for ultimate allegiance, to proclaim that crucified Jesus as Lord of Lords, King of Kings, authority over all authorities.

This offense of the gospel was not lost on the critics of the early church. The pagan Celsus—who asked the early church to consider "what would happen if everybody did that"—likewise understood quite clearly the offensiveness of their prioritization of church over empire, and their insistence that the way of the church be the way of Christ. Celsus recognized that these Christians believed that it is not in the business of empire-building and power-brokering that history is made, but within the community of the apparently insignificant people of God. In spite of Celsus's abusiveness, one can yet detect in his caricature something of the outline of the basic New Testament claim: Christians appear to be, Celsus snapped, likened to "a flight of bats or to a swarm of ants issuing out of their nest, or to frogs holding council in a marsh, or to worms crawling together in the corner of a dunghill . . . asserting that God shows and announces to us all things beforehand." Christians are like "worms which assert that there is a God . . . and that all things have been made subject to us—earth, and water, and air, and stars—and that all things exist for our sake, and are ordained to be subject to us."[18]

Celsus instead wanted Christians, to use modern parlance, to "get real." Your stupid claims about God having now revealed his purposes for human history in this obscure Jew, whom the Roman Empire crucified—give it a rest, come to grips with the way the world really works. If you want to do something useful, then "take office in the government of the country, if that is required for the maintenance of the laws and the support of religion."[19]

Origen's response to Celsus provides an alternative vision, holding up the church as the primary venue through which God brings about his purposes in human history. Origen replied that rather than raising up young people to serve in the administration of the empire, the church instead encourages those "who are mighty in word and of blameless life" to give their lives to service in the church, for the true good of the world. Such a policy, Origen noted, was not intended to escape "public duties." Instead, the practice was simply a pragmatic, realistic one. If we are truly to be of service to the world, it will be by way of the church of God, rather than by way of the empire.

But in time, Eusebius provided justification for believing that perhaps the pagan Celsus was right, after all. Could it be that here, too, deeply rooted Christendom reflexes have more in common with ancient paganism than with early Christianity? To the degree that we continue to prefer the sociological prioritizing of "empire" over "church," to that degree do we continue the legacy of Eusebius and Celsus. And to that degree, we may be like the Gospel of Mark's account of Peter, who knew all the right words—"You are the Messiah," he proclaimed to Jesus (8:29)—but misunderstood their meaning. Until Peter followed Jesus to Jerusalem, witnessed from afar his condemnation and his crucifixion, and saw in person the resurrected Christ, only then could he begin to understand the call to "follow me." It was a call that led him not to the majestic power of the throne room of empire, but to the way of suffering servanthood, and only by that route to the life offered in the kingdom of God.

Reassessing Our Lenses

To question these deeply inbred Christendom reflexes may appear to many as sheer unfaithfulness. To many, these reflexes appear to be very *biblical*, and any critique of them appears to be irresponsible, naïve, and idealistic. But such a cataract, as I have only suggested thus far, is not biblical, but only a set of presuppositions that we impose upon the biblical story. It does not derive from the overarching story of Scripture itself, but from a long tradition that misconstrues our reading of Scripture.

Like Peter and the rest of the Twelve, who walked alongside Jesus during his earthly ministry and yet so often misunderstood his mission, we too must return again and again to the story of Jesus, seeking to make sense of his call to "follow me." Through the discipline of seeking to read Scripture well, we hope that our vision will not be clouded by that cataract which would make us falsely believe that "the end justifies the means," or that we should "spiritualize" Jesus' teachings because of fear of "what would happen if everybody" actually took Jesus seriously. Through submitting ourselves again to the authority of Scripture, we hope to find an alternate reading to that of Eusebius: that it is not through the power brokers of human history that God will effect God's purposes, but through the little minority band of peoples committed to walking in the way of Jesus of Nazareth, bearing witness to the new reality, the new creation, the kingdom of God. And all this requires, besides, great trust: that it is not our task to make things turn out right, but instead to be faithful witnesses. We will have to trust that God will be God, and do what God has promised.

PART 2

What Disciples Believe

The Gospel

Repent, for the Kingdom Is at Hand

> *He is not in his heaven with all well on the earth. He is on this
> earth, and all hell's broke loose.*
>
> Clarence Jordan[1]

The Constantinian cataract makes the "Christian religion" something ultimately unrelated to this world, to time, or history, or human culture, and instead makes it about the "other world." We wait for the "sweet by and by" when we will diet on love and mercy and goodness and God and heaven; but in the meanwhile, "down below," we wait out our time, where we have to put up with violence and hatred and injustice and unkindness and hunger and poverty, fighting fire with fire. Some day will come when we get our "mansion over the hilltop," but in the meanwhile we have to put up with the way things "really are here on earth." While waiting, we might adopt a variety of waiting tactics: some withdraw from "the world" in an effort to maintain their purity and holiness, while others try to "make a difference," but seek to do so by getting their hands on the mantle of power.

But such approaches have little to do with Jesus, on at least two accounts: one, Jesus called his disciples to participate in a kingdom that was invading human history, a kingdom so present you could reach out and touch it, a new order in their very midst. "For, in fact, the kingdom of God is among you" (Luke 17:21). That new kingdom is "otherworldly" only in the sense that it is the will of the "Father who is in heaven." The new kingdom is very "this-worldly" in the sense that the kingdom calls us to participate in God's will and reign even now, in the midst of human history. And it is also "this-worldly" in the sense that we now see, in Jesus, what it means to live life fully according to God's will, in the midst of all the concerns, hurts, and pains of human history. The kingdom is not unrelated to human history, but it is the new reality that redefines human history.

Two, the way of the kingdom was not the way of power and might, but the way of suffering servanthood, a real alternative to the ways of the rebellious principalities and powers that naïvely, if not arrogantly, think they are in control of human history. The Anointed One responds to injustice and oppression and violence and poverty with the only thing that can *really* "make a difference": a patient, unwavering, fearless, self-giving love. Through such means, Christ won victory over the powers: only by a nonviolent love that loves even unto death could the principalities and powers be stripped of their biggest weapon, the fear of death. Because of the powers undone by Christ's death and Christ's way vindicated by the resurrection, we are invited to participate in the kingdom that celebrates that victory and lives out its immediate implications: as he loved, so we love. As he served, so we serve. As he died, so we die. As he was raised, so shall we be raised. In fact, as Karl Barth put it, "we are waiting only until Easter becomes for the world a general event."[2] This is a kingdom that cannot be stopped, for it has been set free from the fear of death.

Participation in *this* kingdom, by definition, could not give way to an "end justifies the means" logic, for the only way we can bear witness to a patient God who forgives seventy times seven is by our practicing such patient forgiveness. The only way we can bear witness to a God who seeks to reconcile all peoples unto himself is by our ministry of reconciliation. The only way we can bear witness to a God who serves is by our serving. The only way we can bear witness to a God who loves even enemies is by loving our enemies. Thus our ethic and our doctrine prove inseparably linked: if we truly believe that the kingdom has come, and is now present in our midst, and is made manifest in the work and ministry of Jesus of Nazareth, our lives must conform to that new reality.

If the gospel be true, then, the most important characters in the unfolding human drama are those faithful witnesses to the truth, those witnesses often deemed to be irrelevant, lacking common sense, unable to see "reality." Moreover, if the gospel be true, then our fundamental identity will be wrapped up in the new kingdom. Full allegiance must be given, shared with no other. There is no dual citizenship, but only complete commitment and obedience. "Let the dead bury their dead," and "those who have put their hand to the plow and look back are not fit for the kingdom," and "no one can serve two masters." Indeed, it is as if we have been called to a holy war.[3] Everything must now be set aside for this one calling. But the war is a war quite unexpected, for it is a war fought for the God who commonly surprises, and does the unthinkable: it is the war of the Lamb in which we are called to participate, bearing faithful witness to the God who conquers through suffering love.

What "Good News"?

All of these claims, of course, assume a great deal about what "gospel" is. To substantiate these claims, I must spend some time discussing the basic story line of the Good News. What is this new thing that is supposedly so good?

"Gospel preaching" sometimes goes this way: the holy Creator God set forth a holy law, which that God demands we keep. In rebellion, we transgressed God's law, and now deserve death. In his mercy, though, God gave his own Son in our place, so we don't have to die. If we believe in this Good News (and/or give intellectual assent to sound doctrine? and/or do the right things in church? and/or grow in personal holiness?), we can be saved from hell and go to heaven. Thus you must decide: what will your fate be when you die?

While such preaching might capture some biblical trajectories, truer to the biblical portrait of Good News is this synopsis: God created a good creation in order to be in relationship. In rebellion, we rejected the offer of relationship, made a hell of God's good creation, and find ourselves enslaved to those things created for our good. In God's mercy, God consistently pursued covenant relationship and sought to redeem the rebellious creation. God offered in Jesus a new beginning, the kingdom of God, the new creation. We rejected him again and killed the Son. Yet our rebellion did not have the last word, for Jesus' obedience even unto death unmasked the rebellious powers of this world for what they are—weak, paltry, concerned only with their own pitiful self-existence. Thus the Father raised him from the grave—and offers that same power of renewal to be at work in his covenant people, embodying the new creation. We may receive the Good News (which comes with the same suffering experienced by Jesus, for the world lives yet in rebellion) and trust that we shall be vindicated and blessed beyond measure by fellowship with God. Or we may continue in our rebellion, left to our own peril, self-centeredness, loneliness, and hell.

Of much offense to our "postmodern" world, the biblical narrative purports to be nothing less than a "metanarrative"—a story that claims to understand the ultimate meaning, purpose, and direction of human history. Many in the so-called "postmodern" world object to "metanarratives" because such worldviews have often been used to violently impose a worldview or set of "values" upon those who do not share those convictions. Nonetheless, the biblical account does provide just such an account of human history—claiming to guide us into the very purpose and meaning of human history. And without an understanding of the basic structure of this narrative, we cannot hope to understand what the "Good News" is that "gospel" preaches.[4]

The canon opens with an account of the creation in Genesis 1, which repeatedly pronounces that God created a *good* creation. Again and again the biblical account pronounces the Creator's assessment of the creation: "it was good," and finally, in finished form, "it was very good." Rather than strife, there was peace; instead of hunger, abundance; rather than lust, contentment; instead of death, life. Unlike other competing creation accounts in the ancient Near East, the biblical account claims that the universe grew out of a loving desire for communion, rather than the violence of the gods. Violence, greed, lust, enmity, and strife are not inherent to created life, but a perversion of it.

This way of characterizing the creation also stands in stark contrast to a Platonic conception of the world—in which physical and earthly existence is inferior to the "spiritual" realm. In various forms of this dualism, the ultimate desire is to be free of the body, the "prison-house of the soul," thereby being freed from the limitations and burdens of physical existence. But the biblical account begins with the *goodness* of bodily and physical creation, created as it is by a good God.

And yet this is, clearly, not the end of the story. For soon things go to hell in a handbasket, and the beginning of that fateful journey begins with rebellion. Though the human was endowed with stewardship, freedom, and abundance, there were limits within the created realm: "You may freely eat of every tree of the garden; but of the tree of the knowledge of good and evil you shall not eat, for in the day that you eat of it you shall die" (Gen. 2:16–17). The fact that none of us will find any fruit from the "tree of the knowledge of good and evil" in our local grocer's produce section should clue us in to the idiomatic nature of the phrase. An idiom is an expression that, if taken literally, misses the point. "It's raining cats and dogs," "You've broken my heart," or, as we often said in Alabama, "I'm fixing to go to the store." So what's the point here? The Hebrew term *yada'* is often translated "knowledge" and carries with it the sense of participation in and intimate knowledge of the thing "known." "Knowledge" is not a mere intellectual holding to a fact, but more the notion of having relationship with someone or something. Thus biblical characters are sometimes said to "know" their wife or husband. That is, the verb "know" carries with it the sense even of sexual intercourse. "Good and evil" serves as an expression meaning all possible things, whether good or bad.

The temptation, then, is *not* to break an arbitrary rule, to eat the cookie the authoritarian parent has forbidden to the child. The temptation is to take the place of God, to submit to no limits, to overreach the proper place of the human as creature. The temptation is sheer rebellion, to usurp God's throne, and thus the text states that the human is tempted with the desire to "be like God, knowing good and evil" (Gen. 3:5). As the human tries to be sovereign, he overthrows the harmony, wholeness, peace, and abundance of the sovereign God's good creation. Hierarchy and domination replace the mutuality of relationship between male and female; violence and oppression shatter the peace and friendship known in the garden; death consumes life. Overreaching his place, the human embodies arrogance and pride, and in disobedience makes a hell out of God's good creation.

In short order, the narrative records the fratricidal killing of Abel by Cain, followed by a genealogy that leads directly to the indictment of human history: "the earth was filled with violence. And God saw that the earth was corrupt; for all flesh had corrupted its ways upon the earth" (Gen. 6:11–12). But the judgment of flood is followed by renewed covenants. Rather than forsaking a rebellious creation, the Creator God refuses to abandon those who do not love in response to love, and following the covenant with Noah, enters into a covenant relationship with Abram: Abram, you follow me, live as a sojourner, and I will give you a land, numerous offspring, and bring a blessing to all peoples through you (Gen. 12; 15). With Abram, God promises to redeem what has been lost, to renew what has been corrupted, to create again what was good but is now fallen (cf. Gal. 3:14).

The remainder of the canon is an outworking of this covenant promise. But the exodus story stands front and center as the foremost story giving the covenant people their primary identity. Repeatedly the Old Testament recounts the deliverance wrought from Egypt—God's powerful hand at work, accomplishing what could not be accomplished on their own strength. They knew deliverance not because they were mighty, not because they deserved deliverance, not because they were a numerous people, and not because they somehow merited God's favor. Quite instead, they were a rebellious, stubborn, ungrateful, undeserving people, but God delivered them anyway, because the God of Abraham, Isaac, and Jacob is a God of steadfast love, keeping covenant, loving even those who do not love in return (cf. Deut. 9:4–7). They were not delivered because they kept the law, for they did not yet have the law. They were not freed because they merited their salvation, for their salvation was something beyond their ability to engineer or accomplish.

But freed from slavery, they were not free to do as they pleased—for licentiousness is but slavery in another guise. Freed from Egypt, they were not free to treat others howsoever they pleased—for this is but imposing the ethic of Egypt upon those more vulnerable than yourselves. Instead God gave Torah, the law, as a new Way, a call to embody an alternative to the nations. The Hebrews were called to embody an alternative to Egypt, where they had been treated as mere human chattel, used as human resources for the grinding machine of Egyptian productivity. The law was never intended as a legalistic system by which a people might make themselves righteous before God; law was, itself, a gift from God, for the Torah contained what was for Israel's own good (cf. Deut. 6:24; 10:13).

That God selected a particular people is of great importance to the biblical story: God did not drop from the sky a text containing "timeless universal principles." Instead, this God entered into covenant relationship with a particular people and called them to embody an alternative to the peoples round about them. Through Israel, all were to come to know the God of Abraham, Isaac, and Jacob as the one true God. Their task was not to "fix" the nations round about them—the sovereign God would do that, in God's way, in God's time. Their task was not to make history turn out right—the sovereign God would do that, in God's way, in God's time. Their task, instead, was to be faithful to that God, faithfully embodying his will for the world.

Adopted as a son at the exodus, Israel turned her back on the loving father, and instead placed her hope in Egypt. Israel turned to Egypt both literally and figuratively: literally, in trusting that military alliances with the likes of Egypt and Assyria would solve its need for security and protection. And figuratively, Israel returned to the ethic of Egypt (e.g., Isa. 31; Hosea 11). Where the Sabbath rest, for example, had been intended as a contrast to the ethic of the slavery of Egypt (Deut. 5:15), the prophet Amos declared that the Sabbath day of rest, though kept in the letter of the law, had became a mere religious hindrance to what the merchants really wanted: to rip off the poor and trample the needy for their own financial gain (Amos 8:4–6). Rather than serving as a light to all peoples, rather than showing the world God's good desires for his creation, rather than hallowing God's name by obeying God's will, Israel defiled the name and adulterated herself with the idols and injustices and oppressions of the unredeemed peoples.

Because of such unfaithfulness, the prophets grieved the injustice, hatred, and oppression that appeared to rule human history. Such arrogance, pride, and ingratitude marked not only the nations, but the covenant people of God as well. That arrogance manifested itself in cruel abuses of humankind, in economic injustice, and in the terrors of war. Rather than trusting in God, Israel trusted in her own power and alliances with those who had mighty arsenals of swords and chariots; rather than submitting to the law of God, which was intended for her good, Israel preferred the ways of the pagans; rather than seeking the good of the weak and vulnerable in her midst, Israel took advantage of them.

Ah, you who make iniquitous decrees,
    who write oppressive statutes,
to turn aside the needy from justice
    and to rob the poor of my people of their right,
that widows may be your spoil,
    and that you may make the orphans your prey!

Isaiah 10:1–2

The prophets, filled with a passion and longing for God's name to be hallowed in the temple *and* the marketplace, pronounced judgment and the coming wrath of God, and called for repentance — they demanded, in the name of God, that the people of God actually order their lives *as* the people of God. No empty profession of religion would suffice. No trampling of the courts of the temple in passionate worship would suffice. No matter how exuberant or charismatic, no matter how emotional or profuse the praise, if the praise was not manifested in every part of the life of the covenant people, then God wanted nothing of it. So speaking for God, the eighth-century prophet Amos condemned northern Israel:

Even though you offer me your burnt offerings and grain offerings,
    I will not accept them;
and the offerings of well-being of your fatted animals
    I will not look upon.
Take away from me the noise of your songs;
    I will not listen to the melody of your harps.
But let justice roll down like waters,
    and righteousness like an ever-flowing stream.

Amos 5:22–24

Though the prophets grieved over the injustice of human history, they did not despair. Instead, they promised and hoped for a coming day in which righteousness would be vindicated and injustice overthrown. In that day, there would be no quarter for the arrogance that leads to exalting oneself above others, comfortable with oppression and glib talk of "collateral damage," as if those created in the image of God are disposable property, or mere numbers to be crunched in some apathetic economic model or military strategy:

The haughty eyes of people shall be brought low,
    and the pride of everyone shall be humbled;
and the LORD alone will be exalted in that day.

Isaiah 2:11

The wealth, ease, and shopping that so often accompanies oppression, the luxury that enables a lack of concern for the weak, would be overthrown:

> In that day the LORD will take away the finery of the anklets, the headbands, and the crescents; the pendants, the bracelets, and the scarfs; the headdresses, the armlets, the sashes, the perfume boxes, and the amulets; the signet rings and nose rings; the festal robes, the mantles, the cloaks, and the handbags; the garments of gauze, the linen garments, the turbans, and the veils.

Isaiah 3:18–23

Similarly the prophet Amos pronounced judgment upon such indulgence:

> On the day I punish Israel for its transgressions,
>   I will punish the altars of Bethel,
> and the horns of the altar shall be cut off
>   and fall to the ground.
> I will tear down the winter house as well as the summer house;
>   and the houses of ivory shall perish,
> and the great houses shall come to an end,
> says the LORD.

Amos 3:14–15

Amos impudently compared the wealthy women of Israel with the fat cows grazing in the verdant pastures of Bashan, and announced their impending doom:

> Hear this word, you cows of Bashan
>   who are on Mount Samaria,
> who oppress the poor, who crush the needy,
>   who say to their husbands, "Bring something to drink!"
> The Lord GOD has sworn by his holiness:
>   The time is surely coming upon you,
> when they shall take you away with hooks,
>   even the last of you with fishhooks.

Amos 4:1–2

But the day did not promise mere punishment and wrath. Though the prophets declared that the unfaithful ways of the people of God would lead them to their own destruction, they did not give way to hopelessness. Much more, the prophets announced a day of redemption, renewal, and new creation. "Sin is not a *cul de sac*, nor is guilt a final trap. Sin may be washed away by repentance and return, and beyond guilt is the dawn of forgiveness. The door is never locked, the threat of doom is not the last word."[5] Thus the prophets declared that in the day of the Lord grief would give way to joy, poverty give way to abundance, and oppression give way to liberation; and their hope was no mere wishful thinking, but the confident expectation that the God of steadfast love, of faithful covenant commitment, would indeed bring about the day. The will of God would be exalted, the knowledge of God would fill the earth, and the abundance and goodness of God would overflow to all who seek his face.

> In days to come
> > the mountain of the LORD's house
> shall be established as the highest of the mountains,
> > and shall be raised above the hills;
> all the nations shall stream to it.
> > Many peoples shall come and say,
> "Come, let us go up to the mountain of the LORD,
> > to the house of the God of Jacob;
> that he may teach us his ways
> > and that we may walk in his paths."
> For out of Zion shall go forth instruction,
> > and the word of the LORD from Jerusalem.
> He shall judge between the nations,
> > and shall arbitrate for many peoples;
> they shall beat their swords into plowshares,
> > and their spears into pruning hooks;
> nation shall not lift up sword against nation,
> > neither shall they learn war any more.
>
> Isaiah 2:2–4; cf. Micah 4:1–3

But what will bring about the transition of the times? One must be careful not to oversimplify the shape of Israel's expectations for the coming reign of God. There were various expectations regarding what would happen when the Messiah or messiahs or prophet or prophets or Son of Man or king would appear. But one thing was sure: the day of the judgment, the day of the Lord would come, and the power of God would vindicate the righteous, and vanquish the unjust. The *parousia* (a word used in the Greek New Testament usually translated "coming" or "appearing" or "presence" or "advent") of the Lord, or of the "Messiah," would occur, and all peoples would stream to the house of God in order to know the will of God. War would be learned no more, injustice defeated, and all nations gathered together in worshipful praise to the Creator.

But there will be no gloom for those who were in anguish. In the former time he brought into contempt the land of Zebulun and the land of Naphtali, but in the latter time he will make glorious the way of the sea, the land beyond the Jordan, Galilee of the nations.

> The people who walked in darkness
>   have seen a great light;
> those who lived in a land of deep darkness—
>   on them light has shined.
> . . . .
> For all the boots of the tramping warriors
>   and all the garments rolled in blood
>   shall be burned as fuel for the fire.
> For a child has been born for us,
>   a son given to us;
> authority rests upon his shoulders;
>   and he is named
> Wonderful Counselor, Mighty God,
>   Everlasting Father, Prince of Peace.
> His authority shall grow continually,
>   and there shall be endless peace
> for the throne of David and his kingdom.
>   He will establish and uphold it
> with justice and with righteousness
>   from this time onward and forevermore.
> The zeal of the LORD of hosts will do this.
>
>   Isaiah 9:1–2, 5–7

On that day, the sovereign God would exalt again his will; the arrogance of human-kind, which led only to destruction, lust, greed, and violence, would be undone, and the compassion of God would fill the earth.

Centuries later, when Matthew writes his account of Jesus of Nazareth, it is this very text from Isaiah to which Matthew refers when he proclaims that Jesus "fulfills" Scripture (Matt. 4:15–16). It is the Good News of the long-awaited reign of the true sovereign that Jesus comes proclaiming. The long-awaited triumph of God has come, Jesus proclaimed. So repent, and believe in the Good News! The Good News is not first and foremost a message that gives one hope for the afterlife; the Good News is not first and foremost a message that one may have inner peace and tranquility; the Good News is not first and foremost that one may experience an "authentic" life; the Good News is, first and foremost, a proclamation that the long-anticipated rule and reign of God has now come in the midst of human history. The Good News proclaims that we may participate in God's new creation if we will repent and accept the new reality.[6] "The Kingdom of God in the New Testament," as Barth put it, "is both the life and the purpose of the world according as they agree with the intentions of the Creator. . . . The end and purpose of the world is the coming of the Kingdom: 'Thy Kingdom come.'"[7]

The Two Aeons

The prophetic vision divides time into two, as it were: there is *this aeon*, and there is the *coming aeon*. (*Aeon* is a Greek word often translated as "age," but that word may sometimes miscommunicate the biblical notion, so aeon will be used here.) The current aeon is marked by rebellion, and consequently, injustice and oppression, sin and death, estrangement and violence; the coming aeon is marked by faithfulness, and consequently, the triumph of justice, the forgiveness of sins, the defeat of death, reconciliation, and peace. The current aeon is marked by hatred and warfare, factions and strife; the coming aeon is marked by the lamb lying down with the wolf, and the child playing over the hole of the asp, yet unharmed (Isa. 11:6–9).

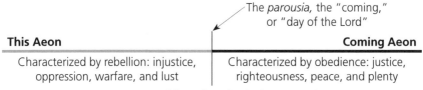

This Aeon	Coming Aeon
Characterized by rebellion: injustice, oppression, warfare, and lust	Characterized by obedience: justice, righteousness, peace, and plenty

The *parousia*, the "coming," or "day of the Lord"

Common Jewish Eschatological Expectation

The New Testament, in continuity with the Old, draws a sharp contrast between *this aeon* and the *coming aeon*, between "this age" and the "coming age," as it is commonly translated. So Jesus spoke of those who will "receive a hundredfold now in this age (aeon) . . . and in the age (aeon) to come eternal life" (Mark 10:30; cf. Luke 18:30). Or again, Jesus noted that "the children of this age (aeon) are more shrewd in dealing with their own generation than are the children of light" (Luke 16:8). Similarly, Luke reports that Jesus proclaimed that "those who belong to this age (aeon) marry and are given in marriage; but those who are considered worthy of a place in that age (aeon) and in the resurrection from the dead neither marry nor are given in marriage" (Luke 20:34–35). And again, "whoever speaks against the Holy Spirit will not be forgiven, either in this age (aeon) or in the age (aeon) to come" (Matt. 12:32).

Paul likewise makes common use of the term: "do not be conformed to this world (aeon), but be transformed" (Rom. 12:2). "Where is the debater of this age (aeon)?" (1 Cor. 1:20). "Yet among the mature we do speak wisdom, though it is not a wisdom of this age (aeon) or of the rulers of this age (aeon), who are doomed to perish" (1 Cor. 2:6). "None of the rulers of this age (aeon) understood this; for if they had, they would not have crucified the Lord of glory" (1 Cor. 2:8). "Do not deceive yourselves. If you think that you are wise in this age (aeon), you should become fools so that you may become wise" (1 Cor. 3:18). "In their case the god of this world (aeon) has blinded the minds of the unbelievers" (2 Cor. 4:4). Jesus "gave himself for our sins to set us free from the present evil age (aeon)" (Gal. 1:4). (See also Eph. 1:21; 1 Tim. 6:17–19; 2 Tim. 4:10; Titus 2:12–13; Heb. 6:5.)[8]

The Presence of the New Aeon

Much ink has been spilt by those who think it imperative that we calculate the timetable for the inbreaking of the coming aeon. But from the perspective of the New Testament, this is a relatively insignificant question—because the more fundamentally important claim is that *the coming aeon has already, in a very real sense, begun.* Even the Son does not know "the time" or "the hour" of the final consummation of the kingdom (Mark 13:32); only the Father, elsewhere called the "King of the ages" (1 Tim. 1:17), knows the times and hours of the final events of redemptive history. And even though that coming aeon remains yet in the future, there is in Jesus' life and ministry something occurring which embodies that future coming reign. The word "proleptic" is a helpful adjective here: "proleptic" is that which represents or characterizes something in the future as having already occurred, or already having been accomplished in the present. Jesus' life and ministry—and subsequently the life and ministry of the church—thus proleptically realizes that coming age, in which the enemies of God will be entirely defeated.

New Testament Eschatology

So Jesus "watched Satan fall from heaven like a flash of lighting" (Luke 10:18), but Satan's ultimate defeat still stands in the future. Jesus' healing of the sick and casting out demons likewise signified the presence of the kingdom: "But if it is by the Spirit of God that I cast out demons, then the kingdom of God has come to you" (Matt. 12:28). Likewise, the resurrection of the dead expected with the coming aeon appears with the resurrection of Lazarus and the son of the widow of Nain; in the ministry and life of Jesus, even the power of death itself is overcome. The demons were aware that in the work of Christ, he was doing what was to be done in fullness in that coming aeon: "What have you to do with us, Son of God? Have you come here to torment us *before the time?*" (Matt. 8:29; emphasis added). When John the Baptizer wondered whether Jesus of Nazareth was the one for whom Israel was waiting, Jesus told John's disciples to report to him the evidence: "the blind receive their sight, the lame walk, the lepers are cleansed, the deaf hear, the dead are raised, and the poor have good news brought to them" (Matt. 11:5).

It might be, then, that our English word "age" does not quite communicate what the New Testament professes: we must not think of "this age" as something that must end prior to the beginning of the "coming age." Instead, we might picture the overlapping of two aeons, of the new having broken into the old; the old still holds onto its pitiful existence, while the new is even now in our midst, its triumph assured. The eschaton, the end, is even *now* in our midst, but *not yet* fully. Thus we have even now "tasted the goodness of the word of God and the powers of the age (aeon) to come" (Heb. 6:5). Similarly Paul proclaims that we have even now been redeemed from this "present evil age (aeon)" (Gal. 1:4); and yet, "we ourselves, who have the first fruits of the Spirit, groan inwardly while we wait for adoption, the redemption of our bodies" (Rom. 8:23). The Father "has rescued us from the power of darkness and transferred us into the kingdom of his beloved Son, in whom we have redemption, the forgiveness of sins" (Col. 1:13–14). This triumph, however, is not yet complete: the final triumph over death and the redemption of our mortal bodies into "spiritual" bodies is yet to come, when God shall be "all in all" (1 Cor. 15:23–49).[9]

Likewise the gift and the presence of the Holy Spirit signifies the proleptic presence of the final purposes of God; after the death, resurrection, and ascension of the Christ to lordship, the Holy Spirit in the life of the believer becomes a sign and anticipation of what will occur in the end. So Paul depicts the gift of the Spirit as the "first fruits" of what is to come: "we ourselves, who have the first fruits of the Spirit, groan inwardly while we wait for adoption, the redemption of our bodies" (Rom. 8:23). Or similarly he describes the Spirit as an "earnest," as a down payment or first installment of what is to come: "it is God who establishes us with you in Christ and has anointed us, by putting his seal on us and giving us his Spirit in our hearts as a first installment" (2 Cor. 1:21–22; see also 2 Cor. 5:5).

Or then Acts 2:14–36 describes the sermon of Peter, which cites Joel 2:28–32; the manifestation of the Holy Spirit Peter takes as a sign that the "last days" have begun—a new era, a new aeon is now underway, moving us that much closer to the conclusion of the story of God's redemption of the world. The "last days" of the "old aeon" have begun. The rays of the new are appearing over the horizon. We may, very late in the night, begin to catch a glimpse of the first rays of the new day—the night is not yet over, but it is on its last legs, and the dawn is beginning. In the same way, the early church heralded the appearance of the new, knowing that they were now to live according to the ways of the new light, rather than the ways of the passing darkness.

But the sick healed and the dead raised were to succumb to sickness and death again; Lazarus died yet again. The sick healed by Jesus and Peter and Paul fell ill yet again. The full defeat of the enemies of God was yet to be realized. So the end, the eschaton toward which all things are moving has not yet been fully realized; the end, the goal toward which all history is moving, in which God will be "all in all" (1 Cor. 15:28), has already been partially realized in human history. But there remain forces and powers hostile to the lordship of Christ, the last of which to be conquered is death. We see it, then, yet again: the kingdom is here "now," but "not yet."

A decisive turn has occurred in human history—the kingdom of God is now in our midst—but its final and ultimate triumph lies yet in the future. The work of God, in forgiving sins, healing disease and affliction, overcoming alienation and estrangement, defeating injustice and oppression—this long-anticipated work of God has now broken into human history and will be completed at the *parousia* of the Lord. (See Matt. 24:3, 27, 37, 39; 1 Cor. 15:23; 1 Thess. 2:19; 3:13; 4:15; 5:23; 2 Thess. 2:1, 8; James 5:7, 8; 2 Pet. 1:16; 3:4, 12; 1 John 2:28.) But, as we have seen, the kingdom of God does not await only out somewhere in the future; the New Testament claims, given the death and resurrection and ascension of Jesus, that the kingdom has already dawned in our midst, has already come upon the scene—the powers and principalities and forces arrayed against the purposes of God have already been unmasked and defeated.

Thus the church lives "between the times," between the inauguration of the kingdom and its final consummation. That very fact accounts for the tension between "church" and "world," between disciples of Jesus and those who refuse to reckon Jesus as Lord. The church, those who walk in Spirit-empowered obedience to the way of Christ, sojourn in the midst of the still-rebellious world; and thus the church has a cross to carry, too. The church, by its very presence, by its very faithfulness, stands as an omen, exists as a judgment upon "the world," the peoples and institutions and powers and systems that continue to walk according to the old order of rebellion against God's way. "Between the times," the church waits, still embattled, beleaguered, struck down, seen as irrelevant to the way things "really work."

For good reason, then, does Paul use the language of birthing to describe our ministry "between the times." Only the pain of a mother in labor with a child suffices to get at the nature of current existence of both the creation and the church: "the whole creation has been groaning in labor pains until now," and we too, who have received the first fruits of the Spirit "groan inwardly" (Rom. 8:22–23). Imagine any mother, say, eight months pregnant, on the telephone with an old friend who had heard the news of the pregnancy, but did not know the anticipated date of delivery: "Do you have your baby yet?!" the old friend might ask. To which the mother would undoubtedly be thinking, "—Yes!—of course I've got a baby, of which I'm reminded on every frequent trip to relieve my bladder, or every time the dear one decides to roll over in the womb, or each time she rakes her sweet little arms across my belly." But then again, she does not yet have her baby. To remain eight months pregnant indefinitely would be nothing short of torment. And so she waits for the day—and the day comes, with pain and tears. The mother's body is transformed, and everything changes. Crying gives way to laughter, cursing gives way to joy, the groaning gives way to life.

In the meanwhile, the expectant mother must live respecting the day. To live without respecting the day would be nothing short of disastrous. A pregnant mother is already a mother. What a horror for a pregnant mother to live a dissolute life, to care nothing for her body or for the baby within, or to abuse her body. In the same way, the church lives respecting the day—the kingdom is not yet fully present, but it's already here—and to live otherwise is nothing short of disastrous.

In the middle of the twentieth century, New Testament scholar Oscar Cullmann provided what is, by now, a very well-known but still helpful analogy. Just after World War II, Cullmann suggested that one might understand the biblical concept of the kingdom of God by analogy of D-Day and V-Day. A war is often effectively over long before the final day of victory—a momentous battle may so turn the tide of the war that it both heralds and brings into reality now the not-yet fully realized victory. And so the Allied forces, in their invasion of Normandy beach, won both the battle and the war on that Decisive-Day; the war was as good as over, though many battles were yet to be fought, many lives yet to be lost, and many belligerents yet to concede defeat. V-Day was not yet in sight, the armistice not yet signed, but the war was over.[10]

It is this proclamation that stands at the heart of the gospel message. The Gospel writers record that in preaching the Good News, Jesus proclaimed the presence of the kingdom: "repent, for the kingdom of heaven is at hand." The long awaited day had appeared, the long awaited rule of God had come, the very kingdom of God was on the scene. "My kingdom is not from this world," John 18:36 recounts Jesus saying. But that his kingdom was not from the world is not the same thing as saying his kingdom is not *in* this world. Indeed, it had invaded the rebellious creation, and consequently all hell broke loose, or so it appeared. The "kingdom" announced by Jesus was no mere "spiritual" idea or a new "religion" or a new "personal relationship with God" or even an "opportunity to go to heaven," but a kingdom that threatened the very fabric of the political and social and religious status quo. After all, that's why the proclamation of the kingdom was always accompanied by the admonition to *repent*. Repentance, *metanoia*, does not mean feeling badly about one's sins, kicking or shaming oneself for one's wrongdoing. Instead, *repentance* means *change*, and without change, without deep, thoroughgoing change, one could not enter and participate in the kingdom.

The Savior

The Slaughtered Lamb

The alternative to how the kings of the earth rule is not "spirituality," but servanthood.

John Howard Yoder[1]

Just try to imagine that the Pattern is called a "Lamb." That alone is a scandal to the natural mind. Who has any desire to be a lamb?

Sören Kierkegaard[2]

Take Up Your Cross and Follow Me

The Christendom cataract makes Christianity a "religion," which we must endorse or "hold" or "believe" in order to have right standing with God, to "be saved and go to heaven." But as suggested in the previous chapter, the New Testament sees things differently. The gospel is not an offer of after-death fire insurance, nor is it even an offer of merely personal peace and serenity in the here and now. More, the gospel invites us to participate in the kingdom of God, that long-awaited rule of God, in which the rebellion, with its corollaries of lust and violence and greed and self-seeking, is undone. The gospel invites us to follow in the way of Jesus, who embodies for us the way of the kingdom.

One thing should be made clear, if it is not already: we are not called to *be* the Messiah, but to *follow* the Messiah. There is, unquestionably, a unique role given to the Son of God who is the Savior and Redeemer; it is ultimately God who will bring about and establish the kingdom, and not we ourselves, and it is not we who can free ourselves from the rebellious principalities and powers, but the redemptive work of Jesus Christ alone. In his death, Jesus as the Anointed, as Son of God, accomplished certain things in behalf of humankind that we were (and are) unable to accomplish ourselves.

But the Christendom model increasingly made Jesus' way of effecting reconciliation irrelevant to the way of Jesus' disciples. The cross of Jesus increasingly became a symbol of legal atonement that could be conveniently separated from our own lives. The cross is looked upon as something Jesus does for us—he dies so we don't have to. The cross is very handy—nay, is celebrated and extolled—for its religious connotations, for its announcement of divine mercy, for its good news of the appeasement of divine wrath. But the cross is compartmentalized, made a handy religious device, shelving the claims that the cross lays upon us. The New Testament, however, makes very clear that the cross is not something reserved for Jesus alone. The reconciliation effected by Jesus' cross was effected by Jesus as Messiah; the cross, however, was not for Jesus alone, but for all those who would follow him.

> If any want to become my followers, let them deny themselves and take up their cross and follow me. For those who want to save their life will lose it, and those who lose their life for my sake, and for the sake of the gospel, will save it. For what will it profit them to gain the whole world and forfeit their life? Indeed, what can they give in return for their life?
>
> Mark 8:34–37

It is common practice to "spiritualize" Jesus' cross in the lives of believers; but Jesus' call to bear the cross is not mere counsel that we should be patient in illness, or persevere in grief, or persist in suffering; the call to bear the cross is not mere spiritual counsel that we must patiently bear the suffering borne by all humanity, whether sickness or betrayal or failed dreams, and whether followers of Jesus or not. Surely our faith graces us with such virtues as perseverance, but this is not what is meant by "take up their cross and follow me." Instead, Jesus would have us know that taking up the way of the kingdom means taking up a cross, that taking up the way of the kingdom means we shall have to bear the brunt of the brutality and fear of a yet unredeemed world. As John Yoder put it so well,

The believer's cross is no longer any and every kind of suffering, sickness, or tension, the bearing of which is demanded. The believer's cross must be, like his Lord's, the price of his social nonconformity. It is not, like sickness or catastrophe, an inexplicable, unpredictable suffering; it is the end of a path freely chosen after counting the cost. It is not . . . an inward wrestling of the sensitive soul with self and sin; it is the social reality of representing in an unwilling world the Order to come.[3]

Taking up the cross means bearing the cost of faithfulness to the way of Christ. As Clarence Jordan put it, "Faith is not belief in spite of evidence but a life in scorn of the consequences."[4] The work of Christ sets "free those who all their lives were held in slavery by the fear of death" (Heb. 2:15), enabling us to live a life of love and service and forgiveness, without fear of the consequences. That new humanity does not live in fear of death, but confident expectation of resurrection, and thus a willingness to die with Christ. If we have thus embraced a willingness to die with Christ, then we can of course expect a willingness to suffer the potential estrangement from family members or old friends or esteemed acquaintances, if not active persecution by the representatives of the powers who believe their security thus threatened.

There is herein a paradox: the cross of Jesus signifies for the disciple both Christ dying in our stead (so that we need not die as slaves to sin, for his atoning sacrifice has undone the power of sin unto death), and Christ calling us to die with him (so that we must be willing to die with him, for the rebellious powers have yet to accept his lordship). That is, the cross proclaims that we need no longer die as a consequence of our sins, and yet we must die, or be willing to do so, because of the world's sins.

Consider in more detail the two sides of this paradox. Often in Scripture, death symbolizes the full outworking of sin and rebellion—"in the day that you eat of it you shall die," proclaimed God in the garden (Gen. 2:17); "the wages of sin is death," proclaimed Paul (Rom. 6:23). What we might call the "natural" outworking of enslavement to the rebellious powers is death. But the power of resurrection now working in the believer frees us from the "law of sin and death," so that we need not "yield our members as servants of unrighteousness," we need no longer live under slavery to sin unto death (see remainder of Rom. 6). We need no longer die because of our sins. And yet living between the times, living while still awaiting the *parousia* of the Lord, in which all the enemies will be undone, the last enemy of which is death, walking in the way of the Lord means that we shall suffer death because of the ongoing rebellion of the world. "The servant is not greater than the master." "If they had loved me, they would have loved you." Because the principalities and powers have yet to submit to God's purposes, and because the final enemy, death, has not yet been defeated, we shall yet have to suffer at the hands of the rebellious powers.

The early church, Clarence Jordan noted, did not preach the ethic of Jesus—it preached the resurrection of Jesus from the dead. Proclaiming resurrection from the dead strikes at the heart of fear, for fear is grounded in self-preservation. And death is the great enemy of self-preservation. If the specter of death be on the horizon, fear will keep us from acting in faith. The message of resurrection proclaims that death has been defeated, and thus we cannot be beaten. The one who is in us, the one who is in our midst, is greater than the one who is in the world. The power of resurrection—and the love, vindicated by the resurrection, in which there is no fear—vanquishes all foes.[5]

Accepting this call to take up the cross is all very different, of course, from what is often meant by "conversion" or "taking Jesus as my personal Lord and Savior" or "getting religion." Too often such "invitations" to "conversion" fail to communicate that receiving Jesus as Lord means joining him on the road to Jerusalem, where the Son of Man is slandered, abused, spat upon, and killed. The invitation to baptism must never be far removed from the stories of the lives of the "saints," or the suffering of the martyrs. Baptism means an embrace of the kind of faithfulness embodied in the Anabaptist martyr Dirk Willems. Captured and imprisoned for various Anabaptist "heresies," Willems had opportunity to escape his captors, and he fled for his life. A deputy (of sorts) pursued Willems; it being winter, some ice had formed across the water over which Willems took flight. The deputy, however, fell through the ice—and when Willems perceived that his pursuer might lose his life, he returned to the scene, pulling the deputy from peril. When the deputy's superior arrived on the scene, the deputy argued that Willems should be released. But when reminded of his oath of fidelity to law and order, the deputy seized Willems and returned him to captivity. In time, "after severe imprisonment and great trials," Willems was slowly burned to death outside the village.[6]

Precisely because we live "between the times," precisely because the kingdom of God has come, but has not yet been fully established in God's still rebellious creation, we must be willing to embrace Jesus' call to bear the cross. To take on the way of the kingdom—of loving enemies, forgiving offenses, sharing wealth—when the world continues yet in rebellion to the ways of God means that we shall suffer. It is in this way that we are to understand the "imitation of Christ." The New Testament does *not* call us to "imitate Christ" in every facet of Jesus' life; we are not called to imitate Jesus the carpenter, taking up manual labor as the only legitimate employ of the disciple. We are not called to imitate Jesus' socioeconomic context, taking up an agrarian lifestyle among peasants. We are not called to imitate Jesus' supposed diet, even if his diet was undoubtedly healthier than the regimen of fast food that often fills our bellies. There is, of course, much spiritual wisdom in living a life in which we have regular periods of manual labor, or times in which we enjoy the peace and tranquility of nature, or a diet of whole grains and fish and fruits and vegetables. "Man shall not live by super-sized combos alone." But any of these characteristics we might identify of Jesus' life are *not* the point at which the New Testament counsels us to imitate Jesus.

The point of imitation of Jesus is found in the cross. It is the cross we are called to imitate, joyfully accepting suffering, joyfully bearing the injustices and oppression and rebellion of our world, because we are living according to the present and coming kingdom, in the midst of a world still rebellious. Ephesians pronounces, for example, that it was through the crucifixion, through the blood of Christ that Jesus made peace, reconciling Jew and Gentile, breaking down the hostility, creating the "one new humanity" (Eph. 2:13–18). Shortly thereafter, the disciples are admonished, "Therefore be imitators of God, as beloved children, and live in love, as Christ loved us and gave himself up for us, a fragrant offering and sacrifice to God" (5:1–2).

Similarly, in Colossians, Jesus serves as the fullest representation, the fullest embodiment of the will and purposes of God, and indeed the very hope of God for his creation (Col. 1:15–20, 24–29; 2:8–15). Furthermore, "God was pleased to reconcile to himself all things, whether on earth or in heaven, by making peace through the blood of his cross (Col. 1:20). Significantly, Paul's suffering is depicted as "completing" the suffering of Christ: "I am now rejoicing in my sufferings for your sake, and in my flesh I am completing what is lacking in Christ's afflictions for the sake of his body, that is, the church" (Col. 1:24).

Similarly, Paul's correspondence to the Philippians proclaims that the very same mind of Christ—the intention of Christ that led him to crucifixion—is to be the same mind in us:

> Let the same mind be in you that was in Christ Jesus, who, though he was in the form of God, did not regard equality with God as something to be exploited, but emptied himself, taking the form of a slave, being born in human likeness. And being found in human form, he humbled himself and became obedient to the point of death—even death on a cross.
>
> Philippians 2:5–8

Examples could be multiplied:

> Therefore, since we are surrounded by so great a cloud of witnesses, let us also lay aside every weight and the sin that clings so closely, and let us run with perseverance

the race that is set before us, looking to Jesus the pioneer and perfecter of our faith, who for the sake of the joy that was set before him endured the cross.

Hebrews 12:1–2

If you endure when you do right and suffer for it, you have God's approval. For to this you have been called, because Christ also suffered for you, leaving you an example, so that you should follow in his steps. "He committed no sin, and no deceit was found in his mouth." When he was abused, he did not return abuse; when he suffered, he did not threaten; but he entrusted himself to the one who judges justly. He himself bore our sins in his body on the cross, so that, free from sins, we might live for righteousness; by his wounds you have been healed.

1 Peter 2:20–24

For this is the message you have heard from the beginning, that we should love one another. . . . We know love by this, that he laid down his life for us—and we ought to lay down our lives for one another.

1 John 3:11, 16

One should not conclude that the "way of the cross" is mere passivity, a trust that God will make everything okay in the "sweet by-and-by," as if the pain and oppression of the world ought not concern us. Quite to the contrary, the New Testament proclaims that it is *through the cross* that God gains victory over the structures of the rebellious world. Or to use more explicitly New Testament language, it is through the cross that God defeats the "principalities and powers," the "rulers and authorities," which perpetuate the enslavement of sin and the oppression of the weak. It was *not* through the *resurrection* that the powers were unmasked and disarmed, but through the *cross*:

And when you were dead in trespasses and the uncircumcision of your flesh, God made you alive together with him, when he forgave us all our trespasses, erasing the record that stood against us with its legal demands. He set this aside, nailing it to the cross. He disarmed the rulers and authorities and made a public example of them, triumphing over them in it.

Colossians 2:13–15

The Principalities and Powers[7]

The Synoptic Gospels make much of Jesus' encounters with various forms of power and authority: the kingdom of God comes with a Messiah who confronts demonic powers, debates with and is framed by the religious authorities, and is ultimately executed by the imperial principalities. The Synoptic Gospels do not develop, however, a systematic accounting of these powers and forces. But in Paul's writings, explicit talk of the "principalities and powers," or "rulers," or "authorities" plays a dominant role. G. B. Caird notes that "the idea of sinister world powers and their subjugation by Christ is built into the very fabric of Paul's thought, and some mention of them is found in every epistle except Philemon."[8] Just a few examples will suffice here: Satan constantly frustrates Paul's missionary endeavors (1 Thess. 2:18; 2 Cor. 12:7). The "elemental spirits of the world" hold Jew and Gentile both in bondage (Gal. 4:3; Col. 2:8, 20). Given the discussion above, it is also important to note that these powers are linked to "this age": "the god of this world (aeon) has blinded the minds of the unbelievers" (2 Cor. 4:4). And the triumph of these powers has begun to be overthrown: "You were dead through the trespasses and sins in which you once lived, following the course (aeon) of this world, following the ruler of the power of the air, the spirit that is now at work among those who are disobedient" (Eph. 2:1–2).

What are these "principalities and powers" or "authorities" or "rulers"? At a minimum, this notion points us to the fact that there is something beyond mere mechanical and materialistic and historical explanations for things—to accept the worldview of the New Testament, there are "powers and principalities and rulers" behind the institutions and religions and empires and tyrants that govern and order our world. A bridge is more than just cables and girders; a religion is more than a set of beliefs; one's psyche is more than the thoughts and experiences organized therein.[9] In other words, the whole is more than the sum of the parts. And there's a "something" about the whole of human history that is more than can be explained by merely looking at the parts, by merely looking at the elements that can be tangibly seen and recounted.

It is this "something," this force or inertia or spirituality, that the New Testament labels the "principalities and powers." In human history, and in and among the institutions and organizations and movements of human culture, the rebellious principalities and powers are at work. But rather than serving humankind according to God's original intention, they enslave; rather than freeing humankind to live the abundant life in communion with its creator, they oppress. The gospel is not merely an invitation addressed to an individual and his or her God. Thank God it *is* addressed to the individual, but thank God it is much more. The Good News for Paul is the renewal of the entire creation, the possibility of redemption of all the principalities and powers, along with the individuals who participate in and are shaped by those orders.

In Paul's day, "principalities and powers" represented a very wide array of forces, systems, and powers in the world, both visible and invisible. Pagan religion, Stoic philosophy, and Greek thought all held to similar notions, though differing on the details: some thought in terms of demonic and angelic forces, some in terms of immanent causes of the world, some in terms of the powers of the state and government, some in terms of the forces of nature. Perhaps common to all these is our word "systems" or "structures." There are all sorts of systems, processes, institutions that order and govern our world, visible manifestations of forces and commitments and values that are not always visible or easily identifiable. In Paul's thought, these principalities and powers work in a variety of systems and traditions. When Paul rebukes the spiritual snobbery of some of the Corinthians (where one may note the link between "this aeon" and the powers), we get a hint at this: "Yet among the mature we do speak wisdom, though it is not a wisdom of this age or of the rulers of this age (aeon), who are doomed to perish. But we speak God's wisdom, secret and hidden, which God decreed before the ages for our glory. None of the rulers of this age (aeon) understood this; for if they had, they would not have crucified the Lord of glory" (1 Cor. 2:6–8).

Here Paul indicates that the "rulers" or the "principalities and powers" were at work in the power of the Roman Empire and the Jewish religious authorities. Romans 13 similarly uses the language of "powers" and "rulers" in reference to the empire. Paul also connects these powers and elemental spirits to the power of religious law (Gal. 4:3), and apparently to astrology, which was thought by many in Paul's day to be a system that exercised control over people's lives (Col. 2:8, 20). To use contemporary examples, we might list the state or politics, the media or national interest, commonly accepted moral norms or educational institutions. Or, to systematize the list, we might enumerate "religious structures, intellectual structures (-ologies and -isms), moral structures (codes and customs), political structures (the tyrant, the market, the school, the courts, race, and nation)."[10]

What are the source and intention and destiny of these powers? Four convictions apparently underlie Paul's beliefs about the powers.[11] Put most simplistically, we may say, from Paul's perspective, (1) that the powers are created by God as good; (2) that they are fallen, and therefore in rebellion against the original purposes of God; in this fallen state, rather than serving humankind, they enslave it; (3) that the powers are used by God for good even in their state of rebellion; and (4) the domination of the powers has been broken by the work of Christ.

First, the powers were created by God for good.

> He is the image of the invisible God, the firstborn of all creation; for in him all things
> in heaven and on earth were created, things visible and invisible, whether thrones

or dominions or rulers or powers—all things have been created through him and for him. He himself is before all things, and in him all things hold together.

Colossians 1:15–17

In Christ "all things hold together." This provides a clue to the purposes of the powers: to help order and systematize human existence. Life cannot be lived without order and structure. Society, culture, and history all require the structures and systems represented by the principalities and powers. Education, family, economic exchange, moral norms, cultural norms and expectations—these are all structures upon which human life is dependent.

Second, these powers have rebelled and are fallen from the original good purposes of God. The powers are meant to serve a role in submission to the will and purposes of God, but they demand submission to themselves; they become, as Walter Wink puts it, "hell-bent" on control, and so become an idolatrous parody upon the authority of God.[12] "Civilization," "democracy," "freedom," "economic well-being" are all values good in themselves, but they become idolatrous. Demanding absolute submission to themselves, they enslave humankind and dominate those they were meant to serve. So Paul often uses the language of "slavery" to describe the plight of humankind. We become enslaved to the structures necessary for life when they claim status as an idol that demands our total submission: created to help us live a life of freedom and love, the powers demand submission to themselves as having absolute value, and so in turn harm and enslave us.

Third, and requiring more comment here: through God's divine control, the powers are used for good even in their state of rebellion. This is the point of Romans 13 (particularly evident when taken in context of Romans 12). God can still use for good those powers that have not yet accepted the gospel. Unlike the Christendom reflex, which assumes that emperors serve as the primary channel through which God works in human history, Paul maintains that the people of God serve as the primary bearers of God's purposes for the world (cf. Ephesians 2–3). Nonetheless, God can and does in his sovereignty use even the rebellious powers, often manifested by emperors and kings and governments, for his purposes. The Old Testament proclaims that God used the Assyrians to punish Israel (e.g., Isa. 7:10–20; 8:7; 10:5) just as God employed the Babylonians as an instrument of wrath upon Judah, while Cyrus was later employed as God's servant sending the exiled Jews back to their homeland. In such cases, Babylon and Assyria—as the rebellious powers so often do, and just as Adam and Eve desired in the garden—think themselves sovereign; but the prophets declare that God alone is sovereign, making use of these empires for his purposes.

The offense of such a claim was not lost upon the prophets—the despised Assyrians?! The evil Babylonians?!—used as agents and servants of God?! It was for good reason that Jonah did not want to preach the possibility of repentance and mercy to the wicked Assyrians living in Nineveh, for this was the city the prophet Nahum (3:1) denounced as the

> City of bloodshed,
>   utterly deceitful, full of booty —
>   no end to the plunder!

The scandal of speaking of Assyria as the tool of God would spark the same emotional offense as calling the Yankees the minister of God while in the midst of the Confederate South during the "War of Northern Aggression," calling Hitler the servant of God while in the midst of London during the German Blitzkrieg, or calling Saddam Hussein the servant of God in the United States today. The Assyrians were no respectable, churchgoing folk, dressed up in their Sunday best, but ruthless destroyers of cities and villages, often decapitating their conquered victims, reducing towns to heaps of rubble. Like predatory lions, said Nahum, the Assyrian "has filled his caves with prey and his dens with torn flesh" (2:12). According to one historian, after capturing a city,

> The king's throne would be set up before the gates of the city and the prisoners would be paraded before him, led by the monarch of the captured town, who would undergo the most agonizing torture, such as having his eyes put out or confinement in a cage, until the king of Assyria set a term to his long-drawn agony. Sargon had the defeated king of Damascus burned alive before his eyes. The wives and daughters of the captured king were destined for the Assyrian harems and those who were not of noble blood were condemned to slavery. Meanwhile the soldiery had been massacring the population, and brought the heads of their victims in the king's presence, where they were counted up by the scribes. Not all the male prisoners were put to death, for the boys and the craftsmen were led into captivity, where they would be assigned to the hardest tasks on the royal building projects, where the swamps which cover so much of Mesopotamia must have caused an enormously high rate of mortality. The remainder of the population were uprooted and sent to the other end of the Empire.[13]

And yet Scripture proclaims that these very same Assyrians, used as tools in the hand of God, bringing about God's purposes, would be judged and punished for their arrogance and violence (e.g., Isa. 10:12–13; 14:24–27; 30:27–33; Jer. 50:17–20; Zeph. 2:13). Just because God has used them in his overarching providence does not mean that they are pleasing to God. And more importantly, just because Assyria is used by God to punish his people, the covenant people are not to become like the Assyrians; just because God employs Babylon for his overarching purposes, God does not subsequently call Israelites to adopt the ethic of the Babylonians.

Instead, they are called to do what God always called them to do—to be the people of God, to "seek the welfare of the city where I have sent you into exile" (Jer. 29:7), to be a channel of blessing to all the nations of the earth by bearing witness to the God of Abraham, Isaac, and Jacob. They are not called to withdraw themselves from the good of Babylon, but to seek its good—not by adopting the ethic of the Babylonians, not by buying into the myth that they need to get hold of the mantle of Babylonian imperial power, and not by defeating the Babylonians through revolutionary violence, but by faithful, obedient witness to their God.

In other words, throughout the biblical narrative God calls his people to embody an alternative vision of community life: the people of God live a community ethic that stands at odds with the unbelieving peoples that surround them. Through being a "peculiar people," the people of God can bear witness to the will of God, as well as bring about transformative change for the cities in which they dwell. Only by being what God has called his people to be can his people really bring about good for the cities in which they dwell.

Similarly, the task of God's people is not to "run things"—that is God's job, for he alone is sovereign. The task of the church is to be the church, a people living under God's governance, a governance embodied most fully in Jesus. So, Paul says, you are to

> Bless those who persecute you; bless and do not curse them. . . . Live in harmony with one another; do not be haughty, but associate with the lowly. . . . Do not repay anyone evil for evil, but take thought for what is noble in the sight of all. If it is possible, so far as it depends on you, live peaceably with all. Beloved, never avenge yourselves, but leave room for the wrath of God; for it is written, "Vengeance is mine, I will repay, says the Lord." No, "if your enemies are hungry, feed them; if they are thirsty, give them something to drink; for by doing this you will heap burning coals on their heads." Do not be overcome by evil, but overcome evil with good.
>
> Romans 12:14–21

But, Paul immediately goes on to say, even the authorities and powers—those who do not return good for evil, even the empires who do not feed their enemies but starve them, even the nation-states who do not give drink to the thirsty but use war to destroy the infrastructure that provides water—even these authorities are used by God for God's purposes (Rom. 13:1–7). God is, after all, sovereign; God can bring good even out of evil. "We know that all things work together for good for those who love God, who are called according to his purpose" (Rom. 8:28). Thus understood, it would not have been possible for the Roman Christians, nor should we think it possible for us, to interpret Romans 13 as authorization for disciples to take up the ethic of the rebellious principalities and powers in the name of "good."

Fourth, since our lives do depend upon the powers, since culture and life are inseparable from them, the powers do not need to be destroyed—instead, their sovereignty and control must be broken, so that both we who are enslaved by the powers, and the powers themselves, might experience redemption. And it is precisely this that Jesus did in his life and his cross: refusing to submit to either the pretensions of the religious authorities of his day or the power of the Roman Empire, Jesus bore witness to the love of God, and he consequently suffered and died. Jesus accepted the rightful authority of the powers—for life is not possible without them—but he refused to submit to their idolatrous claims to sovereignty, and they crucified him. Yet his crucifixion was *not* a defeat, for in his death Jesus maintained his refusal to submit to their idolatrous claims: he would not let their threat of death deter him from living a genuinely free life. "Do you not know that I have the power to . . . crucify you?" asked Pilate (John 19:10). Jesus recognized only the rightful source and sovereign: "You would have no power over me unless it had been given you from above" (John 19:20). Jesus refused to fear even the power of death.

And so in his faithfulness, even in his death, Jesus triumphed over the arrogant powers. The cross was not a defeat, but a triumph, as seen in the text cited above from Colossians 2:13–15. The biggest stick in the arsenal of the arrogant powers was wielded to cow Jesus into submission to their way, and he refused. And in his refusal, he broke their domination. Or as Wink puts it, "What killed Jesus was not irreligion, but religion itself; not lawlessness, but precisely the law; not anarchy, but the upholders of the order. . . . And because he was not only innocent, but the very embodiment of true religion, true law, and true order, this victim exposed their violence for what it was: not the defense of society, but an attack against God."[14] Jesus' obedience showed the powers for what they were: full of pretense and pride, willing to smash any who would threaten their agenda of domination and self-interest. And in his obedience, he stripped them of their delusory ability to oppress.

Thus some day those principalities and powers and rulers will acknowledge his lordship; some day "every tongue" will "confess that Jesus Christ is Lord, to the glory of God the Father" (Phil. 2:11). Meanwhile, all those who live in a way inconsistent with his lordship live foolishly, for the coming kingdom is here already, and the old is even now passing away. "For the present form of this world is passing away," Paul declared (1 Cor. 7:31). To live according to the old age, to accept the supposed "reality" is to stay on a sinking ship. To operate according to the rules of the nation-states and principalities and powers of our world is to try to keep the *Titanic* from sinking by bailing water with a one-gallon bucket. Or better put, to be "chaplain" to this world's unredeemed armies and corporations and banks, to provide a "spiritual presence" that reminds them of "eternal things" without actually calling them to the way of the kingdom, this is like trying to keep the *Titanic* afloat by bailing water with communion cups. It's a useless, futile task—and a foolish one.

The Cult of Power versus the Power of Suffering

The cult of power and might rules the principalities and powers of this aeon. Bowing the knee to self-preservation at any cost, worshippers of this aeon trust not in a God who becomes a Lamb, but the god who destroys enemies, seeks vengeance, and dispenses punishment. Isaiah condemned Israel for trusting in military alliances with Egypt and her unquestioning conviction that horses and chariots would protect. And yet Israel's sin is the sin of all those nations enslaved to the rebellious principalities and powers: reliance upon the cult of might, enslaved to the assumption that might makes right.

But with great consistency in the New Testament, the God revealed in Jesus Christ is a God who wins, who engages and ultimately overcomes enemies, not through might but through suffering, not with a sword but a towel. The very identity of Jesus as Lord or Messiah is authenticated by his *suffering* and *service* (cf. Mark 10:41–45; Luke 24:25–27, 44–49; Acts 3:18; 17:3; 26:19–23), and in that way, he overcomes the rebellious powers.

Consider two examples from Jesus' own life. First, his ministry to the outcast. Confronted with the power of a religion rooted in seeing law as an end, in and of itself, it was taboo to associate with "publicans and sinners." When Jesus, then, began to not only proclaim but embody a kingdom that refused to submit to such taboos, the hostility of the power of law and tradition targeted Jesus. As he refused to either categorize peoples or further alienate the outcast, the whispers began, his reputation became marred, and the opposition stirred. "What sort of man is this?" The Jewish law—created by God to serve, to liberate, but used instead to oppress—became a power against which Jesus had to contend. Repeatedly that power sought to overthrow Jesus, to discredit him, to trap him, to frame him, ultimately to kill him. But by simple obedience, Jesus overcame that demonic power, showing it for what it truly was: rather than upholding God's good purposes of mercy and justice, it was shown to be self-righteous, self-seeking, arrogant, and idolatrous. "Go and learn what this means, 'I desire mercy, not sacrifice'" (Matt. 9:13). Simply by being the Light of the World, simply by his embodying the Father's will—an inclusive love that unflinchingly showered the unmerited forgiveness of God—Jesus revealed the demonic power of those traditions for what it truly was. Just as a battery of overhead lights illuminating a dirty kitchen sends roaches scurrying to find a place to hide, so does the presence of God's Light threaten the works of darkness as they scurry to protect their self-seeking agendas.

On the run, their power and status and security threatened, the powers ultimately wielded their ultimate weapon of death—but Jesus obeyed even unto death. His obedience, his simply being light, led to his suffering. His suffering, his crucifixion, was required not by some abstract universal principle of "justice," as if the heavenly Father had to execute someone for those who violated his arbitrary rules. Instead, the cross was a consequence of being love, and light, and holiness in the midst of a rebellious world of vengeance, and darkness, and lust. The incarnation of a God who loves, and forgives, and heals, and offers life, and does so precisely in the midst of those who live by an altogether different order, could result in nothing but suffering. The death-driven, insane powers of darkness would not let anything threaten their supposed security, and thus they struck out—and in striking out, we see them for what they really are. These powers are no servants, but fear-filled and self-seeking, grasping after their own survival at whatever expense necessary. These are powers that will do "whatever it takes," that assert that the "ends justify the means."

Second, and similarly, consider Jesus' speaking truth to power, exemplified in the cleansing of the temple. In that act, Jesus clearly demonstrated that the nationalistic, self-seeking religion of Jesus' contemporaries offended God: "My house shall be called a house of prayer for all the nations" (Mark 11:17). Armed with an exclusivistic faith, the authorities sought to kill him, just as the hometown folks had sought to kill Jesus when he proclaimed in inclusive love of the Gentiles (Luke 4:16–30). The power of "religion" and "law" are real, tangible forces to be reckoned with. One does not question the "orthodoxy" of any given social grouping—whether local church congregation, or international corporation, or nation-state, or political party, or Christian college, or college fraternity, or Rotary Club—without consequences. Jesus insisted, though, that the law and the practices affiliated with the law were intended to serve humankind, not the other way around: "The sabbath was made for humankind, and not humankind for the sabbath" (Mark 2: 27). Under the power of sin, that which God created for good begins to dominate and oppress, and the only way out is through: that is, the way to overturn the false domination of the powers is to obey God's good purposes, to embody God's redemptive order, and to take the consequences that come from the rebellious powers that continue to hold onto their paltry, rebellious existence.

Our encounters with the powers may come in various ways, and we certainly need not think that such encounters will come only in the form of a patriotic nationalism waging war against "evil," or merely in the form of a Hitlerian tyranny. The powers certainly delude in that way (as I am suggesting in this book, especially in chapters seven and eight), but the rebellious powers may come more subtly. So the preachers remind us that "Satan never shows up in horns with a pitchfork." The delusion may come, for example, in the midst of a moralistic community that is more concerned to show its displeasure with an individual using a "four-letter word" than with an individual who has been enslaved by the self-serving goals of corporate America, or by a community caught in the throes of its own arrogance and self-righteousness. Moralism sees the keeping of particular moral rules (typically to the exclusion of other rules) as the end-all and be-all of "discipleship" or "faith." But such communities often are blinded to the degree to which their religion is death-dealing, precisely because the death-dealing of a moralistic community masks itself in a cloak of self-righteousness. In the name of "faithfulness," of being the "only ones," of walking through the "narrow gate," such narrowness is not of the kingdom, but of a rebellious power that seeks to enslave its adherents. "Woe to you, scribes and Pharisees, hypocrites! For you cross sea and land to make a single convert, and you make the new convert twice as much a child of hell as yourselves" (Matt. 23:15). Instead of offering good news to those enslaved by the powers, moralism's indiscriminate shoveling of shame prompts individuals to hide in fear, burying their failings, their sins, and their hurts, further digging into their hole of bondage. Created for good—do not lust, do not covet, do not bear false witness—the rule is perverted, becomes a power that enslaves, placing its heavy foot upon the neck of those already oppressed.

In the midst of such a setting, walking in obedience to the way of Christ may be perceived as a grave threat: compassionate service to the one alienated from a moralistic community may be seen by that community as nothing short of a denial of the faith. To minister to those with AIDS, to walk alongside the addict, or to serve the homosexual bears witness to a kingdom bigger than our moralistic agendas, and may be perceived as a threat. Similarly, our speaking truth to power in the midst of such moralism effects a moment of crisis. To speak truthfully, for example, about the pretense, pride, and hypocrisy so often buttressed by such religion may effect fruitful change. Or, on the other hand, such a community may lash out. But even should the cross have to be borne in this way, it already signals the defeat of such a power. It signals the power's defeat for those who have eyes to see—for it shows that walking in freedom and truthfulness and Christian liberty is indeed possible and life-giving. And it shows those supposedly "religious" and "faithful" powers to be not a dispenser of God's abundant life and freedom and wholeness and holiness, but a dispenser of death and fear and judgment and hostility.

Of course, we must ever be on guard against a martyrdom complex—our task is not to go out looking to suffer. Our task is to live as a faithful people, and given that the world continues in its rebellion, suffering will come. Our task is to be faithful in spite of the consequences, to walk in obedience scorning the shame, to walk in the new life that is, by definition, perceived as a threat to the darkness. This is, I might put it too simply, what the New Testament means by being the church.

In any case, the New Testament does consistently assert that Jesus overcame the rebellious principalities and powers through his suffering and service, rather than through powermongering and controlling and dominating, even on behalf of the "good guys." Indeed, the New Testament closes with this very assertion: that it is the slaughtered Lamb who is worshiped as the victorious one, triumphing over the enemies of God. John's Apocalypse opens to a glimpse of the majesty of God's throne room. But in spite of such a vision of glory, John is soon reduced to weeping. None can be found to open the scroll, found in the right hand of the one on the throne. The purposes of God for human history are unknown because the scroll is sealed. But one of the elders seeks to comfort John: "Do not weep. See, the Lion of the tribe of Judah, the Root of David, has conquered, so that he can open the scroll and its seven seals" (Rev. 5:5).

This claim that the Lord and his anointed have *conquered* is of great importance in John's Revelation. In fact, all this praise from the heavenly hosts is rooted in an audacious claim: "The kingdom of the world has become the kingdom of our Lord and of his Messiah" (Rev. 11:15).[15] John is not merely asserting that our sins are forgiven so we can "go to heaven"—his vision is of something greater. John—again, along with other New Testament witnesses—does not envision this victory as merely a "spiritual" or "otherworldly" victory, but instead points to the very real, historical defeat of the enemies of God. Our God's rightful claims over his world have been reasserted, reestablished, and renewed. The principalities and powers have been unmasked, and their pretensions exposed. John's use of traditional, military messianic metaphors underscores the manner in which he wants his readers to understand the very real historical and political triumph of the kingdom of God: it is the "Lion of Judah" and the "Root of David" who has triumphed over the enemies of God's people (5:5).[16]

Imagine the delight of church communities pressed down, oppressed in their minority status, hearing the news of John's vision: there is one who has conquered—there is one who has gained victory—there is one who has fulfilled messianic expectations and continues the rule of the throne of David—the *Lion of Judah*, the *Root of David* has defeated the enemies of God's people! But *the one who has conquered*, who stands ready to take the scroll and open its seals *is none other than the slaughtered Lamb*, by whose blood the purposes of God are fulfilled.

In continuity with the teaching of Jesus, John modifies the traditions of a militaristic messiah. The heavenly host does not praise a "Lion of Judah" who conquers as *lions* do, conquest through sheer exercise of raw power, through the ripping and tearing of flesh. Instead, one finds in Revelation a Messiah who conquers through *faithful witness* (1:5; 3:14). Through faithful obedience, the Anointed One bore witness to the true God. In the same way, God's people bear witness to that same God (cf. 1:2, 9; 6:9; 12:11; 20:4) through their obedience to God's commandments (12:17). Such obedience and faithfulness, however, results not in accolades from the powers that be. For those who do not acknowledge the triumph of the slain Lamb, such obedience can only appear as naïve, as ignorance of "how the world really works." And so the powers that be respond with opposition, with persecution, and ultimately with death (2:13; 11:7; 12:17).

But martyrdom—whether for the Lamb or for the people of God—is not defeat. Instead, it becomes the means of victory.

> Now have come the salvation and the power
>> and the kingdom of our God
>> and the authority of his Messiah,
> for the accuser of our comrades has been thrown down,
>> who accuses them day and night before our God.
> But they have conquered him by the blood of the Lamb
>> and by the word of their testimony,
> for they did not cling to life even in the face of death.
>
> Revelation 12:10–11

Strangely though, martyrdom is described as both a conquest for the beast and a victory for the martyrs (11:7; 13:12; 12:11). Surely *death* is, is it not, a *defeat* for the people of God? Surely destruction of one's opponents signals victory for the conquerors? To answer these questions rightly depends upon one's rightful worship. For those who do not worship the true God, the death of the martyrs is a victory for the beast (13:7–8); but for those who share in John's vision of praise, it is the martyrs who are the *true* victors (7:9–14; 11:12; 14:2; 15:2–3). As Richard Bauckham puts it, "the perspective of heaven must break into the earth-bound delusion of the beast's propaganda to enable a different assessment of the same empirical fact: the beast's apparent victory is the martyr's—and therefore God's—real victory."[17]

Awaiting the Triumph of God

The anguish experienced by followers of Christ, or indeed by those who may have received John's Revelation to the seven churches—wondering where is the promise of his coming, wondering why they continue to experience death and injustice—is not a new phenomenon. One of the central dilemmas of the Old Testament is precisely this question: where is the Lord of Hosts, almighty in power, when his covenant people are suffering injustice and abuse? Perhaps the most troubling text in the Old Testament is one of the imprecatory psalms, Psalm 137:

> By the rivers of Babylon—
> there we sat down and there we wept
> when we remembered Zion.
>
> Psalm 137:1

Exile for the people of God upset every facet of life for the people of God: witnessing the destruction of one's culture and symbols of identity, uprooted from home, and subjugated as an oppressed people.

For long years prior to the Babylonian exile in 587 B.C., the prophets had decried the unfaithfulness of the covenant people. They declared the word of the Lord, insisting that the people of God repent and turn away from their injustice, idolatry, and sin—and yet they persisted in their unfaithfulness. In response to such unfaithfulness, the prophet on occasion castigated God for failing to act more speedily:

> O LORD, how long shall I cry for help,
> and you will not listen?
> Or cry to you "Violence!"
> and you will not save?
>
> Habakkuk 1:2

"O Lord," Habakkuk seems to declare, "where are you?—how long will we have to wait on you to get to work bringing about justice? Your people are unfaithful—do something about it!"

So exile created theological problems. Not only did exile lead to social uprooting and political bondage; it likewise raised new problematical questions about God. How was it that the people of God could be carried away into exile, could suffer the abuse and oppression of Babylonian captivity, and God still be faithful to his covenant promises? This was a theological problem apparently not overlooked by Judah's captors: if your God is really much of a god, then why have you been defeated? So the captors, reports the psalmist-in-exile, taunted the covenant people, "Sing us one of the songs of Zion!" (Ps. 137:3). Angry and bitter, their hearts aching at the apparent silence of God, the psalmist forthrightly curses his enemies:

> O daughter Babylon, you devastator!
>   Happy shall they be who pay you back
>   what you have done to us!
> Happy shall they be who take your little ones
>   and dash them against the rock!
>
> Psalm 137:8–9

So the psalmist-in-exile longs for vindication, waits for the triumph of God, for God to break in and do-to-them-what-they-did-to-us. God, if you are really God, why don't you come down here and kick a little . . .

Psalm 2 preserves for us a model of kingship that fits nicely with the cursing psalmist-in-exile. This psalm depicts a commonly accepted model for the coming One or Ones—that Messiah would rule with a rod of iron. Psalm 2 is a "royal psalm," apparently used when a king was crowned in Israel. The Old Testament often describes the practice of "anointing," particularly when God through a prophet selected a king to serve his people (e.g., see 1 Sam. 9:16; 10:1; 15:1, 17). The Hebrew word *messiah* simply means "anointed one," and is equivalent to the Greek word transliterated as "Christ" in English. A "Christ" is a "Messiah," who is an "anointed one." In other words, "Christ" is merely a designation of one appointed for a special purpose by God.

Psalm 2 not only uses the language of "anointing" to describe the king (2:2, 6), but also the language of sonship: "You are my son; today I have begotten you" (2:7). Given such language, some take Psalm 2 as merely predictive of the "Son of God" identified only in the person Jesus of Nazareth. The early church certainly employed this language to identify Jesus (see Acts 13:33). But just as "messiah" was not uncommon language to use for the king, so "son of God" was used to describe at least one king in Judah, King David (2 Sam. 7:14; cf. 1 Chron. 17:13).

Kingship was never God's preferred model of ruling among his covenant people. Nonetheless, when Israel insisted that they have a king in order to be "like all the nations," God consented with this proviso: that the king serve as representative of God's concern for justice and righteousness in the community. God remains the *king*, the true sovereign of Israel (see, e.g., Psalms 24 and 47), but the anointed one receives the task of effecting righteousness and justice in the community of God's covenant people (see, e.g., Ps. 72:1–4).

In this task of effecting justice and righteousness, Psalm 2 prescribes the model of power, imposition, and empire: "Ask of me, and I will make the nations your heritage, the ends of the earth your possession" (v. 8). In other words, the psalmist anticipates that the Messiah will have dominion, and lots of it, and will have no hesitancy about imposing God's will upon the nations: "You shall break them with a rod of iron, and dash them in pieces like a potter's vessel" (v. 9). The desire for "justice" shall be sated with an iron rod—power and dominion, law and order, all effected by Messiah.

What Kind of Messiah?

Oppressed by Rome, there were not a few who longed for a Son of God to come with a rod of iron, subjugating their oppressors and establishing the righteous rule of God. Herein lies the key to the disciples' misunderstanding of Jesus' mission. They were not wrong in expecting a real kingdom that would make a difference in human history, politics, and culture. Jesus corrected them not for expecting a kingdom; he corrected them for their false construal of the *kind* of king who would rule the kingdom, and their false nationalistic and militaristic hopes.

The disciples, indeed, misunderstood; but we have too often misunderstood their misunderstanding. That is, they were not wrong for expecting a "political" kingdom as opposed to a "spiritual" one; they were not wrong for expecting a "this-worldly" kingdom as opposed to an "otherworldly" one. Instead, Jesus announced a kingdom that was *political*—in that "politics," in the classic sense, is concerned with the manner in which real communities arrange their affairs. Jesus announced a kingdom that was *this-worldly*—in that the rule of God was not far off in the heavens, but, even then, invading human history. "The kingdom of heaven is at hand" (Matt. 4:17 NRSV marginal reading).

The misunderstanding arose in their expectation of the *kind* of politics to be employed by Jesus. The misunderstanding arose in their expectation of the shape the kingdom was to take in the midst of this world. And it is this very question that stands at the very beginning of Jesus' ministry—what kind of Messiah will you be? *If you are the Son of God*, then how will you assert and demonstrate your sonship? Matthew, Mark, and Luke all three record Jesus' baptism, following which a voice from heaven proclaims, "You are my Son, the Beloved; with you I am well pleased" (Mark 1:11; cf. Matt. 3:17; Luke 3:22). All three Gospels also subsequently record Jesus being led by the Spirit into the wilderness to be tempted. Picturing Jesus doing battle with an embodied demonic spirit with horns and pitchfork or finding in these accounts spiritual nurture in the midst of our own time of spiritual desolation misses the point. What is at stake in these accounts is what *kind* of "Son," what kind of Messiah, Jesus is going to be. The identity given Jesus at his baptism by the voice from

heaven—"you are my Son"—is the same language used in Psalm 2:7 to designate the king of Israel. Jesus is about to go out proclaiming the present and
coming kingdom of God. So the important question in the temptation accounts
is: *what sort of king will he be?*

So the narrative describes the tempter presenting a number of options, all of
which were real, humanly possible temptations.[18] First, the economic option. "If
you are the Son of God, command these stones to become loaves of bread" (Matt.
4:3). One does not break a forty-day fast with large loaves of bread; Jesus is not being
tempted to satisfy his carnal hunger with a selfish show of divine power. Instead,
Jesus is being tempted with a relevant social option: if you're going to be king, if
you want to quickly galvanize support, be a welfare king. Just feed the people. In
fact, the Gospel of John recounts how, after the feeding of the five thousand, the
people wanted to make Jesus king (John 6:1–15); and so the easy way to messianic
power presents itself here. Merely meet the physical wants and needs of the masses,
and you'll indeed be Son of God.

Second, the tempter presents Jesus with the religious reformer option. Jesus, if
you are to be Son of God, if you are to be king to the people, would not a heavenly
vision of one suddenly appearing at the temple (as Mal. 3:1–3 envisions) lay the
groundwork for you to become leader for the people? If a merely economic agenda
does not work for you, what of a religious one? Jesus could decide, once and for
all, all the important religious questions; he could be the spiritual authority, giving
all the proper guidance and direction on how to please God and find peace within
oneself. Again, Jesus does not discount what we might call "religion." Indeed, he
takes up the traditions of cult and worship and seeks to direct them toward their
originally intended purpose: toward fashioning and shaping a covenant people
who show the world what God wants the world to be. So Jesus refused to reduce
his mission to the banal task of showing the world how to be religious, or how to
do church "right," or how to be a "spiritual person." His mission was much larger,
broader, and all-encompassing; what we call "religion," matters of worship and
ritual and assemblies, Jesus by no means discounted, but they must always be
ordered to the larger purposes of the kingdom of God.

Third, the power option. While Jesus had been proclaimed after his baptism
to be a divinely designated king using the words of Psalm 2:7, here the tempter
does not merely use the title "Son of God" out of context, but refers precisely to
the larger scriptural context for his last temptation: "Ask of me, and I will make
the nations your heritage, and the ends of the earth your possession" (Ps. 2:8). So
Satan takes Scripture apparently at its word: if you are to be king, if you are really
Son of God, then all the nations of the earth can be yours! Jesus experiences the
temptation to which many contemporaries yielded—a Jewish nationalism that

hoped for the militaristic defeat of her enemies. The temptation here is to be emperor, to bend the knee to the idolatrous power of empire. But Jesus refused. "Worship the Lord your God"—give ultimate allegiance only to God, not empire—"and serve only him" (Matt. 4:10).

Jesus would, of course, be declared king; and the official charges posted on his cross would declare his treason: "Jesus of Nazareth, the King of the Jews" (John 19:19). Yet Jesus refused to accept conventional wisdom for the meaning of kingship, refused to accept any of the paradigms of conventional wisdom. His model of kingship, and his vision of the kingdom of God, was not to "make the world safe for democracy" by the exercise of sheer force, was not to effect a "balance of power" through the threat of nuclear holocaust, was not to "rid the world of evil" through a never-ending crusade of "war against terror." He would not rule by a sword, but by a towel.

Three options, three temptations, three victories: Jesus will announce another way, a new way. Rather than the psalmist's model of the king ruling with a rod of iron, employing empire power and nationalistic victory, Jesus identifies with a distinct alternative. "The alternative to how the kings of the earth rule is not 'spirituality,' but servanthood," notes Yoder.[19] Jesus found his alternative in none of the options offered by the kingdoms of this world, but in the prophets of old.

> Here is my servant, whom I uphold,
>   my chosen, in whom my soul delights;
> I have put my spirit upon him;
>   he will bring forth justice to the nations.
> He will not cry or lift up his voice,
>   or make it heard in the street;
> a bruised reed he will not break,
>   and a dimly burning wick he will not quench;
>   he will faithfully bring forth justice.
> He will not grow faint or be crushed
>   until he has established justice in the earth;
>   and the coastlands wait for his teaching.
>
>   Isaiah 42:1–4

The prophet depicts a Servant who comes with such compassion and gentleness that a dimly burning wick, a wick barely able to hold its flame, will not be extinguished. The Servant would disrupt all conventional wisdom, all notions of the way things "really work." "Common sense" and "reality" and "what would happen if" would all be laid aside, unsettling expectations and undoing the prudence of the politicians:

> Just as there were many who were astonished at him
>> —so marred was his appearance, beyond human semblance,
>> and his form beyond that of mortals—
> so he shall startle many nations;
>> kings shall shut their mouths because of him;
> for that which had not been told them they shall see,
>> and that which they had not heard they shall contemplate.
>
> Isaiah 52:14–15

Rather than smashing the nations who stand opposed to God's purposes, the Servant comes as one who is "despised and rejected by others; a man of suffering and acquainted with infirmity" (53:3). Rather than effecting vengeance, or tit-for-tat "justice," the Servant "has borne our infirmities and carried our diseases" (v. 4). Yet such a strategy, given conventional wisdom, could do nothing but lead to dismissal and scorn: so the Servant was "as one from whom others hide their faces," "he was despised, and we held him of no account" (v. 3), for surely such a one who does not "win" is to be accounted "stricken, struck down by God, and afflicted" (v. 5).

> He was oppressed, and he was afflicted,
>> yet he did not open his mouth;
> like a lamb that is led to the slaughter,
>> and like a sheep that before its shearers is silent,
>> so he did not open his mouth.
>
> Isaiah 53:7

Remarkably, in the midst of exile, the prophet had called the covenant people to exercise *self*-judgment, to confess their *own* sins, their *own* complicity in the pain and injustice and unrighteousness of the world, indeed of their own exile. In exile, how easy it would be merely to damn the Babylonians; "no mercy for the Babylonians," and "happy shall they be who pay you back!" and "I wish I could smash your babies like you did ours!" And yet the prophet's depiction of the Servant declares that God's chosen one will actually suffer because of the sins of the covenant people:

> But he was wounded for our transgressions,
>> crushed for our iniquities;
> upon him was the punishment that made us whole,
>> and by his bruises we are healed.

> and the LORD has laid on him
> the iniquity of us all.

Isaiah 53:5–6

If we take the Gospel accounts seriously, Jesus self-consciously rejected the various expected modes of being Messiah and chose the way of the Suffering Servant. Jesus refused to play according to the rules of conventional wisdom, which gets depicted in the Gospel accounts as demonic temptation. But the crowds in Jesus' day, and much of Western Christendom in our day, prefers the demonic attempt at control and mastery rather than the way of suffering service. "We know what it means to be Son of God," they professed, and Jesus failed to fit the bill. So Matthew records a remarkable account of scorn being heaped upon Jesus, precisely because he failed to fulfill their expectations of being Son of God:

> Then two bandits were crucified with him, one on his right and one on his left. Those who passed by derided him, shaking their heads and saying, "You who would destroy the temple and build it in three days, save yourself! If you are the Son of God, come down from the cross." In the same way the chief priests also, along with the scribes and elders, were mocking him, saying, "He saved others; he cannot save himself. He is the King of Israel; let him come down from the cross now, and we will believe in him. He trusts in God; let God deliver him now, if he wants to; for he said, 'I am God's Son.'" The bandits who were crucified with him also taunted him in the same way.

Matthew 27:38–44

"You want us to believe you're the king of Israel, that you're the Son of God," it's as if they said, "then come down from that cross and kick some . . ., and we'll believe you." To such expectations, Kierkegaard said that "to rule the whole world with a scepter is nothing compared to ruling it with a reed, that is, by impotence, that is divinely." Or again, "Just because Christ was upon the cross proves that He was the Son of God. But humanity cannot grasp the divine mind. It would conclude that He was the Son of God if only He had come down from the cross."[20]

So both in Jesus' day and in ours, the preferred mode of effecting "God's will" or "good" or "protecting civilization" or "fighting evil" is that of the rod of iron. The accounts of Jesus' ministry and crucifixion and the Gospel accounts of his own self-understanding show us most clearly that the "God" invoked in "God and country" is not the God of Jesus Christ—because that God is invoked so we might raise up our rods of iron and show our enemies who's who. But Jesus transformed the meaning of "Son of God," and transformed the meaning of "king of Israel." The "crucified God" stands in judgment upon the kings, the corporations, the nations, the emperors, the rulers, the presidents, the prime ministers of this world who seek violently to wield power, to control and dominate.

The Church
The Body of Christ

Suffering, then, is the badge of true discipleship. The disciple is not above his master.

Dietrich Bonhoeffer[1]

I follow him to the cross, but not on the cross. I'm not getting myself crucified.

Robert Jordan[2]

The People of God and Human History

The Constantinian cataract distorts our vision so that we believe it to be the power brokers, the emperors, and the mighty who control human history. Believing that we must make things "turn out right," we seek to get hold of such power for the purposes of the "good" and the "right" and even "God." In Christendom, we try to employ the methods of the rebellious principalities and powers to beat them at their own game.

But one thing the Scriptures make very clear is this: the principalities and powers of this world, the kings and princes and queens and presidents—they do not run the world, though they may think they do. It is not nation-states that run the world or determine the real meaning and purpose of history, but God. And, as a corollary, it is not the unbelieving nation-states but the faithful people of God who are most important on the stage of history. It is not those with worldly might, but the obedient, despised minority whom God chooses to be a light to the nations. The *primary* characters in the flow of history are the weak, apparently insignificant characters chosen by God to walk in obedience to God's covenant promises. We will not "make a difference in the real world" by trying to beat the powers at their own game; we will not "make a positive contribution to culture" or "exercise responsibility" by playing games on the principalities' home turf. Instead, we are called to be a people walking in faithful discipleship to the way of Christ, and thereby to be the salt and light the rebellious world so desperately needs.

The ancient nation of Israel was often tempted to rely upon the might and wealth of the nations to defend herself against her enemies—in fact, she too desired a king to be "like other nations," precisely during a time of social and political upheaval. Perhaps a king, many thought, would provide greater homeland security, more centralized protection against the enemies of Israel (1 Samuel 8). Though monarchy was never God's preferred model of covenant community, God acceded to their unfaithful request. Once having established the monarchy, Israel was often tempted to seek out military alliances as further protection against her enemies. When threatened by Syria and Israel, King Ahaz in Judah toyed with accepting the coercive "invitation" of those two countries to join an alliance against Assyria. And some years later when Hezekiah rebelled against Assyria, he sought an alliance with Egypt, trusting that its military might would save Jerusalem. But the word of the prophet Isaiah denounced what we take as conventional wisdom: it is not by alliances with the geopolitical power brokers, it is not through taking hold of the reins of regional military power, it is not through seeking out a balance of world powers that one can bring about the good purposes of God or bear witness to the will and ways of God. It is, instead, through faithful and obedient trust that God will provide what is needed. The same word of the Lord came to both Ahaz and Hezekiah: trust the Lord, and he will provide. To Ahaz, Isaiah proclaimed, "Take heed, be quiet, do not fear, and do not let your heart be faint" (Isa. 7:4). You may be frightened because of the threats of the kings in Samaria and Damascus—but they are nothing but hot air, "smoldering stumps of firebrands," and before you know it, they will be taken care of. To Hezekiah, the "realist" king who was merely seeking a balance of powers in the Middle East, the prophet declared,

> Alas for those who go down to Egypt for help
> and who rely on horses,

> who trust in chariots because they are many
> and in horsemen because they are very strong,
> but do not look to the Holy One of Israel
> or consult the LORD!

Isaiah 31:1

It is not through the mighty nations, it is not through the wealthy power brokers that you are to be a light to the nations—it is through being the faithful people of God.

The New Testament shares this basic assumption that it is within the people of God that we find a clue to the meaning of history: the gospel proclaims "the plan of the mystery hidden for ages in God who created all things; so that through the church the wisdom of God in its rich variety might now be made known to the rulers and authorities in the heavenly places" (Eph. 3:9–10). Such a bold claim must indeed appear offensive to those who invest their lives and their hearts in empires and nation-building, for empires and nations assume that they hold the key to history, that their agendas are of ultimate importance, and that the good of the world depends upon the maintenance of "civilization." But this is the wisdom of the world, the wisdom of the defeated aeon; it is the cross, instead, that is the wisdom of God.

Jesus does not intend to bear that cross alone. Consistently, the New Testament proclaims that the suffering borne by Jesus can be expected by Jesus' followers: "'Servants are not greater than their master.' If they persecute me, they will persecute you." (John 15:20). The reason for this is clear: the church is the body of Christ, continuing to love, forgive, and reconcile, giving up its prerogatives of power and position, in order that it might serve. "Do you not realize that Jesus Christ is in you?" (2 Cor. 13:5). The church continues to proclaim the presence of the new order of the kingdom of God; the threatened principalities and powers will either receive the Good News and repent, or lash out in defensiveness. Just as Jesus bore the ministry of reconciliation to a lost and rebellious world, so the church has received this ministry of reconciliation and can expect to receive the same treatment. It is Christ who is in us, among us. It is the same Christ who set his face to go to Jerusalem, to be ill-treated, to be killed, who is in the church. The Christ remains in the midst of our rebellious world, for he is in the church—and he continues to suffer. John's Revelation proclaims that the continuity of the church's witness in martyrdom, in participation in the blood of the Lamb, leads to victory (12:11). Just as Jesus was victorious through sacrificial death (5:6), so shall the saints be (7:4–14). We might summarize Revelation this way: in the ring of human history, there's a bleeding Lamb in one corner and a dragon in the other. "Common sense" would tell us we should place our bet on the dragon—but there's a new common sense, a new reality, in which the Lamb turns out victorious. It's the people of God, the church, who are supposed to know that secret, because the mystery has been revealed in Christ.

"Do You Have a Church?"

Born and reared in Talbotton, Georgia, and son of a prosperous banking family, Clarence Jordan was an unlikely candidate to establish an interracial Christian commune outside of Americus, Georgia. Jordan had been a Baptist from his youth; he sang that common children's song:

> Jesus loves the little children,
>   all the children of the world,
> Red and yellow, black and white,
>   They are precious in his sight—
> Jesus loves the little children of the world.

But he saw from an early age that even if Jesus was no respecter of color, the precious little children of Talbotton were not all loved alike. In fact, the same hometown environment that encouraged his culturally acceptable profession of faith—himself having gone to the front of the church one Sunday to receive Jesus as Lord and Savior—likewise taught him that "a nigger was a nigger and must be kept in his place,"[3] as Jordan wrote later in his journal. Such irony struck Clarence with particular repulsiveness one evening: he happened to hear the groans of an African-American acquaintance who was being tortured on the "Stretcher," the Georgia jailer's version of the antiquated rack. "What added irony," as James Mc-Clendon tells the story, "was the boy's knowledge that the administering torturer was the same Warden McDonald who only hours earlier had been lustily singing 'Love Lifted Me' in the Baptist revival choir."[4]

In 1942, having received a Ph.D. in Greek New Testament from Southern Baptist Seminary in Louisville, Kentucky, Clarence set out with his wife to establish an interracial community based upon the Sermon on the Mount. The community was based upon nonviolence and a strict equality of ownership in all goods (taking Acts 2:44 as the basis for the practice). But even more radical for his day, Jordan knew that since the division between Jew and Gentile had been broken down in the gospel, the same was certainly true of black and white. So the community was open to all, regardless of skin color.

By the latter half of the 1950s, the rage of segregationists descended upon Koinonia Farm. The opposition began with the institutional church, when a neighboring Baptist congregation excommunicated Koinonia, given that "said

members . . . have persisted in holding services where both white and colored
attend together."[5] The national press reported more violent forms of opposition,
which began with threatening phone calls and then escalated to bombings, van-
dalism, cross-burnings, Klan caravans, beatings, legal harassments, and shootings
at most anything, alive or not—Koinonia buildings, houses, farm animals, and
residents. An almost complete economic boycott likewise threatened the existence
of the community.

In the early fifties, so it is told, Clarence approached his brother Robert Jordan,
who later became a state senator and justice of Georgia's Supreme Court. Clarence asked Robert to serve as legal representative of the Koinonia community.
Robert responded:

> "Clarence, I can't do that. You know my political aspirations. Why, if I represented
> you, I might lose my job, my house, everything I've got."
>
> "We might lose everything too, Bob."
>
> "It's different for you."
>
> "Why is it different? I remember, it seems to me, that you and I joined the church
> the same Sunday, as boys. I expect when we came forward the preacher asked me
> about the same question he did you. He asked me, 'Do you accept Jesus as your Lord
> and Savior?' And I said, 'Yes.' What did you say?"
>
> "I follow Jesus, Clarence, up to a point."
>
> "Could that point by any chance be—the cross?"
>
> "That's right. I follow him to the cross, but not on the cross. I'm not getting myself
> crucified."
>
> "Then I don't believe you're a disciple. You're an admirer of Jesus, but not a
> disciple of his. I think you ought to go back to the church you belong to, and tell
> them you're an admirer not a disciple."
>
> "Well now, if everyone who felt like I do did that, we wouldn't have a church,
> would we?"
>
> "The question," Clarence said, "is, Do you have a church?"[6]

In the minds of the Robert Jordans of the world, "church" means holding
onto certain "right" or "sound" doctrines, or worshipping in the correct way, or
having the "right" things preached. Jesus is admired, even extolled and praised.
Jesus is taken as my Savior, forgiving me of my sins, so I need not feel badly about
myself; "Jesus" may give me "meaning in life"; "Jesus" may give me "authenticity." Whatever the case, this mode of Christian faith does not embrace Jesus as a
master whom we are to follow, and certainly not follow to the cross. Filled with
such admirers, "church" becomes a community concerned to "do church right."
"Church" subsequently has little to do with discipleship, with faithfulness, with
such transformation that obedience to the Lord is truly enabled.

This way of thinking about "church" can, of course, take a variety of shapes and forms: there are those who set forth a set of "marks of the church" or "doctrines" to which one must hold. If one holds the correct doctrines, and worships in the right way, or baptizes in the right way, or does not participate in a certain list of activities deemed immoral, then one may, after all, be allowed entrance to heaven. "Obedience" is indeed required—there may be a very rigorous personal moral code that supposedly determines one's standing before God. But such obedience required may have little connection to the coming of the kingdom of God that challenges the systems and commitments and institutions of this world that stand in rebellion to the will of God.

There is an alternative model of "church," but the end of which is the same as the former. In this type, a "personal Lord and Savior" provides, to put it crassly, "fire insurance." The "grace of God" provides the necessary insurance that I will not go to hell. Though emphasizing "grace," in this model God remains a legalist after all, who must hand out punishment to *someone* for any infraction of his holy law—Jesus provides his blood, so we don't have to. This grace is "personal," having nothing to do with a new social order, a new kingdom order among humankind. Concerned almost exclusively with "forgiveness," "grace" is equated merely with "pardon," with "getting saved." "Good works" merit us nothing—though they may be construed as something we do out of gratitude for the grace we have received. The primary task of the Christian, in this model, is to "believe" and to express sorrow for one's sins.

Or there may be yet a third model, a variation on the second model: faith in Christ may be less about concern with heaven and hell, and more about inner peace with one's life. One might be called to experience inner "peace" in spite of the contradictions of one's life. When the emphasis upon an afterlife heaven and hell is removed, the same existentialist emphasis is found in the likes of Protestant liberals like Rudolf Bultmann: one is called to respond, as an individual, to the call of Jesus in a way that gives meaning and authenticity to one's life. In this way, too, there can result a disjunction between ethics and faith.

In all these ways, "the church" may end up being the greatest threat to Christian faith, because all these models of "church" proffer cheap substitutes for the gospel. When "the church" presents to the world a second-rate counterfeit, rather than the real thing, the original gets discredited. By playing at religion, rather than walking in the way of Christ, the church becomes its own worst enemy. As Kierkegaard put it,

> The established church is far more dangerous to Christianity than any heresy or schism. We play at Christianity. We use all the orthodox Christian terminology—but everything, everything without character. Yes, we are simply not fit to shape a heresy

or a schism. There is something frightful in the fact that the most dangerous thing of all, playing at Christianity, is never included in the list of heresies or schisms.[7]

In other words, a "cultural Christianity," in which many people ascribe to the "Christian faith," but few walk in discipleship, showing the world what God created the world to be—this is apostasy. "The apostasy from Christianity will not come about by everybody openly renouncing Christianity; no, but slyly, cunningly, by everybody assuming the name of being Christian."[8]

The Body of Christ

But the Clarence Jordans creatively offer us alternatives to such apostasy. In his experiment, Jordan and his friends at Koinonia Farm offer us the reminder that the church must first and foremost be a community of disciples of Jesus, and that the primary agenda of the New Testament is calling us to be such a people. Incredibly, the four Gospels and the book of Acts use the word *mathetes*, or "disciple," over 240 times. A "disciple" is a "pupil," a "learner," an "apprentice," one who typically follows a master or teacher in order to learn how one should live and conduct one's life. Jesus' calling of disciples, "Follow me," plays an important part in the Gospel accounts. Mere "ideas"—even "mere Christianity"—do nothing unless embodied in a community of people, and so Jesus, from the start of his ministry, called disciples to bear the news of the kingdom. Rather than accepting the existing social institutions as they stood, and reforming them from within; rather than seeking to establish top-down control and then dominate the masses; rather than propagating a merely "spiritual" message, Jesus instead set about to proclaim and embody the new order, the new kingdom. And so he called disciples to join him in that endeavor.

Typically, many interpret Acts 2 as an account of the "birth" of "the church," a fair enough interpretation to a great extent. But the assembly of people described there only *continues* the story of Jesus' ministry. Jesus *remained* in their midst; empowered by the Holy Spirit, the Christ remained at work in his body, the church. Just as Jesus had called an assembly of people to follow after him, living, loving, serving, and teaching as he did, the assembly of people baptized and gifted with the Holy Spirit in Acts 2 continues that same ministry. As Jesus called disciples in the Gospel accounts, so Acts records Jesus continuing to call disciples through the Holy Spirit in the gathered church. The body of Christ, following Pentecost, continues the work and ministry of Christ: followers of Christ proclaim the news of the kingdom, they share, they proclaim the forgiveness of offenses, and they reconcile peoples.

An *ekklesia*, the Greek word for "church," is an assembly that gathers together to discern how their common life ought to be ordered. The *ekklesia* that claims Jesus as Lord does the same, gathering together to discern how they might walk in faithfulness to their master. "Church" is, in other words, simply a community of disciples, gathered together to order their lives according to the will of their Lord who lives still in their midst. Such a strategy for church is no sectarian withdrawal from the world—it is, instead, the only and very public hope for the still rebellious world.

While the writings of Paul did not employ the word "disciple," he used another expression that provides an alternative way to get at this way of thinking about "church." Paul's favored analogy for "church" is "body of Christ." (See Rom. 12:4–5; 1 Cor.10:17; 11:29; 12:12–27; Eph. 1:22–23; 3:5–6; 4:4, 12, 16; 5:23, 29–30; Col. 1:18, 24; 2:18–19; 3:15.) There are at least two important aspects of the "body" metaphor to note. First, the "body of Christ" language emphasizes the ongoing nature of the incarnation. When the church is described as the "body of Christ," we get at the fundamental identity of "church"—a community of those under the lordship of Christ, who continue the work and ministry of Jesus. The church is called to be no less than a community that continues to incarnate (to embody) the will of God. In the incarnation, God becomes flesh, taking the form of a servant, working and living among social outcasts and reprobates, touching lepers, running into conflict with the authorities and powers, executed as a common criminal. Then for the *church* to be understood as the *body of Christ* has obvious implications—as he was in the world, so are we to be. Jesus of Nazareth, *the* way, truth, and life—he alone is Redeemer, not we ourselves. Yet the gospel proclaims that the Redeemer does not merely offer us the wonderful grace of pardon, but the grace of power, that we might live as did he, that we might continue to embody the reign of God, that we too might bear witness to the new aeon even now in our midst.

Thus "church," biblically speaking, is much more than "doing church right." Being church means *embodying God's intentions for the world as revealed in Christ.* "Church" is not about showing the world how to be "religious," but showing the world how it is supposed to be a world that reflects the intentions of its creator. The body of Christ, by simply being the church, exhibits to the world "the plan of the mystery hidden for ages in God who created all things; so that through the church the wisdom of God in its rich variety might now be made known to the rulers and authorities in the heavenly places" (Eph. 3:9–10). The church embodies the new social order, the new-world-on-the-way; the church exists as an outpost of the coming kingdom.

To properly understand "church," we must properly understand "kingdom," as discussed in chapter four. Eschatology must undergird our understanding of the church. We must ever hold before ourselves the "end of history," the goal or purpose or final destination toward which human history is moving, the reign of God over God's good creation, in which all rebellion will be defeated. We cannot know what we are supposed to do unless we know who we are; and our identity is known only in light of the story of the people of God. Our task is not to "think positively," but to "think eschatologically."[9] All baptized into Jesus Christ are brought into the "new aeon," the "coming aeon." We do not need to try to "run the world" on the world's terms because, biblically, the "world" is a realm that corresponds to the "present evil age," in which unrighteousness, lust, violence, hatred, and animosity reign; the church, instead, is the community of the Spirit, in which love, joy, peace, patience, and kindness reign. As Richard Hays articulately suggests, such an understanding of the church explains Paul's

> extraordinary affirmation that the purpose of God's reconciling work in Christ is "that we might become the righteousness of God" (5:21). He does not say "that we might know about the righteousness of God," nor "that we might believe in the righteousness of God," nor even "that we might receive the righteousness of God." Instead, the church is to become the righteousness of God: where the church embodies in its life together the world-reconciling love of Jesus Christ, the new creation is manifest. The church incarnates the righteousness of God.[10]

For this reason, the church will often be in trouble — or be seen as an incorrigible rabble-rouser or adolescent mischief-maker. Jesus was executed as such. If indeed "through the church the wisdom of God in its rich variety might now be made known to the rulers and authorities," then the church is charged with a dangerous task: making known the purposes and will of God to rulers, authorities, structures, and institutions that do not *want* to know the will of God. We are charged with "challenging the system." So Martin Luther King Jr., writing from Birmingham jail to the "moderate" clergy who had critiqued King's nonviolent protests of racism in Birmingham, suggested that in the days of the early church, the people of God were "not merely a thermometer that recorded the ideas and principles of popular opinion; it was a thermostat that transformed the mores of society. Wherever the early Christians entered a town the power structure got disturbed and immediately sought to convict them for being 'disturbers of the peace' and 'outside agitators.'"[11]

Or alternately, we might think of our role as analogous to that of the "whistle-blower." We declare to the world that what has been declared to be "real," or "the way things are," or "common sense," is in fact no such thing. Instead, the church declares that the kingdom of God is most "real," that "the way things are" is another name for rebellion, and that the wisdom of God revealed in a crucified Christ is the new common sense. The scandal of the Christ's incarnation remains in the body of Christ, the church.

There is a cost, of course, attached to such professions of faith. But this is the meaning of "take up your cross." I find myself consistently disturbed and unsettled, yet spurred on to greater courage, by those who have refused to waver in the integrity of their faith, even in the face of imprisonment or the threat of death. One of the ways in which the principalities and powers of southern culture (and southern church culture) continue to bear power over me is in what the psycholo gists call "codependency" — my fear of making others angry, or provoking dissent, or, God forbid, of coming under threat of reprimand or sanction. Southerners like me are well schooled in "being nice," in "being polite," and while such social virtues certainly have their proper place, they can become an idol that keeps us from realizing the role that the church should have in stirring up trouble simply by being the church.

This role necessarily follows, however, if we are to be true to the vision of the New Testament of "church" as the body of Christ, as the ongoing enfleshment of Jesus in the midst of messy human history. As Clarence Jordan's experiment shows, the principalities and powers of various stripes may lash out when threatened with the new order found in Jesus Christ, and the shotgun blasts and fire-bombings with which that community was threatened were certainly a reminder that following Jesus is no flippant matter.

One woman, incidentally, who came under fire while visiting Koinonia was Catholic Worker founder Dorothy Day.[12] Dorothy fully believed the church to be the ongoing incarnation of Christ, and along with Peter Maurin had set out in a faithful if haphazard manner to minister in the manner of Christ, bearing fruit in what became a community called the Catholic Worker movement.[13] The purpose statement of the movement, often published in the journal *Catholic Worker* was put thus: "to realize in the individual and society the express and implied teachings of Christ."[14] The love of Christ was not mere sentiment. Let anyone who thinks we suggest a utopian, romantic love come visit us, she once challenged — come, and smell the poverty and vomit, see the oppression and sickness. The love of Christ is no idealism, but an active love concretely exhibited in feeding the hungry, clothing the naked, being present to the oppressed. The teachings of Christ, she believed, were realizable and attainable.

Arrested numerous times for refusing to bow to the authorities in their propa-gandistic fearmongering (she and other Catholic Workers refused to participate in the legally required air raid drills in New York City during the Cold War), she sought to bear witness to a real alternative to the death-dealing state: through both personal charity and a concern for justice. Personal charity was extended in order to meet the real needs of individuals, and Catholic Worker houses have served millions of meals and housed thousands in their "Houses of Hospitality." But individualistic charity, necessary as it is, must be complemented by a challenge to the powers of government, business, and military, which so often facilitate the oppression and plight of the poor.

Seeing firsthand the manner in which the poor get caught in the cogs of the systems that press down upon them, living amidst the poorest of the poor in New York City, Dorothy Day referred to the fallen principalities and powers as "this filthy, rotten system."[15] Few could criticize feeding the poor and clothing the naked, but the challenge posed to such systems was often seen as a real threat. While Dorothy and Peter viewed voluntary poverty as a part of the journey of discipleship, they always believed that involuntary poverty was merely evidence of the ongoing oppressive work of the rebellious powers. Capitalist orders separated economics, social theory, and politics from a concern for the welfare of individual persons and were thus not to be trusted; Marxist orders, on the other hand, placed their trust in a dictatorship of the working classes and supposed laws of history and were likewise an insufficient account of the needs of people. The role of the church, on the other hand, was to be a community of voluntary sharing, a community that truly sought the good of all individuals.

Such "transgression" upon fields into which Christians are thought not to properly stick their noses was also seen in Dorothy's refusal to support the war cause against the Nazis. She was told to leave such issues to the politicians and theologians and keep to her work of feeding the hungry; but she refused, for she would not be party to compartmentalizing the gospel. Jesus, she believed, had a great deal to say about how we should treat our enemies, and the war-making apparatus of "the system" was an insufficient witness to his teaching. Whether in economics or politics, the world needed the "dynamite" of the gospel, Peter professed; the church was called to "blow the lid" on that cask of dynamite, allowing the gospel to make a transformative difference in the world. When the word of God was made flesh, "all hell broke loose," and we should expect no less when the body of Christ continues its work of faithful discipleship.

As "body of Christ," then, the church continues the work and ministry of Christ. But there is a second important aspect of the "body" metaphor, already implied but not explicitly noted: life in Christ is a *corporate* endeavor, not an individualistic pursuit. Our individualistic age and country easily overlooks the corporate nature of the kingdom of God. But since Christ calls the church to show to the world what the world was created to be, this cannot be done on an individualistic basis. Paul's use of the "body" language in 1 Corinthians emphasizes this communal nature of "being church." For him (as for the Hebraic mindset), salvation and redemption and participating in the work of God always occur within a community, as *koinonia*, as shared participation.

Undoubtedly, the New Testament does envision radical individual transformation, which the words "conversion" and "repentance" aptly denote. The person, including the very nature of one's thoughts and worldview, must be changed. Baptism, for example, is no less than putting off the "old self" of sin, and being raised to "walk in newness of life." But the ultimate goal of the gospel is something beyond even individual transformation: the promise of a "new humanity," or a "new creation." The fallen world lives and breathes based upon divisions, separation, and distinctions among peoples. But Paul declared that in Christ, there is a "new humanity," in which the people of God now comprise both Jews and Gentiles, breaking down the barriers of hostility and estrangement that separate peoples (Eph. 2:11–16). Similarly, Paul employs the language of "new creation"—"So if anyone is in Christ, there is a new creation: everything old has passed away; see, everything has become new!" (2 Cor. 5:17). Or again, Paul to the Galatians asserts that "neither circumcision nor uncircumcision is anything; but a new creation is everything!" (6:15). Given that Paul believes the "new creation" to have begun, he describes the Christ as the "last Adam," for death came through the first Adam, but now the life-giving Spirit comes through the second Adam, Jesus (1 Cor. 15:45).

In addition to Paul's use of the "body" language, 1 Peter uses other metaphors: there the church is described as "a chosen race, a royal priesthood, a holy nation, God's own people, in order that you may proclaim the mighty acts of him who called you out of darkness into his marvelous light" (1 Peter 2:9). As "aliens and exiles," as a band of pilgrims in the midst of a world still hostile to the good desires and intentions of the Creator, the church exists as a holy community that abstains from those "desires of the flesh that wage war against the soul" (1 Peter 2:11), and walks in the way of the Christ. Thus even when maligned as evildoers, however unjustly, the church acknowledges that it is to this very thing that it is called—being in the world as the people of Christ means that we will be in the world as was Christ, unjustly accused, unjustly suffering (cf. 1 Peter 2:19–22). As Bonhoeffer put it, "Suffering, then, is the badge of true discipleship. The disciple is not above his master."[16]

A Cruciform Church versus the "Way of Abundance and Power"

In a world of sound bites and thirty-second news briefs, bumper stickers serve as something of a dipstick to measure conventional wisdom. A bumper sticker I've seen in my neighborhood proclaims the spirit of this aeon: "The Way of Abundance and Power Prevails." Abundance and power, idols of religionists and secularists alike, apparently hold the key to the meaning of life, the sum of success in life. Such was the belief even among some of the Christians in the first century, so that Paul rebuked the "super-apostles" (2 Cor. 11:5; 12:11) for their arrogance and failure to understand the true wisdom that is found in the cross of Christ (1 Cor. 1:18–25). Some Corinthian Christians seemingly placed great value in a superspirituality marked by abundance and power. With apparent sarcasm, Paul reprimanded those who believed themselves to be spiritually elite:

> Already you have all you want! Already you have become rich! Quite apart from us you have become kings! Indeed, I wish that you had become kings, so that we might be kings with you! For I think that God has exhibited us apostles as last of all, as though sentenced to death, because we have become a spectacle to the world, to angels and to mortals. We are fools for the sake of Christ, but you are wise in Christ. We are weak, but you are strong. You are held in honor, but we in disrepute. To the present hour we are hungry and thirsty, we are poorly clothed and beaten and home-less, and we grow weary from the work of our own hands. When reviled, we bless; when persecuted, we endure; when slandered, we speak kindly. We have become like the rubbish of the world, the dregs of all things, to this very day.
>
> 1 Corinthians 4:8–13

So Paul admonished the Corinthians to find their wisdom not in the wisdom of this world, the wisdom of this aeon, but in the wisdom of the cross. "For Jews demand signs and Greeks desire wisdom, but we proclaim Christ crucified, a stumbling block to Jews and foolishness to Gentiles" (1 Cor. 1:22–23). Indeed, there is power and abundance in God, but a power that is revealed through the cross: thus the crucified Christ becomes "the power of God and the wisdom of God" (1 Cor. 1:24).

Followers of Jesus must be willing to follow him to the cross, to be crucified with him. We exist as a "cruciform church," as Leonard Allen put it, a community shaped like the cross.[17] The cross — foolishness to the principalities and powers, to the rulers of this age — is actually the wisdom of God, and the way of the church (1 Cor. 2:1–13). The world and its powers — whether religious, political, social, educa-tional, technical — have their forms of conventional wisdom. But Paul proclaimed that the wisdom of the rulers of this age is not the wisdom of God, but indeed is foolishness destined for failure. Instead, it is through the way of the cross — the way of weakness, suffering, and marginalization — that the Christian community is to reenvision all things, and to interpret the meaning of its existence.

So in his letter to the Galatians, Paul put it this way: "May I never boast of anything except the cross of our Lord Jesus Christ, by which the world has been crucified to me, and I to the world" (Gal. 6:14–15). Paul, of course, places himself before the Galatian community not as someone whom they might put on a pedestal and marvel at, but as a model of what they are to be as the church. "Be imitators of me, as I am of Christ" (1 Cor. 11:1; cf. 1 Cor. 4:16; Eph. 5:1; Phil. 3:17; 1 Thess. 1:6; 2 Thess. 3:7).

The boast of Paul, and thus should it be for the church, is crucifixion. "May I never boast of anything except the cross of our Lord Jesus Christ, by which the world has been crucified to me, and I to the world" (Gal. 6:14). Paul clearly believes that the suffering endured by the Messiah is paradigmatic for disciples of the Messiah; those who follow the suffering Christ will walk in the way of suffering, too. Paul uses crucifixion in a number of senses, among which are the crucifixion of Jesus and the crucifixion of "the world."[18] What might it mean to say that "the world" has been crucified, and what does that have to do with the vocation of the church?

For Paul the gospel declared freedom from "the present evil age" (Gal. 1:4). The "evil age" had a power akin to slavery: "Formerly, when you did not know God, you were enslaved to beings that by nature are not gods. Now, however, that you have come to know God, or rather to be known by God," Paul continued, "how can you turn back again to the weak and beggarly elemental spirits? How can you want to be enslaved to them again?" (4:8–9). Some were advocating teachings that Paul believed returned them to slavery to the *stoicheia*, to the "elemental spirits of the world" (4:3). But the gospel pronounces victory over the "weak and beggarly elemental spirits." How foolish—freed from slavery to the powers of this world, it's as if you return with outstretched arms, offering your wrists and ankles to be manacled yet again.

But what does it mean to suggest that the *stoicheia* have been overthrown? While the text does not provide precise answers to these questions, the context suggests a number of possibilities: immediate context suggests that glorying in the flesh has been overthrown (6:13); or more precisely, that glorying in distinctions, whether "circumcision or uncircumcision," is undone. Instead, all that matters is a "new creation" (6:15). Note the subtlety with which Paul treats circumcision. In a context in which some were making circumcision a mark of genuine relationship with the God of Abraham, it might be natural for those schooled in a "freedom from law" to respond with a negative counterreaction: "Ah, you think circumcision is the key, eh? Well, actually *you're wrong*—as a matter of fact, *uncircumcision* is the key to justification and the new covenant!" And so the practice of "church" continues today to be marred and corrupted by such arguments, the body of Christ fragmented and splintered into innumerable sects and denominations, arguing one side or the other: and precisely in the hostility, precisely in the alienation and estrangement, we have lost already, for in this way, "the world" is not crucified, for the barriers and distinctions and hostility continue.[19] So Paul responds by assuring the Galatians that it is neither circumcision nor uncircumcision, but a new creation in Christ.

The larger context (see 5:11; 6:12, 17) suggests a number of other possibilities: "the world" constitutes an order in which suffering and death are avoided—but given that "the world" has been crucified, Paul advocates a willingness to suffer, particularly for the name and sake of Christ. "The world" schools us in self-preservation, self-maximization, and self-realization; "the world" trains us to live and die, to kill and wage war for the "American way of life." But imagine the radical implications of a community that refuses to bend the knee to such systematic training in self-preservation. Paul instead commends a freely chosen acceptance of suffering and even death. In proclaiming that the world has been crucified, Paul appears to be declaring that that old order has been killed, and is on the way out. "For the present form of this world is passing away," Paul wrote to the Corinthians (1 Cor. 7:31; cf. 1 John 2:8, 17).

Another possibility is located in 5:16–24, in which Paul contrasts the "works of the flesh" and the "fruit of the Spirit." The power of those desires that produce the works of the flesh, Paul declares, has been broken. The power of sin to overwhelm an individual, to lead individuals to destroy their bodies, their lives, their selves—this power is broken through the power of God's Spirit, freeing them from the power of these desires. Large, systematic commitments, institutions, cultural values, and family dynamics empower the "works of the flesh" in our world. Addicts of all stripes bear witness to the powerlessness that pervades their lives. "Willpower" proves insufficient, with the addiction bolstered and fostered by vast cultural, social, and religious institutions and inertia. But it is this world, Paul declares, that has been crucified: its power turned off, its batteries drained. So when the addict comes to know sobriety, when the disciple willingly submits wholly to the reign of God and comes to know instead the fruit of God's Spirit, then the church proclaims the crucifixion of the world and its powers.

For Paul, God's grace is always much more than mere legalistic forgiveness of sins; grace is not a mere forensic transaction in which the legal accounts are cleared so we will not be sent to hell in the afterlife. Grace is not merely *pardon*, but *power*: for Paul, the gifts of God's love are manifested not merely in forgiveness (though certainly in forgiveness, which we desperately need), but also in freeing us from lives of "slavery," freeing us to be the people God intends us to be, seen most fully in the incarnation of Christ.

The church, then, is this Spirit-filled community of those who have received the gifts of repentance and forgiveness, who submit themselves to the transformation and renewal found in the power of God's Spirit. Paul's language of slavery

in Romans 6–8 merits some attention here. For Paul, the human problem is not
how to please a legalistic God whose law we have broken. The problem is much
deeper, much more complex: the problem is rooted in the reality of slavery to sin,
a submission to the power of evil that is both personal and social, both individual
and communal. Indeed, for Paul "the whole creation has been groaning in labor
pains until now" (Rom. 8:22). What is needed is some salvation—some *rescue*,
some "redemption"—from the predicament in which we find ourselves.

It is precisely in the work of Christ that that rescue is manifested in human
history. And so rather than having to continue in slavery, we are freed to walk
in the way of Christ. Grace that is merely "forgiveness" is what Paul calls "sin-
ning that grace may abound" (Rom. 6:1). Or it is what Bonhoeffer called "cheap
grace." Grace does not merely provide forgiveness so that we may be forgiven, but
empowerment to be the people of God, to be the body of Christ, to continue the
work and ministry of Christ in human history.

An alcoholic enslaved to drink, for example, commits all sorts of transgressions
in the cycle of addiction. For the alcoholic, lying and deceit become a way of life.
Transparency would threaten to reveal closely guarded secrets; duplicity is always
at hand. For some, theft becomes a practice—ever in need of alcohol, and with
insufficient funds to purchase drink. Relationships suffer, expectations go unmet,
families disintegrate. Jobs are lost, finances suffer, and despair results. The addict
needs, most certainly, forgiveness. For the relationships harmed, for the trusts
broken, for the money stolen—for all these things, the alcoholic needs the grace
of those individuals harmed by his deeds. And such forgiveness is indeed costly,
painful to give, and painful to receive. But were the alcoholic merely to receive
forgiveness—desperately needed though it is—this would not be enough. This
alone would not be good news for the one enslaved to drink. What is needed is
sobriety—freedom from drink, and more, a new life of freedom from duplicity,
pride, fear, resentments, self. The alcoholic needs a new life, a life lived in service
not to one's self, one's desires, one's pride, but in glory to God, in service to others. It is this that the gospel offers, the power to break the enslaving powers and
principalities of the world. Our problem is *not* how to get a get-out-of-hell-free
card; our problem is *not* a legalistic God who must somehow be appeased after
we've broken God's rules. Our problem—or at least Paul believes it to be so—is the
slavery in which we find ourselves, trapped and oppressed by "the way the world
works." We need "forgiveness," but not mere forgiveness—we need deliverance
from the rebellious principalities and powers.

Addicts do not come to know sobriety apart from the fellowship of a recovery
group. In the same way, disciples do not come to know transformation apart from
communion with fellow pilgrims on the Way. In fact, many addicts attest to the

fact that isolation—wanting to be alone, and to be left alone—accompanies their cycle of addictive behavior. (And our world arrays vast amounts of capital, technology, and entertainment precisely to allow us, in ever-novel ways, to be alone in the small little petty worlds of our own making.) But through the cross, the power of the "works of the flesh" is destroyed, and a joyful antidote to addiction offered—real community with friends on the Way.

In looking at possibilities for what Paul means by the "crucifixion of the world," one other important point should be noted. Though Paul envisions "the world" as having been crucified, he is thus all the more angered when various practices—what we might call "religious practices"—are employed to prop up the faltering *stoicheia*. The powers were down for the count, unable to get back on their feet, but "religion" rushed into the ring to pull up the defeated powers, encouraging them to get back into the fight. So whether through advocating circumcision (cf. Gal. 2:12; 5:6, 11; 6:15), adherence to "the law" (2:15–21; 3:1–14), or observance of "special days, and months, and seasons, and years" (4:10), various practices were employed to accomplish just the opposite of their intended purpose: rather than showing the world God's purposes for it, these practices propped up the fallen oppressive order, breathing new life into an old rebellion. And this ticked off Paul: "I wish those who unsettle you would castrate themselves!" he irritably wrote (5:12), apparently in a crass hope that the circumcision knife might slip and, missing its targeted foreskin, slice off quite a bit more.

Whether Paul's anger was "righteous" or not, his anger can certainly be understood—that the very ones who proclaim to know God's will actually support those powers and *stoicheia* that wage war against the purposes of God. The "dominant standards of wealth, wisdom and nobility," Paul Minear notes in his observations on these Galatian texts, "fuel social ambitions and inflame social animosities." And "religion" very often plays the role of perpetuating, rather than questioning, precisely these "standards of wealth, wisdom and nobility." This "religious" propping up of the powers only points us to the pervasive, assumed reality of what Paul calls "the world." Whether it be creating barriers and distinctions among people, schooling ourselves in self-preservation, or pursuing the "works of the flesh," all these things have such a pervasive acceptance that "the world" seems to be a very appropriate designation for them. For these things are simply taken as "reality," as the "way things are," and thus not to be questioned or toyed with. The struggle for survival and security, the ambition in which we school our young, the quest for "the good life" all apparently bear witness to the "reality" of "the world." Further, Minear notes, the world's "inhabitants have every reason to assume [the 'world's'] indestructibility, ignoring the degree to which its longevity depends upon that very acceptance. At every point we must recognize the religious character of this reality: it is grounded in ancient religious traditions, structured by perennial religious needs, expressed in deeply rooted pieties and loyalties."[20]

In spite of the pervasiveness and power of the *stoicheia*, Paul proclaims that all the powers representing "the world," the way of life, the social structures, the religious traditions that represent life in opposition to the kingdom of God—all these have been declared by God to be "weak and beggarly" (Gal. 4:9). There is, even now, a new creation, a new world, a new humanity that proclaims a new way of life—and thank God for it, because the old, "the world," has been crucified. It's on its way out, and the new is already on the way in.

PART 3

What
Disciples
Do

Worship
Why Disciples Love Their Enemies

You have heard that it was said, "You shall love your neighbor and hate your enemy." But I say to you, Love your enemies and pray for those who persecute you.

Matthew 5:43–44

Shadrach, Meshach, and Abednego answered the king, "O Nebuchadnezzar, we have no need to present a defense to you in this matter. If our God whom we serve is able to deliver us from the furnace of blazing fire and out of your hand, O king, let him deliver us. But if not, be it known to you, O king, that we will not serve your gods and we will not worship the golden statue that you have set up."

Daniel 3:16–18

*I*n the heart of London lies one of England's greatest church buildings, West-minster Abbey. Site of the coronation of kings and queens for almost a thousand years, the church is filled with historical artifacts—tombs of monarchs, monuments to prime ministers, tributes to poets. The Abbey is a magnificent architectural witness to centuries of European history and culture. Woven into the warp and woof of this place of Christian worship, however, is the honor paid to warriors. Behind the high altar, for example, one finds the Order of the Bath, dedicated to various knights, an array of swords and flags displayed to represent their pursuit of justice. Two additional monuments appear to serve as cornerstones for the entire edifice. At the far east end of the building one finds the chapel dedicated to the Royal Air Force, honoring their courage and bravery during World War II. At the far opposite end of the building lies an equally revered site: the Tomb of the Unknown Soldier. "Greater love hath no man than this," reads part of the inscription, commemorating the one who "gave the most so that man might serve God, king, country."

There is something profoundly disturbing about such monuments. Yes, Jesus taught that "Greater love hath no man than this, that a man lay down his life for his friends" (John 15:13 KJV). But what such monuments miss is the rest of the story: the Jesus we praise in our places of Christian worship is the Jesus who did not seek to kill his enemies, but love them. The Jesus we exalt taught us not to destroy our enemies, but pray for them. The Jesus we adore demonstrated his bravery not while taking the life of his opponent, but laying down his life for the good of those who hated him.

Worship and Ethics

Two facets of worship are often overlooked. First and foremost, worship is a matter of allegiance: whom shall we deem worthy of glory, honor, and dominion? To whom shall we ascribe ultimate authority over our lives? To whom do we pledge ultimate allegiance? Shall it be the rebellious principalities and powers, which often claim to be God's representative? Or shall it be the one revealed most fully in the slaughtered Lamb? Shall it be the beast of empire, or the God against whom the empires rebel? Shall it be the god of power and domination, or the God who wins through apparent defeat?

But worship is not only a matter of declaring allegiance to one authority over against another. The second often-overlooked facet of worship is the inseparable link between worship and ethics. Worship leads us to become a particular kind of people, a people who reflect the ways of the God we worship. Worship develops, forms, and shapes a particular kind of people. The important question then, is *who* or *what* are we truly worshiping? The New Testament points us, consistently, to recount the story of a God who has delivered through a crucified Messiah. That storytelling, that recounting of God's redemptive work in human history, becomes *our* story, *our* identity, and *our* profession of allegiance. In biblically informed worship we become a part of the people of God who celebrate *this way* of victory, *this way* of conquering, *this way* of defeating enemies. The New Testament celebrates not merely that God has won in Christ, but that God has won in the *crucified* Christ.

The description of worship given in the book of Revelation (already discussed in chapter five) illuminates this relation between worship and ethics. The assembly of God's people, gathered around the throne, giving honor and glory to a slaughtered Lamb, leads to a community of people willing to walk in the way of Christ themselves, trusting that just as God raised the slaughtered Lamb, so shall he raise those who lose their lives in obedience. To ascribe honor to a slaughtered Lamb—unless it be mere lip service—necessarily leads us to obedience to the way of the Lamb. God has conquered, and we praise him. And because he is worthy of our praise, he is worthy—and authoritative—to reveal how faithful followers are to participate in the triumph of God's purposes in human history. Because he has conquered, he is worthy to reveal how the church shall conquer.

The Authoritative One: You Are Worthy, Our Lord and God

The relationship between democracy and Christian faith provides a helpful case study for the moral implications of worship. Christians can, on one hand, be grateful for democratic orders. In fact, many of the practices of a democracy are analogous to practices of the church.[1] For example, the "right to free speech," even with all the difficulties involved in such a "right," is at least related at one level to Paul's instructions for the assembly of the church at Corinth (1 Cor. 14). There Paul instructs that there should be a time and place for all to bring to the assembly their contribution, to contribute their gift and insight to those assembled in the name of the Christ. "Free speech," in a way, respects this practice in which all are allowed to share their insight and perspective. Similarly, the right of the free exercise of religion relates to the freedom entailed in the practice of adult, believer baptism (see chapter ten). Christians can rightly celebrate the respect shown to individuals in liberal democratic orders, especially over against the tyranny of despotic regimes.[2]

On the other hand, the church cannot assume that democracy in the United States is an ultimate value to be preserved at all costs—because there are certain ultimate commitments in democratic political orders that stand at great odds with the Christian faith. In 1990, for example, political commentator George Will gave his approval to the judgment of the U.S. Supreme Court in its decision that "freedom of religion" did not permit Native Americans to violate a state law against the smoking of peyote in their religious services. Whether one believes

Native Americans, or anyone else, ought to smoke peyote in worship is here unimportant. Instead, Will's central thesis—a forthrightly idolatrous claim—is of great concern: "A central purpose of America's political arrangements," Will claims, "is the subordination of religion to the political order, meaning the primacy of democracy."[3]

Will supports this thesis by reciting standard mantras of classical political liberalism. The founding fathers wanted to "tame and domesticate religious passions of the sort that convulsed Europe." How might such a goal be accomplished? By refusing to "establish religion," but instead by "establishing a commercial republic—capitalism. They aimed to submerge people's turbulent energies in self-interested pursuit of material comforts." Religion then, according to Will's interpretation of John Locke, "is to be perfectly free as long as it is perfectly private—mere belief—but it must bend to the political will (law) as regards conduct." Thus the realm in which freedom of religion exists is restricted to thought, to belief, to the mind: "Jefferson held that 'operations of the mind' are not subject to legal coercion, but that 'acts of the body' are. Mere belief, said Jefferson, in one god or 20, neither picks one's pockets nor breaks one's legs."

Whether Will rightly interprets the intentions of the founding fathers, such an understanding of democracy is simply idolatrous. Discipleship is not rooted in "mere belief" that operates in the realm of the "private." Quite to the contrary, discipleship is rooted in a claim regarding the lordship of Christ—and *lordship* is meaningless unless it denotes a claim of ultimate authority. To claim Christ as Lord flies in the face of a constitutional theory that makes "religion" both "private and subordinate."

George Will affords us, however, an opportunity to question whether the church in America has more often interpreted Christianity through the lens of Western political traditions, rather than interpreting those political traditions through the lens of a biblical worldview. Are we to reduce the claim of the lordship of Jesus to "private" realms? Have we allowed our political traditions to indeed "domesticate" our own "religious passions"? Has our own pursuit of economic self-interest led us to keep our religion in its own socially irrelevant sphere?

The gospel is not merely a "belief system," giving mental assent to "sound doctrine" so that one might "go to heaven." The gospel calls us to participate in the kingdom of heaven, to embody the will of God on earth, empowered by the Holy Spirit to do so. We have been called to participate in the new reign, in the new social order proclaimed and made real by Jesus. This is no "religious passion" that we can "domesticate" through the joy of shopping.

The way of Jesus certainly would have us "believe the right things." But this is not "*mere* belief"—Jesus instead called his disciples to see the world aright, to

envision the world in light of the coming reign of God. As it was in the first century, so it is today: if we are to be *realistic* we must come to grips with the central
biblical claim that the kingdom of God has *won*. What is *impractical* is to submit
oneself to those fallen orders, those rebellious empires that are passing away.
As seen in John's Revelation, whether one views history from the perspective
of heaven or earth results in profoundly different conclusions: viewed from the
perspective of the throne room of God, the way of the slaughtered Lamb leads to
victory. Viewed from the throne rooms and Oval Offices of this world, such a way
is foolish, unrealistic, impractical, irrelevant: and so, better to keep such notions
"private," a matter of "mere belief."

John Locke and his contemporaries, however, had good reason to seek to "domesticate religious passions." Locke's own homeland had known decades upon
decades of turmoil, often rooted in such passions. Locke was not too many generations removed from the days of the English Reformation, to which a number of
monuments bear witness in Westminster Abbey. Early in that Reformation, Henry
VIII would execute, on the one hand, Sir Thomas More for not renouncing the
authority of the Roman pope; and, on the other hand, he executed those who would
not uphold the Roman doctrine of transubstantiation. The many executions of
"Bloody Mary" soon followed, as she sought to uphold the authority of the Roman
Church by burning dissenters at the stake; there followed in turn Elizabeth, who
did not share her sister's "Romanist" inclinations, and so used the power of the
sword and the stake to enforce the new orthodoxy.

Mary and Elizabeth now lie buried side by side in the same tomb in Westminster
Abbey; on a plaque in front of the tomb, a prayer reminds visitors of all those who
"laid down their lives" for the sake of God and conscience during the Reformation.
The irony of the prayer is that those who lost their lives during those turbulent
times lost their lives because Christian kings and queens killed those who would
not submit to the monarchs' agendas. That is, it was Mary and Elizabeth, in the
name of Christ, who *took* their lives.

The "religious passions," then, that classical political liberalism sought to "priva-
tize" were those Constantinian-like efforts to establish religion through the power
of the sword. It is no wonder then, that Locke and friends wanted "religion" to be
irrelevant in the ordering of society, given that the mainstream of recent Christian
history had killed so many, and destroyed so much, in the name of its Lord.

Few Christians today appear to think that "religion" should be "established" by
the power of the state. We have, nonetheless, held onto the practice of using the
power of the sword for "good ends." The "good ends" are now no longer religious
doctrines and practices, but—at best—notions of "justice," and—at worst—nationalistic self-interest. Now, rather than using the sword to uphold what was

once thought to be of ultimate importance (such as "church," "salvation," the "kingdom of God"), we make use of the sword for ends we know are not ultimate ("democracy," "free-market economies," and other liberal political values). In the medieval era, heresy was among the greatest of capital offenses; in the modern world, treason replaces heresy as the highest offense. The "lords" who "really matter" are the lords of this world, rather than the Lord of Lords.

Christians and Warfare

All extant Christian writings prior to the fourth century reject the practice of Christians killing in warfare.[4] It is easy to understand why. Why would one want to fight and serve an empire that persecuted you? Why would the church support an order that too often sought its own demise? But the early Christians did not reject killing in warfare simply because it was not expedient to fight for an empire that sometimes persecuted the church.

They rejected killing in warfare, in short, because it violated the way and teaching of Christ. Tertullian wondered, for example, "If we are enjoined to love our enemies, whom have we to hate? If injured we are forbidden to retaliate. Who then can suffer injury at our hands?" Clement of Alexandria proclaimed, "If you enroll as one of God's people, heaven is your country and God your lawgiver. And what are his laws? . . . Thou shalt not kill. . . . Thou shalt love thy neighbor as thyself. To him that strikes thee on the one cheek, turn also the other." Cyprian said, "And what more—that you should not curse; that you should not seek again your goods when taken from you; when buffeted you should turn the other cheek; and forgive not seven times but seventy times seven. . . . That you should love your enemies and pray for your adversaries and persecutors?" Similarly Tertullian acclaimed the command to love our enemies as the "principal precept," while Dionysius of Alexandria said, "Love is ever on the alert to do good even to him who is unwilling to receive it." And again, Justin asked, "If you love merely those that love you, what do you that is *new*?"[5]

Sometimes these early church fathers also raised the problem entailed in taking an oath of obedience to Caesar. Christians are called to serve one Lord and Master, and no other; if we worship the God revealed in Jesus Christ, calling Jesus Lord, and praying for his return, then an oath of allegiance to Caesar as lord clearly raises a conflict of obligation. But these two issues—killing and oath-taking—are not two separate problems, but the opposite sides of the same coin, seen particularly in Tertullian's discussion of Christians, warfare, and government.[6] Allegiance to the lordship of Christ is not merely a new "faith" or "spirituality" or "religion."

Claiming Jesus as Lord results in a particular manner of life, for which Jesus is the authority.

In other words, the claim "Jesus is Lord" was not for them merely a "matter of doctrine," empty of moral meaning. Confessing "Jesus is Lord" means taking Jesus seriously as Lord, as the authority for the believer: Caesar commands us to kill our enemies, and Jesus commands us to love them. Caesar makes use of torture and chains; Jesus calls us to forgiveness and holiness. So Tertullian asked:

> Shall it be held lawful to make an occupation of the sword, when the Lord proclaims that he who uses the sword shall perish by the sword? And shall the son of peace take part in the battle when it does not become him even to sue at law? And shall he apply the chain, and the prison, and the torture, and the punishment, who is not the avenger even of his own wrongs?[7]

Put differently, *faithfulness* to the teachings of the Master is of first importance; everything else must find its place within the sphere of obedience to the Lord. But once the church assumes a position of privilege within society, once the church assumes a mantle of power and "responsibility" within the empire, such "faithfulness" is thought to be naïve: "We must do whatever is necessary in order for the good to win." The "good guys" can now win, and the "good guys" *should* always win. Our task is now to do whatever is "necessary" in order to preserve and uphold the good.

But such logic refuses to worship, to give full allegiance to Jesus as Lord. Disciples of Jesus do not kill their enemies because they believe the gospel. Our worship is why we don't kill our enemies. The Lamb of God, through suffering and death, has inaugurated the new aeon, in which offenses are forgiven, sins remitted, and war is learned no more. The Messiah's proclamation led to the cross—but the cross was only an apparent defeat, not a real one, for on the cross the new kingdom was most faithfully embodied. As Yoder put it,

> Here at the cross is the man who loves his enemies, the man whose righteousness is greater than that of the Pharisees, who being rich became poor, who gives his robe to those who took his cloak, who prays for those who despitefully use him. The cross is not a detour or a hurdle on the way to the kingdom, nor is it even the way to the kingdom; it is the kingdom come.[8]

It is for this reason that Christians ought not kill their enemies. Christian nonviolence is not rooted merely in a few proof texts from the Sermon on the Mount or other Gospel accounts of the teaching of Jesus. Much more, Christian nonviolence flows out of the entire narrative of redemption and follows immediately from worshipping the God revealed in the slaughtered Lamb. Disciples do not advocate nonviolence because of an "optimistic" assessment of human nature. Christians do not advocate nonviolence because they naïvely believe that "being nice to people" always makes people "be nice" in return. Nor do Christians advocate nonviolence because they simply assume that we can "all get along." The narrative of redemption is much more realistic than this.

Both our Scriptures and our history books depict the widespread prevalence of sin; injustice, abuse, and domination are deeply woven into our social fabric. Though the twentieth century began with waves of unbounded optimism, trust in "progress" soon gave way to disbelief and despair. Technology allowed us to build bigger and better weapon systems to kill more people; industrialization allowed us to mass produce those bigger and better weapons; mass media allowed the propaganda-driven mobilization of entire populations to use that technology and industrialization in service of killing their "enemies."

Hitler's anti-Semitic Holocaust remains an indescribable horror of our age. But Paul reminded his Roman readers that they ought not judge others when they thereby condemn themselves: in response to the injustice of others, and in the name of utilitarianism, United States forces likewise decimated Japanese men, women, and children in our firebombing of Tokyo and our nuclear destruction of Hiroshima and Nagasaki. In its Cold War wake, our idolatrous divinization of science and technology brought about such a mindless rush toward mastery and control that we created a world in which we could literally destroy that world. We napalmed children in Vietnam, and we created a world in which MAD—Mutually Assured Destruction, by means of nuclear weapons—was no fictional technothriller acronym, but stated government policy in response to any threatened attack. And in the last decade, we have contributed, according to U.N. estimates, to the deaths of at least half a million children in Iraq.

In light of the sobering reality of ongoing rebellion to God's purposes, Christians cannot naïvely assume that "niceness" will necessarily entail "niceness" in others. The political "realists" are quite right on one score: pacifism is naïve if it assumes that nonviolence will bring about an easy victory over one's enemies. Christians must realize that walking in the *way* of the cross may, indeed, lead *to* a cross. If you are "nice to people," the possibility exists that one may be killed. The way of the cross is a costly, sacrificial way of dealing with injustice, conflict, and rebellion against the ways of God.

But it is not disciples who naïvely believe they can cure the world of war. Very often, it is the purveyors of warfare who exhibit a utopian trust in the power of violence. Thus World War I was called the "war to end all wars," and America's more recent campaign has been too often suffused with the rhetoric of "ridding the world of evil," of "getting rid of terror," and other such utopian dreams. This is utopian nonsense. So Napoleon declared to his Minister of Education, "Do you know, Fontanes, what astonishes me most in this world? The inability of force to create anything. In the long run the sword is always beaten by the spirit." Reflecting upon Napolean's proclamation, Abraham Heschel commented, "Yet, the most astonishing thing in the world is the perennial disregard of the importance of force. What is the ultimate profit of all the arms, alliances, and victories? Destruction, agony, death."[9] So Christians refuse to fight wars not because they naïvely believe they will thus rid the world of war; instead, we do not fight wars because the kingdom of God has come, in which war is banished, in which it is possible to order our lives according to the justice and peace of God.

Christian nonviolence, then, is always rooted in the narrative of redemption. We worship a God who, in Christ, has nonviolently dealt with the injustice, the alienation, the sin, and the unrighteousness of this world. He thus suffered, died, and yet was vindicated, raised victorious from the grave. We have learned in Christ a particular way of dealing with enemies: to love them. In Christ, the long-awaited day of the prophets was revealed—the time has come for beating swords into ploughshares, for putting away our conceit and pride, for abolishing the bow and warfare, for admitting that we are not in control of human history. Unless our lives embody that good news, our worship is in vain.

Worshipping Other Gods

Yet for centuries we have set aside the way of Jesus. Concerned to "run the country," we cannot envision the way of Jesus as being "relevant," or "practical," or "useful." We need, instead, to replace his way with some other ethic that is "effective." Surely, so the reasoning goes, loving our enemies cannot be an effective social or political policy. To "love our enemies," many have concluded, must mean that we have a loving *attitude*, but little more. In the "real world" the way of Jesus cannot be taken seriously.

The way Jesus taught us to love our enemies is replaced then with some other ethic. So the nonviolence advocated by the early church was replaced by a "just war tradition." In this tradition, certain criteria determine when it is acceptable to use violence against an aggressor: Is there legitimate authority? Is there a just cause, a real offense against innocents? Is the war fought with the right intention? Is the war fought only after all honest attempts have been made to resolve the situation without employing violence? Is the war winnable? Are innocent civilians protected in the waging of war? At the heart of such a system lie many of the "Constantinian" assumptions discussed in part one: injustice ought not win; the wrong ought not defeat the right; evil must be overpowered. So we must "make things come out right." The end of "justice" demands that we set aside Jesus' ethic and employ the means necessary to win.

But the just war tradition fails to account for the narrative of redemption: the kingdom of God is no merely "otherworldly" or "after death" reality. The kingdom of God stands triumphant over every ruler, principality, and power—and every realm that stands opposed to the ways of the kingdom is in rebellion against the will of God. The gospel does not merely give us issues and themes and ends for which we ought to be concerned. Instead, the way of Jesus gives us inseparable ends *and* means, both goals and the manner by which those goals are to be realized. We are indeed called to be concerned for the oppressed; but Jesus teaches us the manner in which we ought to seek the good of the oppressed. We are indeed called to respond to injustice; but "seventy times seven" defines the shape of that response. We are indeed called to seek the good of the cities in which we dwell; but that good is to be realized through servanthood. We are indeed called to proclaim truth to power; but the cross ever reminds us of the fate we must be willing to bear when we venture out in such faithfulness. In the final analysis, however, the just war tradition cannot worship a crucified Lamb.

But the just war tradition can also be critiqued historically. Particularly in our modern era, seldom has the just war tradition *worked* in practice. Few "just war Christians" have ever used the criteria to actually decide whether they would or would not fight in a particular war. In fact, I find few among my students who have ever heard a single sermon on the just war tradition. We have a vague assumption that it is legitimate to fight in certain wars, but we do not train ourselves to make the discerning judgments required. Most often, the just war tradition appears to be empty rhetoric. Even when the bishops conclude that a given situation is not legitimated by the just war tradition, the church as a whole appears unprepared to make the moral stand necessary against a government steadfastly preparing to wage war.[10]

Indeed, those who bore the name of Christ were those who often perpetuated the madness of twentieth-century warfare, simply assuming that their country's cause is always the justified cause. Lecturing at a retreat of church workers in Germany, I had a number of occasions to visit with some of the German Christians attending the gathering. On a long walk through the countryside, one dear woman recounted her memories of World War II—nights in the bomb shelter; a morning walk to school after thousands upon thousands of civilians had been killed in bomb raids in her town the night before; a brother in Youth for Hitler. This was not the first conversation during my time there in which "the War" had come up in casual conversation. My curiosity finally got the better of me, so I asked what I had been wanting to ask: "So you all thought you were fighting a 'just war'? That you had 'just cause' to fight?" With a surprised look she turned to me and excitedly responded in her thickly accented English, "Oh yes, of course! Don't you Americans always think that your wars are just?"

Such anecdotes point us to a historical reality: a lazy use of the just war tradition most often provides *rationalization* for Christians killing their alleged enemies. When governments tell Christians to wage war, Christians wage war. When governments tell Christians to pledge their allegiance, Christians pledge allegiance. When governments tell Christians to prepare for the mass slaughter of millions of innocent lives through nuclear warfare, Christians give both their consent and their support. Rather than loving our alleged enemies, we prepare to kill them—and when called to kill them, we do so. Moral laziness does not take the criteria of the just war tradition seriously. And that moral laziness gives way to nationalism, to blind obedience to the nation-state, to bowing down to the idols erected by the fallen principalities and powers. We worship the wrong god.

Shaped by this mold, conformed to the ways of our self-serving world, Christians respond defensively to the notion that the church should challenge the judgments of the nation-state. Ironically, of course, it is not pacifism alone that would require Christians to question the nation-state. The just war tradition itself requires that the Christian church challenge and weigh the judgments of the authorities that call Christians to arms. Yet little to nothing is done to inculcate such moral responsibility.[11] Instead, reflexive nationalism rears its thoughtless head: "If you don't love it, leave it!"

The 1991 Gulf War experience of one particular student appears to be representative of a large number of Christians. "I served in the war in Kuwait," he began, "but I didn't want to be there, I didn't like being there, I disliked the 130 degree temperatures, and I thought being there was wrong. The war was about money, about oil, and we shouldn't have been there, and we didn't accomplish anything, because we still have the same problem. But I went—I did my duty, because I did what I was told to do." Regardless of the accuracy of his judgment of the reasons for the war, I asked whether he *should* have done "what he was told to do." In response, he appeared to have few moral resources for making sense of such a question. That one would defy the will of one's government simply appeared incomprehensible. In order to have those things we value, it was argued, we must rely upon the military to protect us from outside threats. Therefore no one could have such rights as freedom of speech and religion if they did not rely upon the military in order to protect these rights.

This is a great irony of American Christianity: exalting the nation that affords us "freedom of religion," we set aside the way of Christ in order to preserve the religion we supposedly are free to practice. We kill our alleged enemies in order to "worship" the God who teaches us to love enemies. The most important question about our pledge of allegiance is not whether we pledge allegiance to a flag under "one God," but to *what* god we are pledging our allegiance. Perhaps it is, after all, not the God revealed in Jesus Christ we are worshiping, but the god of the nation-state, the god of power and might and wealth.

Worship, War, and the New Aeon

In the prophets' day, as it is in ours, history was filled with violence, hatred, greed, enmity, injustice, and warfare. All sought their own interests, and not the interests of others. Setting false balances in order to profit off the backs of the less well-off—the contemporary analog to "cooking the books" so popular in accounting scandals in our day—accompanied scrupulous Sabbath-keeping and elaborate ceremonies of worship. In their pride, self-interest, and arrogance, they arranged military alliances and trusted in their weapons of war.

But the prophets did not take the greed, violence, and evil of human history as the final word. Human history is indeed a nightmare, filled with corruption, scandals, and wickedness. But this is not the final word or the final state of God's creation; to accept the fallen state of creation as its last state is to blaspheme the God of creation. So the prophets accept no half measures, no "realism" that is satisfied with balancing competing self-interests, but instead insist that God will redeem his creation. Thus the prophets do not merely condemn and judge, but they offer a promise of the coming day of redemption in which the Messiah will come effecting God's salvation, when war will be abolished and greed banished and evil consumed. The "wolf shall live with the lamb" (Isa. 11:6), all peoples will stream to know God and God's will, and peace and justice will reign.

And at the heart of that promise lies the vision of all peoples worshiping together:

> On that day there will be a highway from Egypt to Assyria, and the Assyrian will come into Egypt, and the Egyptian into Assyria, and the Egyptians will worship with the Assyrians.
>
> On that day Israel will be the third with Egypt and Assyria, a blessing in the midst of the earth, whom the LORD of hosts has blessed, saying, "Blessed be Egypt my people, and Assyria the work of my hands, and Israel my heritage."
>
> Isaiah 19:23–25

Such a remarkable promise, given that Egypt and Assyria were the enemies of the chosen people Israel, to be told that the God of the chosen people Israel is also the God of her enemies! Given that the God of Israel is also the God of Israel's enemies, Egypt and Assyria, the prophet envisions no less than Israel, Egypt, and Assyria assembling to worship their common God. "The God of Israel is also the God of her enemies, without their knowing Him and despite their defying Him. The enmity between the nations will turn to friendship. They will live together when they worship together."[12]

Moving beyond Worship Wars

What does it mean, concretely, to worship in a way that makes a difference for a rebellious world at war with itself? The experience of many of us indicates that it might be a bit naïve to believe that we will have much to offer to the world when our own worship assemblies and church communities have themselves become a battleground. The contention and occasional church splits rooted in the tired old arguments over "contemporary" versus "traditional" worship, or the fusses over liking this or not liking that, might be the place we must start. Surely we cannot expect to offer the world a voice of reconciliation when our own church communities serve as the locus for contention rather than peace. Surely we cannot expect to love the enemy whom we have not yet seen when we do not love the fellow church member whom we can see. Our churches must be schools of discipleship, and this necessitates that our assemblies be laboratories for learning to love one another—especially when we are celebrating the love of a God who loves even the unlovable!

In the abstract, such talk sounds pleasant, but in reality, it proves terribly difficult to practice. It is quite easy to sermonize about "love" and "forgiveness" in the abstract. But such love is difficult to practice, because my self-centeredness runs very deep. How often have I preached that we should forgive those who do not merit forgiveness—the murderer, the warmonger, or the terrorist who has decimated or oppressed some third party unknown to me—and yet am offended and resentful when someone doesn't like *me* or *my* preaching?! Third-party "forgiveness" is cheap, requiring nothing of me. When the rubber meets the road, when *I* or *we* must forgive an offense done to ourselves, our profession of faith gets tested. Self-pity, self-absorption, and self-defense work in concert to undercut my feeble efforts to love those who have acted spitefully towards me. It is difficult, quite honestly, for me to love the man who, in response to a sermon in which I used the birth of my second-born son just the previous day to illustrate the love of God, told me, "That was the worst sermon I've ever heard." It is difficult for me to love the woman who, in response to one of the final sermons I preached as a part of that same congregation, took my hand warmly, looked me straight in the eye, and said, "Lee, I just want you to know that when you are gone, I will be glad."

Pride pushes me to react, to strike out, to respond to harshness with counter-harshness. Self-centeredness convinces me that my task is to have all people think well of me. Fear propels me to act and speak defensively. And yet again, true worship is the heart of the matter, for worship can occur only when the heart of the worshiper practices *humility*. Too often, we construe humility as self-effacement, self-humiliation, or maybe even self-degradation. But such practices know nothing of *humility*, for each of these practices continue gazing at the navel of *self*. Humility, instead, casts its vision upon the God who loves us in our rebellion, the God who loves us even in those places deep in the recesses of our soul that we dare not admit. This God seeks to draw us out of our shame and heal our afflictions of soul, constantly willing to forgive, yet seventy times seven. Even more, humility reminds me that the world is not about me, but about God's purposes, God's kingdom. Rightful worship calls us to surrender our will. Embracing an agenda, a cause, or a policy—howsoever "right" and "good," whether for justice or peace—is not the same thing as discipleship. Discipleship calls us to abandon *our* will, surrendered to the Christ, to follow him in his way, to let go of our agendas, and to be about the work of reconciliation and the hard work of forgiveness. True faith means we obey Christ, turning from *our* will, embracing his.

In worship, we gather to bring our failings, shortcomings, and rebellion. If we wrongly envision church as a place where we are supposed to "do church right," then we are unable to come as a people confessing that we, left to our own devices, do little right; our ecclesiology, instead, must always bear witness to Jesus' declaration that the kingdom of God belongs to those who are poor in spirit, who are deeply aware of their insufficiency, their powerlessness, their inability to make any claim upon God, their inability to stake any claim based upon their own rightness.

It is a mark of the rebellious aeon to divide the world simplistically into groups of those who are "good" and those who are "evil," believing that the "good" are in the right to judge, condemn, or kill those who are "evil." Thus an apparently necessary tactic in warfare is the demonization of the enemy, caricaturing the enemy as the very embodiment of evil. This is not the word of the gospel, but the word of rebellion. This is worship of a different god than the One revealed in Jesus of Nazareth. Instead, the God whom we worship comes not to judge, but to give life. We already stand condemned, trapped in the rebellion of our own making, trapped in a slavery of our own devices; it is all of us, all together, dominated by those rebellious forces in our world, who need redemption. Thus Jesus, Paul, and John all proclaim the same thing about the goodness of the love of God and our response to that love: we love because we are loved by a God who loves those who do not merit being loved. "But I say to you, Love your enemies and pray for those who persecute you, so that you may be children of your Father in heaven; for he makes his sun rise on the evil and on the good, and sends rain on the righteous and on the unrighteous," proclaimed Jesus (Matt. 5:44–45). "Indeed, rarely will anyone die for a righteous person—though perhaps for a good person someone might actually dare to die. But God proves his love for us in that while we still were sinners Christ died for us. . . . For if while we were enemies, we were reconciled to God through the death of his Son, much more surely, having been reconciled, will we be saved by his life," declared Paul (Rom. 5:7–10). "Whoever does not love does not know God, for God is love. God's love was revealed among us in this way: God sent his only Son into the world so that we might live through him," wrote John. That is, "In this is love, not that we loved God"—for what is there not to love about One who already loves, who is truly good?—"but that he loved us," we who had no rightness upon which to merit being loved, and instead needed "his Son to be the atoning sacrifice for our sins" (1 John 4:8–10).

In their contexts, all these passages insist that mere profession of faith is insufficient. Mere liturgical repetition of formulaic doctrines will not do. That is, "worship" and real life, liturgy and ethics, are inseparable. After having commanded his disciples to love their enemies because God loves both the "evil" and the "good," Jesus concluded, "Not everyone who says to me, 'Lord, Lord,' will enter the kingdom of heaven, but only the one who does the will of my Father in heaven. On that day many will say to me, 'Lord, Lord, did we not prophesy in your name, and cast out demons in your name, and do many deeds of power in your name?' Then I will declare to them, 'I never knew you; go away from me, you evildoers'" (Matt. 7:21–23).

John, concerned apparently to counter a false teaching that believed God could not indwell human flesh, insists that "every spirit that confesses that Jesus Christ has come in the flesh is from God" (1 John 4:2). As a corollary, John is very concerned that professions of faith also get enfleshed in the life of the avowed believer:

> Whoever says, "I have come to know him," but does not obey his commandments, is a liar, and in such a person the truth does not exist; but whoever obeys his word, truly in this person the love of God has reached perfection. By this we may be sure that we are in him: whoever says, "I abide in him," ought to walk just as he walked. . . . Those who say, "I love God," and hate their brothers or sisters, are liars; for those who do not love a brother or sister whom they have seen, cannot love God whom they have not seen.
>
> 1 John 2:4–6; 4:20

The opposite of love, for John, is not *apathy*—pointing us yet again to the fact that "love" ought not be construed as a *feeling*, but as an action, self-sacrificially acting for the good of another. Instead, the opposite of love is slaughtering the hated one, as Cain did Abel (1 John 3:12).

Paul similarly makes a connection between our worship of the God who loves all peoples and our everyday lives: indeed, he construes the entirety of our lives as worship: "present your bodies as a living sacrifice, holy and acceptable to God, which is your spiritual worship" (Rom. 12:1). True worship means living not according to the rebellious world and its ways—"do not be conformed to this world (aeon)" (12:2)—but living according to the new way revealed in Jesus Christ. This means we "hate what is evil," and "hold fast to what is good" (12:9). But this does not mean that we then employ whatever means we find "necessary," but instead that we hold, above all, to the good revealed in Jesus Christ. That is, our worship calls us to keep inseparable our doctrine and our ethics. We know *how* to love, we know *how* to "hold to what is good" by the concrete example of Jesus' love. Thus Paul goes on to counsel, "Do not repay anyone evil for evil," "never avenge yourselves," "if your enemies are hungry, feed them," and "Do not be overcome by evil, but overcome evil with good" (12:17–21).

"We're All Bastards, but God Loves Us Anyway"

In worship, we ascribe praise, adoration, glory, and honor to a God who loves enemies, who loves the unlovable, who loves us. We celebrate the God who, with infinite patience, brings us out of our own rebellion, frees us from our slavery. We exalt a God who loves us, embraces us, not with a cheap third-party forgiveness, but at great cost, with much suffering. In great contrast to the angry Nashvillian who suggested that the proper antidote to school shootings was not to "turn the other cheek," but to "execute the little bastards," the gospel proclaims, according to the pithy summary of Will Campbell, "We're all bastards, but God loves us anyway."

Campbell, a southern, Baptist, Yale Divinity School–educated minister, worked tirelessly as, according to his own self-description, a "southern liberal" in the civil rights movement. Believing that the gospel had much to say to issues of segregation and racial hatred, Campbell often worked as a gadfly, prodding and irritating the Christian institutions that should have taken seriously the new humanity found in Christ, but did not. When an agnostic friend named P. D. East insisted that Will boil the gospel down to some simple formula P. D. could understand, in ten words or less, Will finally summarized this way: "We're all bastards, but God loves us anyway."

Sometime later, P. D., Will, and Will's brother Joe happened to be together when they heard the tragic news that one of Will's friends, a young man named Jonathan Daniel, had been murdered. The young divinity-school student had been working in a voter-registration effort in Lowndes County, Alabama. The sheriff's office had jailed Jonathan for his efforts to get out the black vote. After his release, Jonathan and a Catholic priest, also just released, stopped with two black students at a small local grocery store to get a cold drink; before they finished their soft drinks, a deputy named Thomas Coleman arrived, pulled out his shotgun, and fired at the four as they left the store. The first shot killed Jonathan instantly; the second shot mortally wounded the priest.

After hearing the news on television, P. D. and Joe stood by quietly as Will made calls to the Department of Justice, the American Civil Liberties Union, and a lawyer friend in Nashville. Fuming and angry, Campbell recounts that he "had used words like redneck, backwoods, woolhat, cracker, Kluxer, ignoramus and many others." And as evening fell, drinking some beer and eating some cheese, P. D. wanted to talk theology, wanted to talk about Campbell's summary definition of the gospel. P. D. refused to let the gravity of the situation deter his interrogation of Campbell. So he started in on him:

> "Was Jonathan a bastard?"
>
> I said I was sure that everyone is a sinner in one way or another but that he was one of the sweetest and most gentle guys I had ever known.
>
> "But was he a bastard?" His tone was almost a scream. "Now that's your word. Not mine. You told me one time that everybody is a bastard. That's a pretty tough word. I know. Cause I *am* a bastard. A born bastard. A real bastard. My Mamma wasn't married to my Daddy. Now, by god, you tell me, right now, yes or no and not maybe, was Jonathan Daniel a bastard?"
>
> I knew that if I said no he would leave me alone and if I said yes he wouldn't. And I knew my definition would be blown if I said no.
>
> So I said, "Yes."
>
> "All right. Is Thomas Coleman a bastard?"
>
> That one was a lot easier. "Yes. Thomas Coleman is a bastard."
>
> "Okay. Let me get this straight now. I don't want to misquote you. Jonathan Daniels *was* a bastard. Thomas Coleman *is* a bastard. . . . Which one of these two bastards does God love the most? Does he love that little dead bastard Jonathan the most? Or does He love that living bastard Thomas the most?"[13]

Will Campbell recounts that dialog as a moment that "made a Christian out of me." From that time forward, he included in his ministry not only oppressed blacks, but Klansmen too. He saw that Klansmen were oppressed too by the principalities and powers, captured by the rebellious aeon, needing the redemptive love of God to invade their lives, to free them to go love as God loves. The point of the gospel is not that we love the "good people," and hate the "bad people," but that we love as God loves, inclusively, extravagantly. As Dorothy Day put it, citing her friend Father John Hugo, "we loved God as much as the one we loved the least."[14]

The fear deep within us rebels at such love, balks at such indiscriminate grace, recoils at such wholesale forgiveness. Such love appears to cut across the grain of our souls, appears to rip out our very core. Such love refuses to take sides, refuses to play the power games, refuses to simplistically see one class of people as "good" and others as "evil." Such love, we come to see, is not syrupy sentiment, but the hard work of self-sacrificially giving for the true good of another, who desperately needs to be loved. The forces of hatred cannot be conquered by yet more hate. The rebellious principalities and powers will not be undone by us trying to play their game. Victory comes only through love.

It will not do, in other words, simply not to kill our enemies. To adopt a stance of refusing to kill our enemies, of course, *would* be a radical conversion for the Christian church in the Western world. But even such a radical transformation would not be sufficient. It will most certainly not do to hate the war-makers and their military-industrial complex. It will not do to scoff at nationalism and patriotism. Instead, following Christ means we embrace both centurion and zealot alike, calling each to the life-giving way of the kingdom, in which we celebrate the grace and abundance of a God given freely and extravagantly to us all. For us to give such love to the rebellious world, we must come to know that we have first been loved with such extravagance. "We love because he first loved us" (1 John 4:19). We, like the woman judged a sinner by the Pharisee Simon, the woman who fell down at the feet of Jesus, worshiping him with tears and anointing him with oil, we too must first come to realize the depth of our own rebellion, the depth of our own perverseness, the depth of our own woundedness. Our worship, too, must regularly remind us that "our sins are many," that we desperately need an unmerited love, a bountiful forgiveness. Out of such faith and such worship, our Lord may say to us, too: "Your faith has saved you; go in peace" (Luke 7:36–50).

Baptism

Why Disciples Don't Make Good Americans (or Germans, or Frenchmen)

As many of you as were baptized into Christ have clothed yourselves with Christ. There is no longer Jew or Greek, there is no longer slave or free, there is no longer male and female; for all of you are one in Christ Jesus."

Galatians 3:27–28

One is either a good German or a good Christian. It is impossible to be both at the same time.

Adolf Hitler[1]

The Politics of Baptism

When "everyone was a Christian," the means by which "everyone" became a "Christian" was infant baptism. The late medieval world saw the development of the regular practice of paedobaptism, and this practice stood at the heart of the full flowering of the Constantinian church. The radical change the apostle Paul attached to baptism in Romans 6—putting to death the "old man" and being "raised to walk in newness of life"—no longer could be said of baptism. *Everyone* was baptized—even though not everyone walked in that new way of life enjoined by the gospel. Infant baptism thus stood at the heart of the Christendom project. Though the pews may have been filled, discipleship was not for the ordinary person in the pew. Instead, it was reserved for the religious in the monastery.

In the sixteenth century, a group of so-called "radical reformers" questioned the practice of infant baptism on a number of grounds. Typical among these reformers were the Swiss Brethren, led by Michael Sattler, previously a Benedictine monk. After being convinced by Luther and fellow reformers that there was need for fundamental reform in the practice of the Christian faith, Sattler had forsaken his calling as a monk, and had married. But Sattler took their efforts at renewal further than the so-called "magisterial reformers." Reformers like Luther, Calvin, and Zwingli continued, in many respects, Constantinian Christianity, seen most clearly in their dependence upon the "magistrate," the governing authorities, to carry out the reforms of the church. Just as Augustine of Hippo had done not long after the rise of Constantine—using the coercive power of empire to bring to "repentance" those whom he believed to be preaching error—so did the sixteenth-century magisterial reformers.

For the Anabaptists,[2] baptism represented the point of entrance into a community of faith that had "been taught repentance and the amendment of life." According to the Schleitheim Confession, a document considered by many to serve as a classical statement of Anabaptist distinctives, baptism was to be given "to all those who desire to walk in the resurrection of Jesus Christ." Baptism must not serve as an empty symbol of entry into a state-run church; baptism epitomized *discipleship*, and infant baptism cut out the very heart of the New Testament vision of the practice. Instead of baptizing a culture and calling it "Christian," the Anabaptists desired that the church baptize those who sought to walk in the way of Jesus.[3]

For these "radicals," the primary mark of identity became the baptized community. For them, identity, oneness, and social grouping revolved around the baptized believers. Those who voluntarily chose baptism—not those who were told by the state to receive it—these gathered around to break the one bread and drink the one cup "in remembrance of the broken body of Christ." Those who have received baptism, those who partake of the "table of the Lord" must not simultaneously partake in the "table of devils." Baptism inducts one into a community with certain specific requirements, a community of discipleship: "all those who have fellowship with the dead works of darkness have no part in the light," they asserted.

This understanding of baptism, therefore, meant embodying a real difference between "church" and "state," or "church" and "world." Alliances that required setting aside faithfulness to Jesus' way marked unfaithfulness. "Church" and

"Christianity" could not be reduced merely to receiving the sacraments or properly understanding doctrine, to proper worship or rightly preaching the word. Nor could "Christianity" be reduced to being a "good Christian citizen." "Faith" required, enabled, and freed one to walk in the way of Christ; baptism without discipleship was thus not Christian baptism.

Consequently, the baptized renounce the way of violence and punishment, sword and judgment, they argued. Christians do not exist in "two realms" simultaneously—Christians are to submit to the lordship of Christ, and he taught "you shall not resist evil." The magistrate, under the ordering of God, punishes the wicked. But the disciple employs only the way of the Master, and so exhorts the wicked to "go, and sin no more." Rather than passing judgment in "disputes and strifes about worldly matters," the baptized takes the way of the Christ, "who did not wish to decide or pass judgment between brother and brother concerning inheritance, but refused to do so. So should we also."[4] If the magistrate requires the Christian to take up the sword in defense of neighbor or country, then the disciple again follows the way of Christ, who taught us that "the princes of this world lord it over them etc., but among you it shall not be so." Of perhaps most importance for the Anabaptists, a rejection of the sword was rooted in citizenship: the "rule of government" concerns a citizenship that is of "this world." Those baptized into Christ, however, have a different citizenship, one from heaven.

Such heresy, it was thought, had to be stopped. Adult believer baptism was seen as a threat to the very fabric of society, a threat to civilization as they knew it—and indeed, it was. So Luther suggested that the Anabaptists should concern themselves with attacking the pope rather than Christendom:

> They take a severe stand against the pope, but they miss their mark and murder the more terribly the Christendom under the pope. For if they would permit baptism and the sacrament of the altar to stand as they are, Christians under the pope might yet escape with their souls and be saved, as has been the case hitherto. But now when the sacraments are taken from them, they will most likely be lost, since even Christ himself is thereby taken away.[5]

Luther saw that if baptism became a matter of individual, voluntary choice—if individuals are given the opportunity to refuse baptism—then fewer would be baptized, fewer would be "Christians," and thus more souls "lost."

In time, Sattler was arrested by the authorities, charged with acting "against imperial mandate," for rejecting infant baptism, for refusing to "swear to the government," and for refusing to war against the enemies of the empire.[6] Found guilty, he was sentenced to death: " 'It has been found that Michael Sattler should be given into the hands of the hangman, who shall lead him to the square and cut off his tongue, then chain him to a wagon, there tear his body twice with red-hot tongs, and again when he is brought before the gate, five more times.' When this is done to be burned to powder as a heretic."[7] Sattler's death was one of many: hundreds were imprisoned, tortured, strangled, burned, or beheaded. Christians of both Catholic and Protestant stripe killed them, and did so in the name of Jesus.[8]

Baptism and the New Humanity

In the New Testament, baptism signifies many different things: "remission of sins," the "gift of the Holy Spirit," death to the "old self." But often overlooked is Paul's assertion that baptism inducts one into a new humanity: "As many of you as were baptized into Christ have clothed yourselves with Christ. There is no longer Jew or Greek, there is no longer slave or free, there is no longer male and female; for all of you are one in Christ Jesus" (Gal. 3:27–28). At the heart of baptism lies an astonishing claim, an astonishing reality: all the division, all the social groupings, all the forms of identity that serve to categorize, divide, estrange, and alienate one from the other—these are broken down. There is, for those who have been clothed with Christ in baptism, a new identity, an identity that transcends race, economic class, ethnic grouping, and citizenship. Paul's passionate rebuke of Peter (Gal. 2:11–21) flows from his conviction that there must be no barrier between Jew and Gentile. Thus John Barclay notes that the issue for Paul with the Judaizers is "not legalism (in the sense of earning merit before God) but cultural imperialism—regarding Jewish identity and Jewish customs as the essential tokens of membership in the people of God."[9] The antidote to such imperialism is a proper understanding and practice of baptism, seen as that act in which God transcends and nullifies the hostility and estrangement.

It is baptism that theologically requires us to question the definition of our pronouns. Chapter three discussed how the Constantinian cataract leads us to think of the "we" and "our" in terms of the empire or nation-state. Baptism, however, requires us to configure our "we" and "our" in terms of the baptized community. Baptism bears witness to the constructive response to all those who think Jesus irrelevant to the "way things really work." That response is this: we are to be the church, a baptized community, walking always in the way of Christ, offering the hope of redemption to a world trapped under the domination of those principalities and powers desperately clinging to an illusion of control.

Simply practicing adult believer baptism as an end or point of righteousness in itself misses the point. Though some groups reject the practice of infant baptism, they have nonetheless retained the social and political meaning once attached to infant baptism. That is, "being baptized" once one reaches the "age of accountability" serves simply as a cultural or familial or ethnic expectation, thus ignoring the countercultural intent of transcending family, culture, race, and ethnicity.

Too many twentieth-century American churches perverted adult believer baptism, for example, by making it yet another place to perpetuate the racism of the surrounding culture: separate baptisteries for the "whites" and the "coloreds" symbolized that, even in the midst of much wrangling over "sound doctrine" with regard to baptism, baptism was quietly transformed into a mockery of the gospel. In 1960, Carl Spain, professor of Bible at Abilene Christian College, stood before an assembly of thousands of Caucasian members of my own racially segregated Churches of Christ, a community that has held tenaciously to the practice of adult believer baptism. And Spain began to castigate: himself raised in a small, segregated Texas town, Spain had witnessed firsthand the mockery of racist baptism that resulted when a "white preacher" took it upon himself to preach to the town's African Americans.

> A few years later, the Negroes of the community got to hear the gospel from a man of their own race. But the Lord didn't seem to understand about the white folks' problem, or if He did, He didn't seem to care. And the gospel seed that a white man had sown in the Negro heart was watered to life by a Negro preacher. And the Lord gave the increase, but He didn't time it just right. He forgot that the poor Negro folks who were to be baptized didn't have anything but a tent, and the white folks had the only available baptistery. So, in the excitement of becoming the white folks' brothers and sisters in the Lord, the happy preacher didn't see anything wrong about asking if they could come over and use the baptistery.
>
> The Lord had moved in the hearts of a few white Christians in such a powerful way that they said that their Negro friends would be more than welcome. But the blue-blooded members of the Royal Order of the Master Race, including many members of the church of Christ, the Baptist, the Methodist, and Presbyterians protested violently. They preferred death to such a fate as this. Before the baptismal service was over, police came to put a stop to it. . . . The Lord's church was branded as a communist front organization where whites and Negroes socialized as brothers. The community systematically boycotted the business establishments of some of the Christians for months, nearly causing them to go bankrupt.[10]

Paul may have thought that being clothed with Christ in baptism meant "neither Jew nor Greek," but baptism was not to be allowed to trump "white and black."

Centuries upon centuries after the Constantinian shift, this small Texas town showed that the remnant of Constantinian Christianity remained. "Church" and "Christianity" were relegated to a small, socially irrelevant sphere: church was concerned with "sound doctrine," "rightful worship," or the "New Testament pattern." Proud of its faith, proud of its "keeping to the old paths," proud of its orthodoxy, such culturally enslaved Christianity failed to understand a very elementary meaning of baptism: all those who have been baptized into Christ have been freed from the power of the old order.

Ephesians 2 echoes similar themes. Those who are "in Christ Jesus" (and in the Pauline view, being *in* Christ means having been "*baptized into* Christ," Gal. 3:27), though they once were "far off," "aliens from the commonwealth of Israel," and "strangers to the covenant," now they have "been brought near" and "granted access in one Spirit to the Father." Being "in Christ" means that the "dividing wall," the "hostility" has been "broken down." All those things that have divided, separated, estranged, and alienated have been removed: Christ Jesus is "our peace." His purpose is to "create in himself *one new humanity* in place of the two, thus making peace" (Eph. 2:15, emphasis added).

A similar claim is made in 2 Corinthians 5:16–21: all those in Christ are part of a "new creation," are inducted into a "new world" (NEB). Baptism inducts one into a new humanity, a new social order, a new way of existing in the world. We once, Paul says, viewed people from a "human point of view," but no longer—because in Christ, the "old has passed away; see, everything has become new!" (v. 17). When social groupings are given worth in and of themselves, they become means to count who is in and who is out. Race, denomination, family, and citizenship can all become a lever for exclusion—and subsequently, a means of oppression. Family feuds, church sectarianism, institutional racism, and modern warfare all have a common denominator: *us* against *them*. The supposed sins, failings, and offenses of *them* become warrant for denigration, oppression, and persecution.

And here lies the good news of baptism: baptism does not induct us into a group that seeks to wield power and control over others; baptism does not establish us as a people who can now tell the world how they must live their lives. Baptism, instead, makes us ambassadors for Christ; baptism grafts us into a ministry of reconciliation, that just as "in Christ God was reconciling the world to himself, not counting their trespasses against them" (2 Cor. 5:19), this same message of reconciliation and forgiveness is entrusted to us. The baptized go forth with a new identity: a people preaching reconciliation and forgiveness. Harbingers of the new humanity, the baptized go forth to sow peace.

Jesus, Family, and Nation

It was this same message that made Jesus so offensive to his contemporaries. The proclamation of the kingdom of God carried with it a non-nationalistic twist that sent many Jews over the edge: the very notion that Gentiles would be included among the elect was enough for those gathered in Jesus' home synagogue to lead him to the brow of a hill where they sought to stone him (Luke 4:16–30). Jesus likewise rebuked the self-righteous nationalism that would have prayed for fire to come down and consume the inhospitable and hated Samaritans (9:51–56); similarly, Jesus made the unclean Samaritan the model of neighbor love (10:25–37).

Given the laxity with which many take their history and ethnic identity in the Western world, it is perhaps difficult for us to imagine the depth of identity attached to "Jew and Gentile" for a faithful Jew. There were the *Jews*, and then there was everyone else. Acts 10 recounts Peter describing the depth of this unquestioned "reality" to the Gentiles assembled in Caesarea: "You yourselves know that it is unlawful for a Jew to associate with or to visit a Gentile" (v. 28). The Gentiles were "profane" or "unclean." And so it took a vision three times revealed to Peter, plus another vision to the Gentile Cornelius, plus a miraculous manifestation of the Holy Spirit poured out upon Gentiles, before Peter granted baptism to the Gentiles.

Jesus more often than not offends family sensibilities. If your father has just died, don't let that get in the way of following me: "Let the dead bury their own dead" (Luke 9:60). One who does not "hate father and mother, wife and children, brothers and sisters, yes, and even life itself, cannot be my disciple" (Luke 14:26). Likewise, having just taken a wife is no excuse for not following after the Master. Similarly, Jesus often offended notions of loyalty to the nation by eating with tax-collectors, those disloyal Jews who, in their service to Rome, epitomized the betrayal of Israel. It is of no small significance that Jesus had a tax-collector among the Twelve.

We are here getting at what is perhaps most scandalous about the gospel: that the enemy, the one who does not love you, the one who hates you—this one is to be valued equally with one's family members and one's nation. Instead of an exclusive love, which declares "You shall love your neighbor and hate your enemy," Jesus commands an inclusive love: "Love your enemies" (Matt. 5:43–44). What good is it, Jesus asks, if you love those who love you?—even sinners do that. What good is it, Jesus asks, if you are polite to those who are polite to you?—even unbelievers do that. We are called to love as the Father loves, loving those who do not deserve to be loved, loving even those who hate us.

Clarence Jordan tells of the inscription on a tombstone in Mississippi that reads, "Here lies J. H. S. In his lifetime, he killed 99 Indians, and lived in the blessed hope of making it 100, until he fell asleep in the arms of Jesus."[11] The "arms of Jesus" provide cultural sanction for the killing of those outside our group; you kill an "Indian," or 99 of them, and "live in the blessed hope" of rounding it out to an even one hundred, and it's something to boast about—because "Indians" are not of us, they are not in the in-group, they are not like us. And one's religion—the "arms of Jesus"—is taken to give sanction to such an endeavor. But at the heart of the teachings of this Christ—at the heart of baptism—is the claim that all such social groupings have been overcome. That through the blood of Christ, *reconciliation* rather than *estrangement* becomes the standard; love rather than hatred; forgiveness rather than prejudice; inclusivity rather than exclusivity. Loving your neighbor, loving your race, loving your own group—this is a limited love, which Jesus commands us to move beyond.

And precisely here we see why God gifts us with the Holy Spirit in baptism: the love to which God calls us is no simple, realizable goal apart from redemption in Christ. The love that follows from participation in the new humanity is a gift of God's power. As Paul put it in his Corinthian correspondence, "For in the one Spirit we were all baptized into one body—Jews or Greeks, slaves or free—and we were all made to drink of one Spirit" (1 Cor. 12:13). Paul's use of the word "creation" elsewhere underscores this point: throughout the canon of Scripture it is always God alone who *creates*. No human is ever the subject of the verb "create." A new creation is no humanly realizable matter—it is the work of God, the gift of God's grace realized in the death, burial, and resurrection of Christ, and received by the believer in baptism. The old life—"slavery" Paul calls it in Romans 6 (vv. 6, 20)—is put to death, and we are raised to walk in a new life, the life of the Spirit, walking in the power of the One who will bear the fruit of love in our lives.

Nationalism, Patriotism, and Other Works of the Flesh

Nestled into my four-year-old's end-of-year preschool program some months after the beginning of the war on terror was the popular evangelical Christian song "Our God Is an Awesome God." Sung by a delightful assembly of two- to five-year-olds, and orchestrated by a group of teachers who had blessed my four-year-old in innumerable ways the past year, the song came as no surprise, given that the preschool operates as a ministry of a local church. What was jolting about the song was the subtlety of its context: "Our God Is an Awesome God" sung by children all wearing white T-shirts bedecked with handsomely painted U.S. flags, the children standing in front of a large painting of the "Grand Ol' Flag" comprised of red-white-and-blue children's handprints. Other visual cues, the banners and the small flags waved by the two-year-olds, only complemented the actual content of the program itself. Both preceding and following "Our God Is an Awesome God" was a medley of patriotic songs intended to stir the souls of all present, especially when performed in the innocence of childhood. In a very subtle way, the message of "Our God Is an Awesome God" had been transformed: "America's God Is an Awesome God."

Such displays suggest to me that many (most?) Christians in the Bible Belt apparently consider patriotism, and its first cousin, nationalism, to be manifestations of the fruit of the Spirit, a "natural" consequence of love for our awesome God. "What's wrong with patriotism?" one of my university students asked. "Shouldn't we be proud of our country?" This way of putting the question is like asking, "Shouldn't I be proud of my family?" Well, yes, of course, one would hope that one has a particular affinity for one's family. And of course, all families, like nation-states, have certain incidents or character flaws or dysfunctions of which one is not "proud," but these things need not mitigate one's love for that family.

But this way of putting the question misses the theological problem: ultimately the problem with patriotism is its very limited, sectarian nature. In baptism, Christians become part of a community that transcends all racial, cultural, national, geographical, and natural boundaries. In nationalism, we narrow our concerns, commitments, and allegiances to a nation-state whose agenda is not the kingdom of God. In baptism, we give up our lives so that we might be filled with the fruit of the Spirit, ready to die for the sake of the kingdom. In nationalism, we protect our lives to fulfill a narrow, limited set of concerns, ready to kill for the sake of the nation-state. In nationalism, our ultimate identity lies in being "American." In baptism, our ultimate identity lies in being disciples of Christ—"There is no longer Jew or Greek, there is no long slave or free, there is no longer male and female; for all of you are one in Christ Jesus" (Gal. 3:28).

Consequently, we must not limit our concerns for safety for "our own"—our own ethnic group, our own social class, our own race, our own nation-state. When Paul asserted that all fundamental markers of identity, particularly those that buttress separation or estrangement, must be submitted to our identity found in Christ, he included three of the most powerful sources of estrangement in his day: ethnicity, gender, and socioeconomic class. Since Paul wrote before the advent of the modern nation-state, we should add "nationality" to the list, for it is, in the contemporary Western world at least, the most revered source of identity and separation from others. But Paul insists that Christ comes first; everything else must either find its place underneath his lordship or be cast aside.

Nationalism inverts this relationship, having us (whether theoretically or practically) place national citizenship as the first marker of identity. Blood, country, and homeland are powerful symbols that are made to serve as gods. The god of "God and country" is a nationalistic tribal deity that does not baptize into the Spirit of Christ, but the spirit of homeland security; this god baptizes not in the blood of the Lamb, but the blood of soil and country.

Perhaps Hitler better understood than many Christians the allegiance Jesus required of his disciples, when he declared that "One is either a good German or a good Christian. It is impossible to be both at the same time." But the old Christendom cataract wants to make common cause out of such allegiances, and in effect subordinates "Christianity" to the agenda of the empire. Thus one commonly hears American Christians suggest that we would not be able to "practice our faith" or have "freedom to worship" unless we had the United States. So, the logic proceeds to an idolatrous civil religion at its best: we must revere the nation-state, we must exalt the nation-state, and we must kill for the nation-state, so that we may worship as we please. "I fought in the war so you can have the liberty to stand up there and preach about nonviolence," some retort. Well, no, quite to the contrary, Jesus died to free us from fear and self-centeredness, and our faith in his resurrection frees us to preach nonviolent love of enemy.

After insisting to the Galatian Christians that our baptism provides our ultimate and sole point of reference, that all particularities about ourselves must be submitted to the lordship of Christ, Paul subsequently encourages believers to walk in the Spirit. That is, he calls them to be transformed into the image and way of Christ by submitting to the renewal possible in the Spirit. Just after Paul reminded the believers that "There is no longer Jew or Greek, male nor female, bond nor free, but all one in Christ Jesus," he also admonished them to "Live by the Spirit . . . and do not gratify the desires of the flesh" (5:16). That is, this identity in Christ is not a mere assertion that I have been "saved" or "born again," a mere legal standing that I'll "get to go to heaven" when I die, but is actually a new identity, leading to a new life: the old is marked by the "works of the flesh," and the new is marked by the "fruit of the Spirit."

Paul doesn't mean by his oft-used designation of "flesh" some sort of dualism that presupposes the innate inferiority of bodily, physical, or material concerns as opposed to the realm of "spirit." Taking cues from various places in his writings, we might put it this way: you can live your life in a way that is merely concerned with "flesh," with bodily and physical existence and pleasures, or you can live your bodily life in a way that is oriented toward the purposes of God. Your life and the use of your body can be animated by the concerns of "flesh," mere appetites, or your life and the use of your body can be animated by the concerns of God's purposes, God's Spirit.

One might paraphrase or colloquialize Paul this way: "A life driven by fleshly appetites leads you to do this kind of stuff: sleeping around, messing around with stuff that will screw up your life, sexual compulsiveness, pursuing success in the corporate world, self-centered religion and 'spirituality,' militarism, trying to outdo people, jealousy, always irritated and angry, arguing and bickering, patriotism, nationalism, wanting a car or house as nice as your neighbor's, addictions of whatever stripe, wasting your life on stupid stuff, and any sort of junk like that. I'm telling you, just like I told you before, if you're living out this kind of life, you simply cannot be an heir of God's rule, because this kind of crap doesn't come from God."

How does nationalism or patriotism fit into such a list? First, "nationalism" and "patriotism" seem fair enough substitutions for "dissensions" and "factions," because the concern of nation-states always starts with "national self-interest." And our own nation-state, in pursuit of that self-interest, doesn't mind the posturing, the threatening, and the killing of those who get in its way. The prevailing policy of all recent presidential administrations, for example, is a "realism" that forthrightly promotes "national self-interest" as a most fundamental criterion of foreign policy-making. Second, it is self-interest or self-centeredness that lies at the heart of all these "works of the flesh." Greed—for money, "success," sex—is all about "me." My wanting what you have is "envy." Anger at my not getting what you have is "jealousy." My desire for self-justification leads to "quarrels." And a primary component in addictions, whether it be alcohol, or rage, or pornography, or "success," is self-centeredness.

Nationalism and patriotism are self-centeredness writ large, community habits that prepare us to do "whatever is necessary," as our politicians put it these days, to "preserve our cherished way of life." The self-seeking inherent in patriotism led Tolstoy to assert, "patriotism cannot be good. Why do not people say that egoism may be good?"[12] Political philosophers, perhaps, have given "egoism" of various stripes more legitimacy than it had in Tolstoy's day, and subsequently, nationalism appears all the more credible. Employing all means at its disposal—public education, national holidays, churches, culture, media, and, yes, my child's Christian preschool—nationalism has rooted its alleged "naturalness" deep into our souls. So deeply rooted is it, I suppose, that we think patriotism to be a fruit of the Spirit, rather than a work of the flesh. That we appear blind to the self-centeredness of these very "natural" practices is merely an updated guise of old Christendom habits, in which church gets subordinated to empire. We begin to believe it necessary, for our very survival, to pledge our allegiance to the empire, rather than constantly holding before ourselves our exclusive allegiance to the kingdom of God.

Stuart Briscoe recounts his conversation with an elderly German man who had fought in World War I with the Germans, in the days in which war was fought in trenches, not with high-tech "smart bombs" that allow distance from the enemy, but in hand-to-hand combat. For months on end, soldiers would live, fight, and die in trenches full of mud, blood, and filth, with no need for a global positioning satellite to locate the enemy, for the enemy was just across the field. On one particular cold, clear Christmas Eve, the fighting had stopped thanks to the annual Christmas truce. While huddled down in his trench, the old German man recounted, he suddenly heard from the enemy's trenches a loud, sweet tenor voice [that] began to sing "The Lord Is My Shepherd," and the sound floated up into the clear, moonlit air. Then . . . from the German trenches, a rich baritone voice tuned in, singing "Der Herr ist mein Hirt. . . ." For a few moments, everybody in both trenches concentrated on the sound of these two invisible singers and the beautiful music and the harmony. The British soldier and the German soldier sang praise to the Lord who was their shepherd. The singing stopped, and the sound slowly died away.

"We huddled in the bottom of our trenches and tried to keep warm until Christmas Day dawned," he said. "Early on Christmas morning, some of the British soldiers climbed out of their trenches into the no man's land, carrying a football." One soldier carried a round football. These English soldiers started kicking around a football, in a pickup game in no man's land, between the trenches. Then the old man said, "Some of the German soldiers climbed out, and England played Germany at football in no man's land on Christmas Day in the middle of the battlefield in France in the first World War. . . . The next morning, the carnage began again, with machine guns and bayonet fighting. Everything was back to normal."[13]

"Everything was back to normal." This is a frightening indictment of our notions of normalcy, of "reality." From the perspective of the waters of baptism, such "reality" is perverse, a strange reckoning indeed of "normal." One antidote to this aeon's obsessions is baptism. The church celebrates, first and foremost, the new humanity made possible in Christ, received in the waters of baptism. Baptism inducts us into a new humanity, and what the baptized offer the world is altogether different than what the enslaved world has to offer itself.

Our offer begins with a very minimal, but fundamentally important, refusal. That is, we first simply refuse to kill each other. In other words, we actually take our identity in Christ more seriously than our identity with the empire, the nation-state, or the ethnic terror cell whence we come. So the Mennonite poster hanging on my office wall suggests: "A Modest Proposal for Peace: LET THE CHRISTIANS OF THE WORLD AGREE THAT THEY WILL NOT KILL EACH OTHER." And we refuse to kill not only each other, but the enemy, too.

While this minimal refusal not to kill could be a mask for self-serving cowardice on the one hand, or self-serving strategic withdrawal on the other, it is not so for disciples of Christ. For this minimal refusal simply flows from our baptism, which allows us to offer the world much more than a promise that we will not kill them. Having died to the "old self," that self which is dominated by fear of death, we are now free to live to God, to live for God, and thus to live for others. Freed from the works of the flesh, we begin to embody the "fruit of the Spirit," offering the world what it truly needs: "love, joy, peace, patience, kindness, generosity, faithfulness, gentleness, and self-control" (Gal. 5:22–23). In self-giving love, we seek the good of the wealthy and the poor, the "upwardly mobile" and the "white trash," the

American and the Iraqi. The educated and the illiterate, the articulate and the dumb, the pretty and the not-so-pretty, the Hispanic and the Asian, all together are invited to participate in the new humanity, to participate in that great joy of simply being the new-world-on-the-way. Washed, cleansed, and marked with the Spirit as one of God's own, each of us is inducted into the new humanity, gifted by God, and thus given a role in God's kingdom, to go forth and serve the world. This is no unrealistic utopian idealism; it is the only thing that can possibly make a real difference in the violent, rebellious world in which we live.

Empowered by the Spirit, the baptized racist not only overcomes racism, but boldly advocates love of the "other." The baptized patriot not only overcomes the narrow confines of a sectarian worldview, but calls former compatriots to meet the needs of the foreigner and the children of supposed enemies. The baptized upwardly mobile not only comes to live by trust and thus simplicity of life, but calls others to live the adventuresome life of untroubled generosity. The baptized terrorist not only puts away hatred and revolutionary violence, but calls the oppressed neighbor, in creative yet nonpassive ways, to love the humanity of the oppressor, too. The baptized soldier not only refuses to drop bombs upon either Christian or non-Christian, but proclaims a willingness to lay down one's life in service to the mission of reconciliation. The baptized preacher not only forsakes the idolatry of church growth and institutional "success," but speaks truth to the powers, knowing it may cost kudos and career. The baptized church worker not only forsakes petty, politicized church games and maneuvering, but forthrightly calls congregations to repentance, to works of justice, and mercy, and prayer, and the heavier matters of the law. The baptized religious sectarian not only puts away arrogance and conceit, but actively celebrates and participates in the activity of God found in the midst of those Christian communities once cavalierly dismissed as apostate.

The baptized go forth to sow the seeds of the kingdom and trust that the sovereign king will bring forth a bountiful harvest.

Prayer

*Why Disciples Trust God rather
than Their Own Calculations*

*Intercession is spiritual defiance of what is, in the name of what
God has promised. . . . History belongs to the intercessors, who
believe the future into being.*

Walter Wink[1]

*To be a Christian and to pray are one and the same thing; it is
a matter that cannot be left to our caprice. It is a need, a kind of
breathing necessary to life.*

Karl Barth[2]

*W*hether from working in, working against, or working through institutions,
one quickly becomes aware that such systems generate an inertia and energy that
is larger than the sum of the parts. Human history is that way, too, and it was the
"rulers" or "authorities," the "principalities and powers" that best summarized for
Paul that something which makes up more than the sum of the parts we can see,
touch, and make sense of. Thus, when embarking upon the way of Christ, our

way will be caught up in the battle with those powers, just as occurred to Jesus. But the weapons for that warfare are not the weapons used by the kingdoms and nation-states and terror cells of this aeon; the weapons granted by God are fundamentally different. Jesus always made it clear that the real enemy was not who we suspect is our enemy. The real enemy cannot be defeated by swords and power and wealth and might.

So just before Paul admonished the Ephesians to "Pray in the Spirit at all times in every prayer and supplication" (Eph. 6:18), he had reminded them that "our struggle is not against enemies of blood and flesh, but against the rulers, against the authorities, against the cosmic powers of this present darkness, against the spiritual forces of evil in the heavenly places" (v. 12). For this warfare, something more potent is needed, something more powerful. So, "be strong in the Lord and in the strength of his power" (v. 10), by putting on "the whole armor of God" (v. 11)—truth and righteousness, the proclamation of God's peace, and the Word of God. The warfare imagery makes one thing clear: this is serious business, not to be taken lightly.

Daniel and the Lions' Den, and Other Such Nutty Tales of Prayer and Obedience

As the Old Testament tells the story, Daniel was at the peak of his career: already at a position of great power within the empire, Daniel's prospects were outstanding. Given his track record, the king planned to appoint Daniel over the entire kingdom. But one seldom achieves such approval and prominence without an envious spirit near, and so it was with Daniel. With no skeletons hidden in Daniel's closet, his enemies found no mud they could sling, and so they conspired plan B—to require a test of allegiance. So they flattered the king—"O King Darius, live forever! . . . whoever prays to anyone, divine or human, for thirty days, except to you, O king, shall be thrown into a den of lions" (Dan. 6:6–7). Their flattery effective, the king signed the irrevocable edict, and Daniel—who faithfully prayed to the God of Israel three times a day—was set up for a fall.

Informed of the edict, Daniel serves as a character faced with that perennial conflict between compromise and faithfulness, a character faced with the full force of an idolatrous principality arrayed against him, subtly but coercively demanding submission. One can imagine the thought process Daniel might have employed: "What good will I be to my people and to my God if I lose either my position or my life?" Or, "To have a presence requires compromise." Yet Daniel did not succumb to the temptation of alleged "effectiveness," and sought first and foremost to be a faithful witness. Simply by *praying*, Daniel rebelled against "law and order," rejecting the counselors and ethicists who would have him adopt a simple utilitarian calculation of "effectiveness." Utilitarianism suggests that in order to know what is "right," we should attempt to calculate the greatest happiness for the greatest number of people, or the greatest pleasure for the greatest number of people. Then, depending upon the anticipated outcome of our action, we should do what is "right" based upon those calculations. We should do what brings about, as best our calculations can tell, what will be "effective." But Daniel did not employ such calculations, and chose to pray instead. And it was away to the lions' den for him.

The account of Daniel reminds us that living by faith means living dangerously. To heed God's call, to obey God's command, to walk in God's way requires a willingness to move beyond a cold, calculating prudence. Walking in the way of Christ ought not be confused with an adolescent rashness or irrational zealotry. And yet, on the other hand, the logic of a people gathered by faith in the resurrection of Jesus from the dead cannot be reduced to mere "prudence" or "efficiency" or "reason" or "maximizing profit" or "personal safety." Put in terms of ethics, living by faith questions our tendency to reduce everything to what *we* can calculate will be the outcome of our actions. When ethicists employ utilitarianism, they attempt to weigh the results of an action. Will the good of the action outweigh the bad? Will the happiness and pleasure outweigh the grief or suffering? And if the bottom line of calculations favors "good" or "happiness" or "pleasure" or a "positive cost-benefit analysis," then the act under consideration is thought to be "right." We "do evil that good may come."

While there are certainly places where weighing the foreseeable consequences of our actions is both helpful and necessary (whether to put up a traffic light at a particular intersection, say, or how to use the available medical resources in a given community), utilitarianism often becomes a sly, subtle way to set aside our calling to faithful obedience.[3] "Effectiveness" or "realistic expectations" or "what is possible" or "what is safe" or "whatever is necessary"—all these catchphrases subtly rely upon a calculation of intended results, trusting that human wisdom can determine the best course of action, even if it means setting aside faithful witness to the way of the kingdom.

Some versions of "Christian realism" counsel the Christian to set aside the way of Christ in order to take account of "reality"—or at least, it is claimed, one must do so if one wants to make a relevant contribution to the realms of politics, economics, and public culture. The Christian does not inherit an ideal world, but the realities of violence and power and greed and ethnic hatred. In such a "real world," the Christian is counseled to calculate the result of applying force here, or violence there, sanctions here, or debt enforcement there. This is the old

Christendom cataract, encouraging the Christian to do "whatever is necessary" in order to bring about "justice," or proximate levels of justice, or the "reduction of loss of life." Such ways of thinking are quite right to remind us that violence and oppression and injustice are matters to be taken with deadly seriousness. But the difficulty with such approaches is this: they set aside a central canon of Old and New Testament alike, that trusting obedience resides at the heart of covenant relationship with the God of Abraham, Isaac, and Jacob, and the God of Jesus. In fact, *precisely* when it appears that obedience is irrational, when obedience could not possibly be "effective," when obedience could not possibly lead to the "good guys" winning—precisely then is obedience lauded as worthy of honor. The "Faith Hall of Fame" in Hebrews 11 points to just such an expectation—precisely when we cannot see how our deeds of faithfulness can possibly effect good, then we are to obey.

By faith Abel offered a sacrifice by which "he received approval as righteous," but "he died" (Heb. 11:4). However, "through his faith he still speaks." Noah, warned about "events as yet unseen, respected the warning and built an ark" (v. 7). Then there is Abraham, who was called to leave home and family, "not knowing where he was going" (v. 8). Abraham forsook his homeland, and with it all that made for security and position and power, and went to a land he knew not where. By this same kind of obedient faith, Abraham lived as a sojourner in tents, looking for the promises that were not made manifest in his lifetime; he trusted, he obeyed, even when he was "one as good as dead," so that he received children of promise; and by this same obedient faith, he offered his son Isaac (vv. 8–12, 17–19).[4]

God raised up Moses through the faithful obedience of Moses' parents—"not afraid of the king's edict," they hid the child rather than kill him. And Moses himself rejected the privileges of being a part of Pharaoh's household—but why not use the power of Pharaoh, the power of empire to bring about the purposes of God? Because he did not look at what could be seen with human sight, he did not trust in what human logic could calculate. He was, instead, "looking ahead to the reward," and persevering, he "saw him who is invisible." Because he trusted the promises of God more than he feared the power of Pharaoh, he obeyed and stood before Pharaoh to demand, of all impertinent things, that he free the Hebrew slaves. "Unafraid of the king's anger," Moses "considered abuse suffered for the Christ to be greater wealth than the treasures of Egypt" (vv. 23–28).

The crossing of the Red Sea, the conquest of the city of Jericho, the reception of the spies by Rahab—these all point to the heart of biblical faith, in which the covenant people trust the promises and commands of God, even when it appears that the promises of God themselves will be defeated. Potential examples abound, says the writer of Hebrews. There is Gideon, Barak, Samson, Jephthah, David,

Samuel, the prophets—all people of God who trusted and obeyed, even in the face of torture and death. They "suffered mocking and flogging, and even chains and imprisonment. They were stoned to death, they were sawn in two, they were killed by the sword; they went about in skins of sheep and goats, destitute, persecuted, tormented—of whom the world was not worthy. They wandered in deserts and mountains, and in caves and holes in the ground." Yet in spite of their faithfulness, they "did not receive what was promised" (vv. 36–39). They are among those obedient ones who "died in faith without having received the promises, but from a distance they saw and greeted them" (v. 13).[5]

This kind of faith is strange; it makes no sense to the unbeliever, to the one who does not trust the promises of God. This kind of faith makes one a stranger, a foreigner, even in one's own homeland. "They confessed that they were strangers and foreigners on the earth" (v. 13). In their desire for a "better country," they did not yield to the temptation to be "effective" at all costs, to do "whatever is necessary" to "make things come out right." And because of such a faith, "God is not ashamed to be called their God" (v. 16).

The ultimate necessity, in other words, is to bear witness to the lordship of Jesus. And the means to *that* single end is an obedience enabled by the power and grace of God. The consequentialist ethic of nation-states requires calculating, predicting the future based upon models of human psychology and behavior, working out the proportionate reasoning to determine if our action will cause more or less harm than not acting. But the difficulty with such consequentialist logic is neither its rightful concern for the consequences of our actions nor its hope to bring about a "more just world." The difficulty, instead, is that consequentialist models fail to take into account the gospel, in which the power and grace and goodness of God to redeem rebellious humankind is at work in the fallen world. Faith demands that we trust that God can actually redeem apparently unredeemable situations.

So Abraham received a child even beyond the age of conceivable child-bearing "because he considered him faithful who had promised" (Heb. 11:11). For Abraham trusted in a power of God that moves beyond human ability to calculate the means needed to reach a certain end: Abraham knew that Isaac was the son of promise, the one through whom would come numerous offspring, yet he did not succumb to the temptation to set aside obedience in the name of God's promise. Abraham did not make it his responsibility to "make things come out right"; he did not take it as his calling to see that the promises of God worked out in history if it meant his disobedience. In fact, in his willingness to sacrifice the son of promise, Abraham was willing to obey in a way that, to all appearances, frustrated the very design and promises of God. But that willingness was grounded in his trust that "God is able even to raise someone from the dead" (v. 19).

Prayers for the Power of God

In September of 1994, Cindy Hartman entered her home in Conway, Arkansas, where she encountered a burglar. After he ripped the phone cord out of the wall, he demanded that she go into a closet. Hartman fell to her knees, requesting that she might pray for him. And she did, and she said to the intruder: "I want you to know that God loves you and I forgive you." In response, the burglar actually extended an apology, and to an accomplice waiting in a pickup truck outside, yelled, "We've got to unload all of this. This is a Christian home and a Christian family. We can't do this to them." After unloading the furniture from the truck, returning it to the home, the burglar removed the bullets from his gun, gave Hartman the gun, and left.[6]

For some reason, the story strikes me as humorous. Perhaps it's the unexpected response of the burglars — as if they might have continued to rob the woman had she been a Muslim or a Jew. Or perhaps it's simply the jarring incommensurability between an act of violence and an act of faith-filled prayer that evokes my laughter. Perhaps my laughter is not too unlike that of Sarai when, long past the age of bearing children, she laughed at the prospect of pregnancy.

Though Sarai's laughter was taken as a mark of unbelief, perhaps we disciples can practice a faithful laughter — with joyous lives, filled with a lack of too-great seriousness, we know that we serve a God who does the impossible. We know that the deadly seriousness of calculating and depending upon our own strength and our own methods is simply laughable, insufficient, and naïve. With godly laughter, we can proclaim that the error of consequentialist and realist modes of thought does not lie in their rightful concern with practical, "this-worldly" matters. Their error lies in their lack of trust in the fact that God rules the nations, that God raises the dead, that God's power can redeem utterly hopeless situations. Their error lies in their refusal to really pray. This is the logic of unbelief, rather than the logic of "practicality." The Christian doctrine of redemption proclaims that rebellious humans, and the larger constructs of rebellious human history, *can* change, that the love of Christ, embodied in compassion and forgiveness and generosity and kindness and love and self-sacrifice, can effect momentous change in the lives of both individuals and institutions. The church professes that the God of both creation and redemption actually works in the lives and hearts of men and women to bring about God's will and purposes.

The closing benediction of Hebrews prays in just this way, asking that the redeeming power of God, a power that raises the dead, will work in the lives of believers to bring about God's purposes and plans:

Now may the God of peace, who brought back from the dead our Lord Jesus, the great shepherd of the sheep, by the blood of the eternal covenant, make you complete in everything good so that you may do his will, working among us that which is pleasing in his sight, through Jesus Christ, to whom be the glory forever and ever. Amen.

Hebrews 13:20–21

This same type of prayer — that the God who raises the dead, and who has raised Jesus the Messiah from the grave, may be at work in you, making you complete, making you more like Christ, and giving you the faithfulness of Christ — is commonly prayed in the Pauline letters. When writing to the Corinthians, Paul reflects upon his suffering — "for we were so utterly, unbearably crushed that we despaired of life itself" — and requests that the Corinthian believers share in the work of praying for deliverance, "so that we would rely not on ourselves but on God who raises the dead. He who rescued us from so deadly a peril will continue to rescue us" (2 Cor. 1:8–10). Similarly, Paul in the letter to the Ephesians prays

that the God of our Lord Jesus Christ, the Father of glory, may give you a spirit of wisdom and revelation as you come to know him, so that, with the eyes of your heart enlightened, you may know what is the hope to which he has called you, what are the riches of his glorious inheritance among the saints, and what is the immeasurable greatness of his power for us who believe, according to the working of his great power. God put this power to work in Christ when he raised him from the dead and seated him at his right hand in the heavenly places, far above all rule and authority and power and dominion, and above every name that is named, not only in this age but also in the age to come. And he has put all things under his feet and has made him the head over all things for the church, which is his body, the fullness of him who fills all in all.

Ephesians 1:17–23

The Pauline epistles do not depict a cheap salvation by grace by which we are "forgiven" by giving mental assent to "Jesus as my Lord and Savior," but a gospel that proclaims the power of resurrection working among us and in us, that Christ himself now works in us. So for this, the letter to the Ephesians continues its prayer:

For this reason I bow my knees before the Father, from whom every family in heaven and on earth takes its name. I pray that, according to the riches of his glory, he may grant that you may be strengthened in your inner being with power through his Spirit, and that Christ may dwell in your hearts through faith, as you are being rooted and grounded in love. I pray that you may have the power to comprehend, with all the saints, what is the breadth and length and height and depth, and to

know the love of Christ that surpasses knowledge, so that you may be filled with all
the fullness of God.

Ephesians 3:14–19

Prayer that depends upon the power of resurrection will not be bound by human
logic and feasibility studies and business plans and projections of profit margin. The
working of God cannot be constrained by the political pundits and the realists and
the Wall Street financiers who take their pronouncements upon human nature as
the last word, the very wisdom of the ages. Their logic may indeed befit "this present aeon" but fails to take into account either the faith of Easter or the Good News
that the "coming aeon" has already broken into human history. The behaviorists
and utilitarians fail to take into account the very basic claim of the gospel, that the
God who raised Jesus Christ from the dead is now at work redeeming humankind
from its bondage to self and sin. What we need are not better consequentialist
models of predicting social phenomena in order to maintain a coercive "peace,"
but unceasing prayer that God will act to consummate the kingdom, and that we,
in the meanwhile, might bear faithful witness to the kingdom already present in
our midst. Thus the prayer for the Ephesian believers concludes with an assertion
of the incalculable nature of the power of God:

Now to him who by the power at work within us is able to accomplish abundantly
far more than all we can ask or imagine, to him be glory in the church and in Christ
Jesus to all generations, forever and ever. Amen.

Ephesians 3:20–21

Even when such prayers do not refer explicitly to the power of Christ's resurrection, Paul's prayers are most typically concerned with the power of God
being made manifest in the believer so that the believer matures in Christ, being
transformed into the likeness of Christ. In other words, he prays that God's power
will enable the believer to walk in faithful obedience, overcome temptation, and
be preserved blameless until the day of his appearing. So prays the prayer for the
Colossian believers:

For this reason, since the day we heard it, we have not ceased praying for you and
asking that you may be filled with the knowledge of God's will in all spiritual wisdom
and understanding, so that you may lead lives worthy of the Lord, fully pleasing to
him, as you bear fruit in every good work and as you grow in the knowledge of God.
May you be made strong with all the strength that comes from his glorious power,
and may you be prepared to endure everything with patience, while joyfully giving
thanks to the Father, who has enabled you to share in the inheritance of the saints

in the light. He has rescued us from the power of darkness and transferred us into the kingdom of his beloved Son, in whom we have redemption, the forgiveness of sins.

Colossians 1:9–14

Similarly, the prayer for the Philippians:

I thank my God every time I remember you, constantly praying with joy in every one of my prayers for all of you, because of your sharing in the gospel from the first day until now. I am confident of this, that the one who began a good work among you will bring it to completion by the day of Jesus Christ. It is right for me to think this way about all of you, because you hold me in your heart, for all of you share in God's grace with me, both in my imprisonment and in the defense and confirmation of the gospel. For God is my witness, how I long for all of you with the compassion of Christ Jesus. And this is my prayer, that your love may overflow more and more with knowledge and full insight to help you to determine what is best, so that in the day of Christ you may be pure and blameless, having produced the harvest of righteousness that comes through Jesus Christ for the glory and praise of God.

Philippians 1:3–11

Cultivating the Life of the Spirit

Such prayers help us avoid two common pitfalls: one, the heresy that we need not really obey Christ; two, the heresy of the religion of the "self-made man." On the one hand, such prayers do not assume that walking in the way of Christ is an unrealistic, unattainable utopian ideal. The calling of Christ is at the heart of Paul's prayers and gospel, boldly declaring that we might be transformed into the image of Christ (cf. 2 Cor. 3:12–18). And yet, on the other hand, such prayers do not fall prey to a belief that simple willpower provides us the capacity to be obedient followers of Christ. Paul does not pray for willpower, but for God's power. Paul does not enjoin some sort of moral perfectionism, or moralistic works-righteousness, or "self-made man" religion. Through God's grace and power alone do we have any hope.

All the members of the body of Christ are "on the Way," needing maturation in Christ. None of us "have arrived." We will not be sustained on the Way through sheer willpower, but only through the sustenance and grace and empowerment of God. There remains much space for growth and transformation, and indeed the more along the path of light we tread, the more the Light reveals our defects and insufficiencies and failings. One may enter a room and be impressed with the orderliness and cleanliness of that room. Were one to install, however, a battery of high-wattage spotlights in that same room, one might be able to easily identify numerous areas needing immediate attention and housekeeping.[7] And so it is, walking in the way of the light. We will not arrive until the day comes, but that does not mean we are not on the Way. As we seek God, we progressively come to know victory over the powers that once dominated our lives and are increasingly given over to true freedom, which is slavery to Christ.

"The chief act of the will is not effort but consent," says Thomas Keating, providing an axiom that serves as a key to discipleship.[8] This is, indeed, nowhere clearer than with regard to prayer. In our consumerist, individualistic age, prayer can become yet another outlet for exercising our discretion of "choices," laying before God what we want God to do for us, telling God how we want God to run the world and fix our problems and provide simple solutions for what ails us. In a world consumed with consumption, obsessed with having, eating, experiencing, owning, and controlling "more," a prayer of Jabez may quickly become construed as permission to make God the great vending machine in the sky. But this fails to account for the true heart of prayer: laying ourselves before God, submitting our will to God's will.

The "Our Father" thus begins asking that the *Father's will* may be done. All of prayer must flow from this one starting point—that we submit ourselves and our will and our intentions to the will and intention and ways of God. If we take Jesus' model prayer seriously, then all our prayers should be first and foremost centered upon our prioritized desire that God's kingdom be established, in all its fullness. In prayer, we stake our lives, our selves, our cause upon God's cause, and are invited by Jesus, we are commanded by Jesus, to rattle God's cage, to stir God up, to prompt God to be about the work of establishing the kingdom.[9]

The cross, as Stanley Hauerwas has somewhere said, frees us from the conceit that we must run the world. So does praying the Lord's Prayer. Such prayer not only frees us from our petty agendas and obsessive concerns; it also frees us from the arrogance that we may calculate the ultimate consequences of our actions. In prayer we seek God's rule and reign to come in greater fullness, throughout our own hearts and throughout the Earth. That rule and reign has come, and will come, not through our engineering its appearance, but through the power and will of God.

What is true of human history is likewise true of our own personal history: it is God's power upon which we throw ourselves. We fall or flourish upon this one point. Shall we give over our will to God, or shall we seek pitifully to maintain our own "right" to run (and so to ruin) our own lives, and the lives of those around us? The accounts of the life of Jesus, or the biographies of the lives of the saints, suggest that upon this one point, all stands or falls. Indeed, many disciples can identify particular moments of crisis, moments of very grave decision, in which their will was yielded to the Father, often with great struggle or fear and trembling. But such accounts also suggest that this crisis of submitting one's will to God is seldom, if ever, a once-and-for-all decision. It is instead the daily outworking of personal discipleship. Daily, we seek God's will, and yield our own; daily, we seek that God may provide what is needed for the day. "Give us this day our daily bread," give what is needed today to sustain our lives and our faith, that we might live another day in dependence and trust in the gracious provision of the Father — free us from anxieties about tomorrow, and free us from resentments about the past, and grant what is needed just today.

Thus in his comments upon the Lord's Prayer, Karl Barth notes that the first three petitions of the prayer — hallowed be thy name, thy kingdom come, thy will be done — point us toward the all-encompassing nature of our existence as disciples. We are simply called "to concern ourselves with God's affairs . . . with the coming of his Kingdom, with the doing of his will. . . ." Having therefore completely given ourselves over to God's cause and God's purposes, we then pray: "Here we are, engrossed in thy cause. . . . We have no other task; this is our care. . . . Therefore, to thee we hand over our existence — to thee, who hast invited and commanded us to pray, to live for thy cause. Here we are. It is now up to thee to concern thyself with our human cause."[10]

So Barth points us to a kind of prayer that is a practice of the heart and life, in which our entire existence becomes oriented toward the will and kingdom of God. Thus it makes great sense for Paul to exhort, "pray without ceasing" (1 Thess. 5:17). Similarly the Ephesians are taught to "Pray in the Spirit at all times" (Eph. 6:18), and the Colossians encouraged to "Devote yourselves to prayer, keeping alert in it with thanksgiving" (Col. 4:2). Disciples live and move each day out of a repository of constant prayer, constantly bringing ourselves consciously before God, beseeching him to be present, praying "not my will, but thine." Or, as Thomas Kelly suggests, we pray, "Open thou my life. Guide my thoughts where I dare not let them go. But Thou darest. Thy will be done."[11]

Such prayer necessarily undergirds what Kelly calls a life of "holy obedience." He wisely counsels disciples, "don't grit your teeth and clench your fists and say, 'I will! I will!' Relax. Take hands off. Submit yourself to God. . . . For 'I will' spells not obedience."[12] Life in Christ does not mean a white-knuckled determination to "do the right thing," for very often "doing the right thing" flows neither from a love of God nor from a desire to see the will of God made manifest, but from a desire to exalt ourselves before God and humankind. "Doing the right thing" may flow more from fear than love — fear of shame, rejection, or abandonment, or fear of reprisal from the rebellious principalities and powers of the world. But prayer undercuts this desire for control of others, control of ourselves, and control of what others and God think of us.

To pray good prayers regularly, not in rote recitation but in earnest sincerity, opens one to profound renewal. To pray such prayers, such as the Prayer of Abandonment by Charles de Foucauld, requires great courage besides:

> My Father,
> I abandon myself to you.
> Make of me what you will.
> Whatever you make of me,
> I thank you.
> I am ready for everything
> I accept everything.
> Provided that your will be done in me,
> In all your creatures,
> I desire nothing else, Lord.
> I put my soul in your hands,
> I give it to you, Lord,
> With all the love in my heart,
> Because I love you,
> And because it is for me a need of love
> To give myself,
> To put myself in your hands unreservedly,
> With infinite trust.
> For you are my Father![13]

The principalities and powers of marketplace and government, investment banking and economics, education and culture, all school us to balk at such an "out of control" lifestyle. Cultural forces such as these incessantly foster an illusion of control — or perhaps more accurately, they deliberately foster a *delusion* of control. Prayer, on the other hand, schools us to revel in trust rather than "autonomy," to delight in godly submission rather than ruthless competitiveness, to find joy in dependence upon God rather than dependence upon our own paltry efforts at controlling the world around us. One would be naïve, of course, to think that this daily submission of our selves to God always comes with "happiness" — for it may come with lonely prostration upon the ground, sweat falling as if it were great drops of blood. Three times Jesus prayed, "My Father, if it is possible, let this cup pass from me; yet not what I want but what you want" (Matt. 26:39), and yet the Father's will required that the Son drink the cup of anguish, and he was shortly led away to be tried and crucified. Obedience such as this, this obedience unto death, followed only from the Son's former willingness, in all earnestness, to pray, "your will be done."

Wrestling in Prayers on Your Behalf

To the Colossian believers, Epaphras was commended as "always wrestling in his prayers on your behalf, so that you may stand mature and fully assured in everything that God wills" (Col. 4:12). Prayer ought not be construed as an individualistic practice, in which the believer comes alone before the throne of God. Even when—especially when—the pains and struggles and hurts of life assail us, when the threats of principalities and powers and the delusions and lies of this rebellious aeon assail us, we gather with other believers who will pray when we cannot. Prayer is a communal event, in which we pray together, struggling together, bearing one another up before God, praying that God's power and sustenance will sustain, nurture, protect, and make us whole. We never pray alone, but always in communion with one another. "We pray to God that you may not do anything wrong—not that we may appear to have met the test, but that you may do what is right, though we may seem to have failed. . . . This is what we pray for, that you may become perfect" (2 Cor. 13:7, 9). "Pray in the Spirit at all times in every prayer and supplication. To that end keep alert and always persevere in supplication for all the saints. Pray also for me" (Eph. 6:18–19).

So in prison Paul writes to the Philippians, "Yes, and I will continue to rejoice, for I know that through your prayers and the help of the Spirit of Jesus Christ this will turn out for my deliverance" (Phil. 1:18–19). Previously to the community of disciples in Thessalonica, Paul had written, "Night and day we pray most earnestly that we may see you face to face and restore whatever is lacking in your faith. . . . Beloved, pray for us" (1 Thess. 3:10; 5:25). Or again:

> To this end we always pray for you, asking that our God will make you worthy of his call and will fulfill by his power every good resolve and work of faith, so that the name of our Lord Jesus may be glorified in you, and you in him, according to the grace of our God and the Lord Jesus Christ. . . . Finally, brothers and sisters, pray for us, so that the word of the Lord may spread rapidly and be glorified everywhere, just as it is among you, and that we may be rescued from wicked and evil people; for not all have faith.
>
> 2 Thessalonians 1:11–12; 3:1–2

This struggling together in prayer, seeking the Lord's transformation to invade our lives so we might live according to his purposes, assumes a high level of honesty and openness among fellow disciples. When churches pervert the gospel so that it becomes moralistic rule-keeping, shame is often heaped upon those who fail to meet narrow, provincial expectations. Consequently, "church" takes the shape of yet one more perverted principality and power, enslaving rather than serving. "Church" becomes a community of "nice people" who come together to hear sermons and sing songs and do their religious thing, when the reality underneath the nice exterior is always much more messy, filled with hurts, pain, and dysfunctions; caught under the power of delusions about sex, power, and money; trapped in servitude to those institutions and cultural norms and principalities that traffic in such contraband.

If we are to be a people struggling in prayer with one another, we must expose our hurts and defects and wounds to the healing light of God's kingdom. That light alone dispels and dissipates the darkness of rebellion. "My yoke is easy, and my burden is light" (Matt. 11:30), Jesus proclaimed, reminding us that the burden of my going my own way, of insisting upon control of my own life, of harboring and nurturing my lusts and greed and envy and resentments is a much heavier burden to bear, full of pain and deadly consequences. When the weight of such burdens brings us to the point of despair, we might run with open arms to embrace the gift of honesty about the brokenness of our own lives. But the offer of embrace we hold at arm's length, because of the threat of shame and condemnation.

Often burdened under a cloak of shame, many individuals desperately need the liberation of sharing their deepest secrets, of knowing the communal grace of shared prayer and struggle. On our knees together, we have no vantage point from which we might look down upon the disciple next to us. Struggling in prayer together, we know our own need for God's strength and our fellow's encouragement and are less likely to judge our brother or sister.

Unless our own lives reflect the renewal possible in God's new creation, unless the power of God's Spirit is bearing fruit in our own lives, we shall have little to give to a world groaning under the delusions of darkness.

> He who attempts to do things for others or for the world without deepening his own self-understanding, freedom, integrity and capacity to love, will not have anything to give to others. He will communicate to them nothing but the contagion of his own obsessions, his aggressivity, and his ego-centered ambitions, his delusions about ends and means.[14]

So we seek God, striving to offer the entirety of our lives as a prayer itself.

Communion

Why Disciples Share Their Wealth

Forgive us our debts, as we also have forgiven our debtors.
Matthew 6:12

In this life a man gets about what he is worth. . . . The world owes a
man nothing that he does not earn.

Russell Conwell,
Baptist minister and author
of "Acres of Diamonds"[1]

*W*ith some trepidation on a Sunday afternoon in 1994, my wife and I made our way to Sunday dinner at the home of a relatively newly married couple. Having made our way to the bus stop to catch a *matatu*—as the privately run buses are called in Nairobi—we rode the brief distance to Mathare Valley. According to some word-of-mouth reports I received while in Nairobi, Mathare Valley was at the time reckoned one of the largest contiguous slum areas in the world. "Slum," of course, means different things to different people. At Mathare it meant over-

165

population, open sewage, mud-and-stick-and-boards-and-tin housing; little access to drinking water or toilets, but overexposure to crime and drug and alcohol abuse; few employment opportunities; and lots of despair.

Another friend who had grown up in Mathare had previously guided me through the area, and on that first visit to Mathare my friend told tales of his youth—the time the open sewage in the street was diverted by heavy rains, so that it ran through the middle of the muddied dirt floor of their one-room shack; how in the early days poor squatters built shacks of cardboard boxes, and when wanna-be landlords set out to build a concrete-block structure from which they might snatch a bit of rental income, they would set a cat on fire, setting the creature loose to run through the squatters' huts, burning them out; how he and his friends abused various substances in feeble attempts to escape the pain of their lives—and so many lives were only further demolished by bottles of glue and slum-made moonshine; how his father had been murdered by a claw hammer–wielding hit man, whom my friend suspected had been hired by his grandmother, coveting her son's small parcel of land out in the country.

We soon arrived at our stop, a precinct of Mathare not so desperately poverty-stricken as other areas. Our friends' home was a simple concrete-block room, opening onto a small courtyard of sorts, where was situated the shared water spigot. There we were welcomed to Sunday dinner, sat down to break bread, laughed and prayed, and communed in the name of the Lord. That simple meal—of unleavened bread called chapati, rice, a bit of meat, and soft drinks—may have literally cost them days' worth of wages. There was neither money nor room enough for a table around which we might gather, but surely it was a Lord's Supper at which we broke chapatis, for at that meal was the grace of God mediated to us. Ultimately, it was not our friends who were host and hostess, but Christ the host, whom we had asked to be present in our midst. And Christ's grace and Christ's presence *were* made manifest, in the cheerful giving, the simple sharing, and the joyous eating, for this brother in Christ—from a tribal background stereotyped for its manipulating and grasping—generously gave, with gladness and at cost to himself, without expecting payment in return.

Grace

"Grace" denotes the freely given gifts and favor of one who is not obligated to give or act in such a way; those who receive "grace" receive "unmerited favor" or undeserved gifts that are of benefit to the recipient. Many Christians rightly celebrate "God's grace" as the operative principle establishing personal relationship with God; but many appear unwilling and intransigent when it comes to grace serving as an operative principle in various spheres of real life. Compartmental-izing grace in this way, grace becomes merely a "religious" principle or merely a "spirituality" that remains in its own socially and politically irrelevant sphere. Grace may be the way that God works with us sinners, but in the "real world" of politics and criminal justice and business, "merit" and eye-for-an-eye and like-for-like are seen as the operative principles. Market values replace gospel values, and grace is told to stay in its place.

In business, for example, the underlying and operative principle becomes one of supposed "merit." In various sorts of health-and-wealth gospels, wealth and power simply result from good morality and obedience. In the early twentieth century, for example, Russell Conwell, the well-known minister for the Philadelphia Baptist Temple, toured the countryside delivering his famous lecture "Acres of Diamonds." His six thousand public addresses of that lecture, when combined with the royalties of the book, profited Conwell eight million dollars. Conwell relied greatly upon the work of Henry Ward Beecher, who had declared that poverty is largely the product of sin, while wealth is largely the product of virtue. Conwell, more blunt than Beecher, went on to proclaim that it was a duty to seek wealth: "I say that you ought to get rich, and it is your duty to get rich." Further, "to secure wealth is an honorable ambition, and is one great test of a person's usefulness to others," he repeatedly proclaimed. "Money is power. Every good man and woman ought to strive for power, to do good with it when obtained."[2]

Conwell's viewpoint appears little different from his contemporary, Bishop William Lawrence of Massachusetts, who claimed, "in the long run, it is only to the man of morality that wealth comes. . . . Godliness is in league with riches."[3] Conwell perhaps stated his faith in the merit undergirding the accumulation of wealth when he asserted, "*in this life* a man gets about what he is worth. . . . The world owes a man nothing that he does not earn."[4] This old Christendom reflex compartmentalizes life into two unrelated spheres: wealth, accumulation, and power, supposedly proceeding from "merit," operate in the one. "Grace" and "unmerited favor" supposedly operate in the other. Consequently, Christians are thought to operate in these two worlds, the one world of "spirituality" and "church" in which "grace" serves (thank God!) as the operative principle, so I might go to heaven, and the other world of the market and business in which "merit" serves as the operative principle. All the while we assert that so long as we don't get too "attached" to "material things," as long as we "set our sights on heaven," as long as we have an attitude of "detachment from wealth," then the this-worldly pursuit of honor, prestige, and accumulation of capital will not affect our "spiritual walk." That early president of Yale, Ezra Stiles, perhaps prophetically described how American Christians would go about "business" and "religion":

We are ardently pursuing this world's riches, honors, powers, pleasures; let us possess them, and then know that they are nothing, nothing, nothing. They serve a temporary gratification, evanish, and are no more. But we cannot be dissuaded from the pursuit. Death, however, kindly ends it. Let us think that we have two worlds to live for, proportion our attention to their respective interests, and we shall be happy forever.[5]

Subtly and piously, "Follow me" gets divested of any meaning whatsoever, except maybe occasionally "Follow me to church," where we are given justification for accepting the world's ways and world's institutions just as they are. This kind of piety, crudely put, might be reduced to this: "Love Jesus and get rich."[6]

One winter in the early 1970s, nearing Christmas, my father-in-law was working as a reporter for WSM television in Nashville. Having just completed a story at the state capitol building, he heard a call on his scanner: a "10–52–64," the "10–52," he told me, indicating someone had been shot, and the "10–64" indicating someone dead. The location of the scene of the apparent crime was not but a few miles away, in a public housing complex, where the police had discovered an elderly man dead in his apartment. But as they began to investigate, it turned out that the original suspicion was all wrong. There had been no shooting. Instead, the man did not have electricity, and so had frozen to death. What had originally been thought to be a gun wound was no gun wound at all, but the wound from a rat gnawing on the old man's body. As my father-in-law exited the apartment complex, he happened to see the glow emitted from a sign, perched for the Christmas holidays atop one of Nashville's high-rises, announcing "Peace on Earth."

Such an event serves as a parable for a compartmentalized grace: the heart-warming religious message, "peace on earth," that somehow never gets connected to the real world of a poverty-stricken old man. Instead, it is assumed that in the "real world," market values and merit and reciprocity ought to determine the nature of social relations. The very naïveté of such a view makes us unable to see the graces sustaining our day-to-day existence. Furthermore, if Jesus is Lord of all realms and spheres, such a neat compartmentalization of the way of Christ must be rejected. Instead, disciples of Jesus must question the prevailing notions of "merit" and "earning" that underlie some of our most cherished cultural institutions—for such notions often result in our ignoring, if not oppressing, those to whom Jesus was particularly concerned to minister. Grace must not be constrained to the sphere of "religion"; disciples must seek to embody economic, social, and political practices of grace.

For a start, this would mean we cast a suspicious eye upon the subtle health-and-wealth assumptions undergirding many segments of American Christianity. We have deep roots in some of those early Puritan convictions that assumed wealth simply to be the product of godliness and poverty the result of sin. Such a subtle assumption may belie our need to rationalize our own comfortable lifestyles and the relative ease with which many of us accumulate the luxuries we do. Not until we profoundly question such an assumption will we be able to minister fully as the body of Christ. Not until we catch a glimpse of the grace undergirding our own existence will we have a desire to share those blessings with others. Not until we realize that *we do not deserve* all that we have can Christians ever begin to get a grasp of the biblical vision of economics. We live, we exist, we breathe by grace.

Consider the simple example of education: I have a good education because I had parents who valued education, who were supportive and nurturing, who taught me in the home, who taught me habits of personal discipline, who supported my grammar and secondary education, who provided a college education, and who encouraged me in my desire to pursue graduate studies. I merited none of this, at least not any more than poor children who grew up without the privileges into which I was born. The children whom my sister-in-law Lisa teaches in an inner-city elementary school in Nashville, for instance, have few such privileges. The child who lives with his mother who earns her living by prostitution is, needless to say, not in an environment that facilitates healthy intellectual or social development. The domestically abused child must spend time simply learning how to survive, when the child could be spending that time learning to read. The child of two parents working minimum-wage jobs will not have the same benefits—health, education, culture—of the child in suburbia whose father works a salaried position and whose mother works full-time at home.

The Gospel of Luke particularly describes the gracious economic practices that stood at the heart of Jesus' ministry. In fact, Luke points to a short Scripture reading and homily Jesus delivered in his hometown as the programmatic statement of Jesus' ministry. Jesus read a text from Isaiah 61:1–2:

> The Spirit of the Lord is upon me,
>   because he has anointed me
>   to bring good news to the poor.
> He has sent me to proclaim release to the captives
>   and recovery of sight to the blind,
>   to let the oppressed go free,
>   to proclaim the year of the Lord's favor.
>
> Luke 4:18–19

With Jesus comes the Good News of jubilee, of release from the oppression of debt, release from the oppression of captivity, and release from the oppression of illness.

Jesus thus envisioned his ministry in continuity with the proclamation of the prophets, who in turn had articulated the concern of the law for the poor, the weak, and the oppressed. There is evidence that when Jesus announces "the year of the Lord's favor," he is proclaiming a year of jubilee, a practice of economic grace, prescribed by the law. Leviticus 25 stipulates that every seven years the people would observe a Sabbath year, in which they would allow their fields to remain fallow. Just as the daily gathering of manna in the wilderness structured the Hebrews' lives around a practice of trust, so the Sabbath day and Sabbath year functioned similarly. If you work six days and rest the seventh, if you sow six years and let the land lie fallow the seventh, God will provide. Or so Jesus asserted in the Sermon on the Mount—"I tell you, do not worry about your life, what you will eat or what you will drink. . . . Look at the birds of the air; they neither sow nor reap nor gather into barns, and yet your heavenly Father feeds them" (Matt. 6:25–26).

In addition to this commitment to a Sabbath year of rest, Leviticus 25 stipulates yet a more radical vision of wealth and its use: every seven cycles of seven years, every fiftieth year, land that had been "bought" was to be returned to its original holder. Or to put it differently, land is not to be bought and sold, but only *used*. The land is not *mine*, it is *God's*; I do not *buy* it, but only pay for the privilege of using it. "Capital"—in this case, land—belongs to God, and no other. It is therefore always to be graciously shared among all who have need. (See also the assumption of Sabbath economic practices in Lev. 27:16–25; Num. 36:4; Neh. 10:31; Ezek. 46:17.)

This biblical vision stands in sharp contrast to the notion of "private property" undergirding prevailing capitalist orders. Private property, within certain parameters, assumes that use, disposal, and control of that property is accountable to no higher authority than the owner. It is *mine*. Yet Torah approaches wealth from an entirely different perspective—it is *not* mine, but God's, to be employed in pursuit of God's gracious order, in which we must be particularly mindful of the weak and vulnerable. Consequently, our notion of unrestricted use and control of our own private property gets sharply bounded, if not altogether reconfigured, by numerous other practices. Deuteronomy 23:24–25 stipulates that one may wander into a neighbor's vineyard or wheat field and eat their fill, so long as they do not carry any away. Leviticus 19:9–10 required the particularly "inefficient" practices of leaving unharvested the edges of a field of grain and leaving the produce dropped on the ground during harvesting; these practices were intended for the good of "the poor and the alien" (cf. also Lev. 23:22). This same admonition in Deuteronomy 24:19–22 includes as an explanation for the laws regarding gleaning, "Remember that you were a slave in the land of Egypt; therefore I am commanding you to do this." That is, you have received grace—therefore, you shall show grace.

Such practices of economic grace are further reflected in Deuteronomy 15, where the law prescribes the regular practice of remitting debts, so that every seven years, all debts were to be released. In the community of remission of debts, "There will . . . be no one in need among you" (Deut. 15:4). The people of God are commanded not to "be hard-hearted or tight-fisted toward your needy neighbor. You should rather open your hand, willingly lending enough to meet the need, whatever it may be" (Deut. 15:7–8). The passage cited by Jesus, and so oft-cited by those who disparage the notion that the church must be concerned with gracious economic behavior, is in its original context a reason for ongoing service to others: "Since there will never cease to be some in need on the earth, I therefore command you, 'Open your hand to the poor and needy neighbor in your land' " (15:11). In our culture, property is often referred to as one's "holdings," a metaphor connoting a closed fist, a tight grip. But the law's insistence that God's people be openhanded, freely giving and forgiving, merely reflects the grace they have already received—their kind and generous treatment of slaves must reflect the treatment they received from God. "Remember that you were a slave in the land of Egypt, and the LORD your God redeemed you; for this reason I lay this command upon you today" (15:15).

It is, in other words, insufficient to "spiritualize" the disciple's relation toward wealth: that is, the point of the gospel with regard to money is *not* that we should simply "not set our heart on money," but that we should proactively seek to use the wealth at our disposal for the good of God's kingdom. This is not a call to poverty—though the practice of voluntary poverty may most certainly bear witness to the nature of God's kingdom—but a call to share the abundance of God's kingdom in a way that reflects the graciousness of God. "For the Christian, the bottom line can never be the bottom line."[7] Or better yet, the bottom line must be redefined in terms of the kingdom of God.

Table Grace

The Gospel accounts make plain Jesus' continuity with Torah's concern for economic grace. In the kingdom of God, disciples are called to sell possessions and give to the poor. The rich young ruler is told to sell all that he has and give it to the poor, and come follow Jesus; the rich man who ignores poor Lazarus at his gate wakes up in perdition; blessings are pronounced upon the poor, and woes are pronounced upon the rich; and the forgiveness that comes with the kingdom comes with one requirement—if you wish God to forgive your debts, then you must forgive others their debts. The coming kingdom requires the economic grace the Creator had always desired would mark his good creation. Repeatedly, use of money is addressed in the gospel message so that Richard Foster suggests that "Jesus spoke about money more frequently than any other subject except the kingdom of God."[8]

In the kingdom of God, the table provides an especially important place for practicing grace, as John Mark Hicks has suggested.[9] At table with the Lord, grace is an ever present cohost, sharing five loaves and two fish, giving banquets for the poor and disenfranchised, reconciling sinful women and men to God and the ways of God's kingdom. The Good News of God's jubilee is particularly prominent in Luke's narrative when Jesus sits at table, eating and drinking. The classic Sunday School tale of the short tax collector Zacchaeus typifies this:[10] Jesus goes home with Zacchaeus and there (presumably) at table it is justice and concern for the poor that evidently dominates the discussion. Or at least that is the case if we judge by Zacchaeus's jubilee-like response, in which he declared, "Look, half of my possessions, Lord, I will give to the poor; and if I have defrauded anyone of anything, I will pay back four times as much" (Luke 19:8). To this, Jesus responded, "Today salvation has come to this house" (19:9)—that is, the kingdom of God has come even to the house of a tax collector, particularly in the form of sharing one's wealth.

The Zacchaeus story highlights not only the connection in Luke between table and sharing of wealth; in addition, the story points to the manner in which Jesus turns upside down acceptable table etiquette among the people of God. The very fact that Jesus would deign to dine with such a one as a tax collector, one who epitomizes the most reprehensible of Jews, traitorous to Jewish identity, collaborating with the Roman Empire in their conquest—such an act upended acceptable table etiquette and prompted the grumbling of the crowds. "He has gone to be the guest of one who is a sinner" (Luke 19:7; cf. similar account in 5:30). Similarly, while Jesus was dining with a rather inhospitable Pharisee who failed to provide the expected services of a host, "a woman in the city, who was a sinner," imposed herself upon Jesus, bathing Jesus' feet with her tears, drying his feet with her hair. To this scene, the host said to himself, "If this man were a prophet, he would have known who and what kind of woman this is who is touching him—that she is a sinner" (7:36–39). But Jesus, in response, makes it clear that the table, in his ministry, becomes a place to proclaim the Good News and the presence of the kingdom, dining with all, regardless of supposed degree of merit or righteousness, and sharing the Good News of repentance unto life (7:40–50; cf. 5:29–32). The table becomes a place of gracious reconciliation, rather than estrangement, so that accepted mores of acceptability, merit, and righteousness get turned over.

Similarly, when Jesus was dining with a leader of the Pharisees, Jesus recommended a new table etiquette—rather than seeking preeminence, position, and respectability, take the lower place at the table (Luke 14:1–11). And more, when you give a banquet, do not invite those who are able to repay you, but precisely those for whom the prophets were so concerned—"invite the poor, the crippled, the lame, and the blind" (14:12–14). This parable stands in stark contrast to the account of the rich man and Lazarus, recorded later in Luke's narrative (16:19–31): "There was a rich man who was dressed in purple and fine linen and who feasted sumptuously every day. And at his gate lay a poor man named Lazarus, covered with sores, who longed to satisfy his hunger with what fell from the rich man's table; even the dogs would come and lick his sores" (vv. 19–21). The rich man's table, kept to himself, led him to perdition, as he ignored the one at the gate; so Jesus counsels that the table should be the place of gathering together those who are ever so conveniently "overlooked," and thus victimized. Those who embody the Good News of the kingdom in such a way, Jesus declared, would receive their reward at the consummation of the kingdom, "for you will be repaid at the resurrection of the righteous" (14:14).

To this, one of the dinner guests responded, "Blessed is anyone who will eat bread in the kingdom of God!" (Luke 14:15; and cf. the other allusion to this by Jesus recorded in 13:29). That is, Jesus' words remind this table guest of the anticipated messianic banquet, the eschatological feast, that coming meal that symbolized the triumph of God's justice and righteousness, when death would be defeated and tears wiped away. Isaiah had prophesied:

> On this mountain the LORD of hosts will make for all peoples
>> a feast of rich food, a feast of well-aged wines,
>> of rich food filled with marrow, of well-aged wines strained clear.
> And he will destroy on this mountain
>> the shroud that is cast over all peoples,
>> the sheet that is spread over all nations;
>> he will swallow up death forever.
> Then the Lord GOD will wipe away the tears from all faces,
>> and the disgrace of his people he will take away from all the earth,
>> for the LORD has spoken.
>
> Isaiah 25:6–8

When the dinner guest articulates his eagerness to participate in the eschatological banquet, Jesus apparently looks around the table at all the upright, wealthy, and respectable Pharisees, guardians of the law and tradition—and tells another parable, the punch line of which indicates that the messianic banquet would have a much different guest list than those presently gathered around the table. It's not that the likes of the Pharisees would be excluded by the host, but that they would exclude themselves—"For I tell you, none of those who were invited will taste my dinner," the host declares (Luke 14:24). Instead, "the poor, the crippled, the blind, and the lame" would be invited, and would come to the table (v. 21).

Yet another occasion when Jesus upsets respectable table etiquette also occurs at a Pharisee's home. The host, "amazed to see that [Jesus] did not first wash before dinner" (Luke 11:38), finds himself confronted by Jesus: "Now you Pharisees clean the outside of the cup and of the dish, but inside you are full of greed and wickedness" (11:39). Giving a tenth of one's income—even scrupulous tithing, of tithing "mint and rue and herbs of all kinds" (v. 42)—fails to be sufficient in the kingdom of God, for all those things can be done quite well while still "full of greed." Jesus' point is not to abolish the tithe as a requirement for his followers, but to up the expectation that all of our lives and our entire use of wealth should reflect "justice and the love of God" (11:42). Jesus goes on to assert that religion that cleans the "outside of the cup and the dish" but fails to forsake one's greed and desire for preeminence, in the end, leads to murder. The prophets declared the will of God—for justice that cares for the needs of the poor; for righteousness that extends to every facet of communal life; and for peace defined not as the mere absence of conflict but as the presence of self-giving love and communal wholeness—and for such words from the Lord they were persecuted and some put to death. "You are witnesses and approve of the deeds of your ancestors; for they killed them," Jesus declared (11:48).

Jesus as Gracious Table Host

Three times in Luke (9:12–17; 22:14–23; 24:28–35), Jesus himself hosts a table. In Luke 9:12–17, Jesus feeds the hungry crowd of 5,000. Under Jesus' lordship, in Jesus' care, the paltry offering of five loaves and two fish—akin to the smallness of a mustard seed, over against the great need—is transformed into something beyond their imagination. Of great significance, Luke brackets this account with two questions, both of which are concerned with the identity of Jesus. Herod, who had killed John the Baptizer, wondered, "who is this about whom I hear such things?" (9:9); and immediately after the feeding, Luke repositions the account of Peter's confession so as to emphasize the identity question, with Jesus asking, "Who do you say I am?" (9:20). This way of telling the story indicates an answer to those questions: Jesus is the one who sits at table, breaking bread with us.

The Last Supper constitutes the second account of Jesus serving as table host (Luke 22:14–23). Significantly, Luke uses the same words to describe Jesus' deeds as host in both occasions. Before feeding the 5,000, Jesus, "taking the five loaves and the two fish, . . . looked up to heaven, and blessed and broke them, and gave them to the disciples" (9:16). And at the Last Supper Jesus similarly "took a loaf of bread, and when he had given thanks, he broke it and gave it to them" (22:19). The Last Supper—a real meal, not merely a symbolical eating of bits of bread or sips of wine—Jesus instituted as something done "in remembrance of me." When you eat together with me as table host, when you eat your common meal together, sharing your provisions with one another—"Do this in remembrance of me." This is the meaning of the "words of institution"—you remember me, you participate in the ongoing redemptive work of God when you sit at table with one another—as I sat at table so often with you—sharing provisions, eating with the marginalized, reconciling the alienated back to the Father. Jesus here counsels not mere cognitive recall, but the kind of "remembrance" that always accompanied the Passover meal—a renewed participation in the redemption wrought by God. The Lord's meal becomes occasion for celebrating the deliverance wrought in Jesus, the kingdom now present at the table. Indeed, "I tell you," Jesus says, "that from now on I will not drink of the fruit of the vine until the kingdom of God comes" (v. 18).

On the next occasion Jesus eats and drinks with his disciples—the kingdom of God has come in the resurrection of the Lord!—he also serves a third time in Luke as table host (24:28–35). On the road to Emmaus, two disciples of Jesus were walking along, downcast and saddened, their anticipations dashed by the crucifixion of Jesus: "we had hoped that he was the one to redeem Israel" (v. 21), for they too did not know how to process a crucified Messiah. Jesus appeared—but they did not recognize him—and recounted how the prophets had declared that the way of the Messiah was first suffering, and only then, glory. Arriving at their destination, Jesus walked on, "as if he were going on" (v. 28). When they urged him to stay with them, he joined them at table—and strangely, took the place of host. So yet a third time Luke recounts, "he took bread, blessed and broke it, and gave it to them" (v. 30). All this time, they had not recognized him—but then, when he took the bread, blessed it and broke it, "*Then* their eyes were opened, and they recognized him" (v. 31, emphasis added). When the two recounted the experience, joyfully declaring the resurrection of Jesus, "they told what had happened on the road, and how he had been made known to them in the breaking of the bread" (v. 35). Jesus was revealed to them in the breaking and sharing of bread, in fellowship at table. Only then, in the breaking of bread, did they recognize him.

Just prior to Jesus' ascension, Luke records Jesus' instruction to his disciples to wait in Jerusalem, to "stay here in the city until you have been clothed with power from on high" (24:49). When on the day of Pentecost the promise of a manifestation of God's Spirit was fulfilled, Luke records Peter preaching to the Pentecost crowds; in response, those who welcomed his message were baptized, and that day about three thousand persons were added. They devoted themselves to the apostles' teaching and fellowship, to the breaking of bread and the prayers.

Awe came upon everyone, because many wonders and signs were being done by the apostles. All who believed were together and had all things in common; they would sell their possessions and goods and distribute the proceeds to all, as any had need. Day by day, as they spent much time together in the temple, they broke bread at home and ate their food with glad and generous hearts, praising God and having the goodwill of all the people. And day by day the Lord added to their number those who were being saved.

Acts 2:41–47

Given all the emphases of Luke's Gospel accounts, it is not surprising that the "breaking of bread," the eating of the Lord's Meal, would be accompanied by the practice of liquidating possessions and distributing goods as there was need. At table with Jesus, the kingdom of God had been proclaimed and embodied, in the practices of reconciliation and sharing; the table embodied the new order of the kingdom, and as the early church ate together, sharing provisions with one another, they too proclaimed and embodied the new kingdom. Acts 4 similarly recounts:

Now the whole group of those who believed were of one heart and soul, and no one claimed private ownership of any possessions, but everything they owned was held in common. With great power the apostles gave their testimony to the resurrection of the Lord Jesus, and great grace was upon them all. There was not a needy person among them, for as many as owned lands or houses sold them and brought the proceeds of what was sold. They laid it at the apostles' feet, and it was distributed to each as any had need.

Acts 4:32–35

The account of Acts does not require communal living as the required norm for walking in the way of the kingdom (though such a practice can undoubtedly bear witness to the kingdom, especially in our day of radical individualism); nor does the account suggest that the community of believers renounced ownership of goods as a dogmatic prescription. While some Platonic conceptions (which undergird the early Christian heresy of Gnosticism) understand matter and thus wealth as inherently evil, Christian and Jewish understandings depict God's creation—and therefore wealth—to be good. But both the Old and New Testaments likewise insist that wealth is properly used to *meet existing needs*. Renunciation of property ought not be conceived of as an end in and of itself, something sought as a sign of spiritual superiority. Nor does Scripture, and nor should disciples, romanticize poverty. Scripture depicts involuntary poverty as oppressive, and very often it depicts such poverty as the result of societal injustice. Similarly, the amassing of wealth in the face of need is depicted as unjust. God provides wealth not for personal gratification and luxury, but for meeting needs. "God is able to provide you with every blessing in abundance, so that by always having enough of everything, you may share abundantly in every good work" (2 Cor. 9:8).

Thus Acts 2 and 4 should not be read as the assertion that the disciples in Jerusalem once and for all divested themselves of all their possessions and "had done with lesser things." Instead, the practical needs of the community and the voluntary willingness of the members of the community drove the practice of sharing (as evidenced particularly by Acts 5).[11] The fellowship (or *koinonia*) of the early community (Acts 2:42) should not be understood then merely as a warm feeling of goodwill toward a fellow believer, but as much more. *Koinonia* denotes "partnership"—so the sons of Zebedee, for example, are said to be *koinonoi* with Peter in their fishing business venture (Luke 5:10). Thus some years later when Paul organizes a collection for the disciples in Jerusalem consequent to a famine in Judea, he encourages the Corinthian believers to remember the example of Christ, who "though he was rich, yet for your sakes he became poor" (2 Cor. 8:9). Thus, the Corinthians should give in such a way as to meet the needs of the fellow believers: "it is a question of a fair balance between your present abundance and their need, so that their abundance may be for your need, in order that there may be a fair balance. As it is written, 'The one who had much did not have too much, and the one who had little did not have too little' " (8:13–15). By such gifts, Paul professes, one exhibits their confession in the gospel of Christ. That is, by the "generosity of your sharing"—by the generosity of your *koinonias*—you show that you do, indeed, own the good news of Jesus (9:11–13).

In most churches today, we cannot see the significance that the "Lord's Supper" or "communion" or "Eucharist" or "Mass" had to the early church—the Lord's Supper was indeed "supper," or a meal, in which believers came and shared their lives and their provisions. The meal was at once a practice of thanksgiving (or *eucharist* in Greek) for the redemption offered in the new covenant, in the body and blood of Jesus; simultaneously, the meal was an economic practice, a practice of "communion" with fellow believers, sharing their means. Eating together at the Lord's table serves as a concrete form of "fellowship," of partnership in the Lord.

The grumbling that soon arose indicates the great significance the early church placed upon the common meal (Acts 6). Some of the Grecian Christians believed that their widows were getting shortchanged in the daily distribution of bread. Precisely in response to this need, the Twelve initiated a new institutional structure: they appointed seven men to wait on tables, so that the need might be met. Thus with the widows, Luke provides yet another instance in which the early church embodied the jubilee, sharing its provisions, meeting the needs in its midst.

Paul's rebuke to the Corinthians for their manner of eating and drinking the Lord's Supper (1 Cor. 11:17–34) further highlights the social significance of Eucharist: apparently following the social etiquette of the day, in which the table served as a place of social stratification, the Corinthian Christians ate the Lord's Supper in such a way that the poor were placed at the margins, away from the food and drink—"one goes hungry"—and the wealthy gorge—"another becomes drunk" (v. 21). If this is the manner in which you eat and drink together, Paul chastises them, then "it is not really to eat the Lord's Supper" (v. 20). The Lord's table knows no such class distinctions, knows no such economic stratification, knows no such social disparities, and so it cannot be the *Lord's* Supper that they eat. If it is merely their hunger and thirst they wish to quench, then they have their homes in which they could do that; but as it is, they "show contempt for the church of God and humiliate those who have nothing" (v. 22).

The Early Church and Table Grace

The separation of a common meal from the Eucharist occurred early in Christian history. By the second century, the bread and wine were separated from a meal, losing sight of the many-faceted significance of sitting at table with the Lord and one another. The economic practice—sharing daily subsistence with one another, and the very natural outgrowth of sharing wealth with one another—was lost from the Eucharist. Nonetheless, the witness to this practice continued in the form of *agape* meals for a number of centuries. Other reminders and commitments to economic grace continued in the early church, particularly seen in the early church fathers' unanimous indictment of the accumulation of wealth.

So the *Didache* (an early manual of church practice and discipline, dated to late first or second century) counsels *synkoinonein*, that is to "co-koinonize," to copartner in all things: "thou shalt not turn away from him that is in want, but thou shalt share (*synkoinonein*) all things with thy brother, and shalt not say that they are thine own."[12] Do not follow, the *Didache* further counsels, the "way of death" in which lies adultery and murder and those "not pitying a poor man, not labouring for the afflicted, not knowing Him that made [the afflicted], . . . afflicting him that is distressed, advocates of the rich, lawless judges of the poor, utter sinners."[13]

Similarly, the *Epistle to Diognetus* asserts that disciples "have a common (*koinen*) table,"[14] and exhorts believers to show in all things the grace God has shown them:

Do not wonder that a man may become an imitator of God. He can, if he is willing. For it is not by ruling over his neighbor, or by seeking to hold the supremacy over those that are weaker, or by being rich, and showing violence towards those that are inferior, that happiness is found; nor can any one by these things become an imitator of God. But these things do not at all constitute His majesty. On the contrary he who takes upon himself the burden of his neighbour; he who, in whatsoever respect he may be superior, is ready to benefit another who is deficient; he who, whatsoever things he has received from God, by distributing these to the needy, becomes a god to those who receive (his benefits): he is an imitator of God.[15]

While the early church presupposes the practice of private property, the notion was always sharply constrained by the overriding concern for proper *use*. What constitutes proper use? The most commonly prescribed criterion is *sufficiency*. That is, believers should use for themselves what is necessary for their needs — and the remainder should thus be viewed as superfluous and then shared with others whose needs have not been met. Others suggest the criterion of *usefulness* — that is, money ought not be spent on useless or extravagant things. If a thing can be just as useful and simultaneously less extravagant or luxurious, all the better. Clement, for example, reminds the early church that one can actually cut better with an iron knife than one made out of gold.[16] Regardless of the criteria employed by the early church fathers, all fundamentally agreed that their faith required them to share wealth.[17]

Business Ethics?

If indeed the New Testament and the early church fathers call disciples to understand wealth as something not to be amassed but shared, as something that we do not earn or possess but merely steward, then the existing social order in our consumerist, capitalist-driven world will by no means support such a practice. Faithfulness in this regard will require creative and thoughtful critique of existing economic practices, and creative and thoughtful construction of alternative economic practices. But this already begs many questions, jumping over assumptions deeply embedded in many Christian traditions that may first need to be uprooted.

One such assumption is the Protestant notion of an "ethic of vocation," in which it is assumed that the task of the Christian is not to question or critique existing social structures, such as economic or political practices. The Christian, instead, brings certain values (such as the importance of "being honest") or attitudes (such as "love") or traits (such as industriousness) to those existing social practices. But the existing social practices or vocations are not questioned in and of themselves. When the reformer Martin Luther went about his task of recovering the Good News of salvation by grace through faith, he did not, for example, recover the teachings of Jesus as something that had concrete political and social relevance. Instead, he continued the Augustinian tradition of interiorizing, of spiritualizing, the ethic of Jesus. For Luther, there exist two spheres, or two "kingdoms," each ordained by God, that pertain to different ends and make use of different methods: the church employs the methods of Jesus to attain spiritual ends, and the state employs the method of sword and court to attain civil ends. So Luther restricted the teaching of Jesus to the spiritual realm, while the civil realm employs an ethic rooted in an authority other than that of Jesus. The Sermon on the Mount, for example, pertains to one's personal attitudes and actions within the kingdom of Christ, says Luther, while the use of the sword, or the use of the court, is legitimate when acting as a participant in the kingdoms of this world, or as a member of secular society.

Luther thus sets up what theologians call an "ethic of vocation": the ethic of one's job depends not upon the Sermon on the Mount, or any other teaching of Jesus, but upon the ethic rooted in that job itself. So Luther asserted, "Do you want to know what your duty is as a prince or a judge or a lord or a lady, with people under you? You do not have to ask Christ about your duty. Ask the imperial or the territorial law. It will soon tell you your duty toward your inferiors as their protector. It gives you both the power and the might to protect and to punish within the limits of your authority and commission, not as a Christian, but as an imperial subject."[18]

Consequently, Luther helped establish a line dividing two spheres of activity: the spiritual and the civil. These two different spheres do not designate different classes of people, but different spheres of activity within each individual Christian life: "Thus, when a Christian goes to war or when he sits on a judge's bench, punishing his neighbor, or when he registers an official complaint, he is not doing this as a Christian, but as a soldier or judge or lawyer. At the same time he keeps a Christian heart."[19] Social order serves as one of Luther's great concerns, and he concludes that Christians ought to participate in the preservation of this order. But in this task, the "spiritual" teaching of Jesus is not binding. In order to deal with sin, the power of the sword must be utilized: "For without [secular government], this life could not endure."[20] Or, in other words, "What would happen if everybody did that—what would happen if everyone obeyed Jesus' commands?" Though Luther reacts against much medieval Christian practice, his ethic, in many ways, further supports (if not deepens) the old Christendom cataract.

An "ethic of vocation" serves ultimately to circumscribe the ethic of Jesus: existing social orders are left to define and determine their own ethic. However much Luther may not have intended it, there is built into this ethic a social conservatism: the existing social order, the status quo, serves as the authority for what we are to do in our vocations. This does not mean for Luther that the church is to be flatly subservient to the state. But these are two very different realms, requiring different ethics.

The same disjunction between the "church" and the "secular" continues to reign in much Christian practice. "He's really a very serious Christian," someone once told me about a very high-profile businessman in Nashville, "but you just wouldn't know it by the way he practices business." Here indeed is the "ethic of vocation" in its present garb: one might be very "spiritual," one might be a "faithful church member," but business is business. In spite of the fact that Jesus taught so much about sharing wealth, the Christian banker is thought to legitimately help institutions hoard it. In spite of the fact that Jesus taught forgiveness of debts ("unless you forgive, you will not be forgiven"), the Christian businessperson is thought to legitimately prosecute those who cannot pay their debts. "It's just good business" seems to be a self-evident maxim that trumps serious engagement with the responsibilities of discipleship; "Sorry, that's just not good business practice" serves as a way for Christians to leave their "convictions" at the church building, or certainly not bring them to the marketplace.

"Business" is seen as an endeavor with a very specific *telos*, a very specific goal or end: to make a profit, to maximize the profit margin, to provide a return to those who invest capital in the venture. This does not mean, of course, that business is without ethics. Indeed, the proliferation of business ethics courses—particularly in Christian colleges—professes that business can be done ethically. Business ethics thus teaches young businessmen and businesswomen to be honest, to avoid manipulating underage consumers through unscrupulous marketing (maybe), and to keep within the limits of domestic and international law.[21]

There is much good to be said about honesty and the avoidance of manipulative advertising to minors; but this "ethic of vocation" fails to bear witness to the kingdom of God, which is an altogether different order. To seek the interests of others before oneself; to refuse to profit off the needs of the poor; to prioritize maximizing the good of one's customers and employees rather than the maximization of profit; to see wealth as a stewardship used for the good of the impoverished rather than as private property to be held for one's own luxury or benefit—these practices all constitute a very different order than "business ethics," in pursuit of a very different *telos*, a very different end. But it is quite easier, and much more widely practiced, to accept an "ethic of vocation" so that we need not carry this goal, this purpose, into the marketplace. Out of fear of the cost to ourselves—"What would happen if everybody did that?"—we much prefer to limit such goals and purposes to the realm of church, and be "good Christians" in the marketplace by simply being law-abiding and nice.

Christianity and Capitalism

Since the goal of Christian faith is to bear witness to the order of the kingdom of God, and the goal of capitalism is something else altogether, discipleship necessitates our forsaking the notion that capitalism is God's economic order. It simply is no such thing, no more than a nation "making the world safe for democracy" through an overbearing militarism is the kingdom of God. The temptation to identify "our" economic system with God's will is the same temptation we've witnessed since at least the time of Eusebius — to identify God's will with a system of power and success that nominally supports Christianity. But meanwhile the concrete meaning of Jesus is laid aside.

Too often, arguments over economic orders restrict the appropriate considerations to too narrow a realm. Often, the tired debates present a continuum running from socialism to capitalism, and then require us to pick a spot somewhere on that continuum as being the "most Christian." This argument is now, of course, irrelevant, because of the late-twentieth-century downfall of socialist orders.[22] But this way of putting the question misses the point anyway. If there is a significant distinction to be made between "church" (as the community that proclaims and embodies the lordship of Jesus) and "world" (as the community that refuses to accept his lordship and lives in rebellion to the Creator's intention for the creation), then Christians cannot pick and choose among unredeemed economic orders and then ascribe God's favor to one particular unredeemed economic system.

This distinction between church and world necessarily leads us to make a distinction between the economic practices of God's kingdom and the economic systems of the unredeemed principalities and powers. Capitalism ultimately leaves the use and disposal of capital to the self-interest of individuals, corporations, and nation-states. One of the assumptions of free enterprise and free-market systems is the absence of any substantive "common good." That is, capital and its use need not be oriented toward the good of the local community, or toward the good of the larger human community. It does not matter, for example, if the immense resources indiscriminately poured into a community's hosting a professional sports team could be much more faithfully invested in the education of and care for the vulnerable in the community. What "matters," it is thought, is "what the market will bear." Western economic systems begin with the assumed goodness of the free play of self-interest, trusting that the "invisible hand" will guide the interplay of self-centered motives for the ultimate wealth of all.[23] But, as Peter Maurin put it, disciples must be "go-givers" rather than "go-getters."[24] Nonetheless, the stereotypical language of some Christian college freshmen betrays the degree to which the alleged gospel of capitalism dominates our worldview, rather than the Good News of Jesus: "I want to major in something that will allow me to get a good job and make a lot of money." In this worldview, college degrees are not precious stewardships entrusted to college students for the purpose of serving the kingdom of God, and thus the world, but a marketable commodity that will allow them to attain individualistic goals and whims, the necessary precursor to which is "making a lot of money."

Capitalism, however, is not entirely individualistic. There is, of course, one necessary "common good" in which the participants in the capitalist order are expected to participate—the mere *survival* of the capitalist power. Bumper-sticker patriotism—"United We Stand"—makes sense only in a time of warfare against some real or perceived enemy, for the very point of Western liberal democracies is that we are *not* "united" upon anything, except the survival of the order that allows us to live in "freedom," pursuing our own individualistic self-interest. For this reason, capitalism benefits from war-making, for war-making provides some common enemy that will keep the order from fragmenting into three hundred million frayed individualistic agendas. It is for this reason that a "war on terror," a war in which we shall supposedly rid the world of "evil," is so convenient, for it provides an endless war to provide *some* point of unity and common purpose in the capitalist nation.

Ministry of Grace

The church offers the world a hopeful alternative—rather than accumulation and murderous defense of one's spoils, the church extends the invitation to eat together at the Lord's table. There, we all acknowledge the immensity of God's grace and the immensity of the debts forgiven us; there, as the bread is broken, we receive grace to be broken in behalf of our neighbor; there, where the wine is poured out, we receive grace to be poured out for the world. Eucharist is simultaneously sacrament, sign, and sustenance. It is sacrament, for it is the place where we eat with our Lord in the kingdom, receiving God's grace and empowerment. It is a sign, for it symbolizes to the world our partnership, in which all peoples, regardless of supposed merit or rank or status, gather to break bread together. It is sustenance, for there we share bread and wine, for to the degree that we truly eat meals together, the Lord's Supper becomes a very tangible economic sharing, which gives rise to a fellowship, to a partnership, in which we surely care for one another's very real needs, whatever they might be.

If we as a baptized people, as the new humanity, do share communion together, then practices of jubilee or grace will inevitably become part and parcel of our life together, and part and parcel of our offer of God's Good News to the world. How jubilee or grace get played out in concrete terms will obviously vary with the context, but there are innumerable possibilities of what shape such economic practices might take. Whether it be a Habitat for Humanity that extends to the poor an opportunity for home ownership, sharing the capital and the labor necessary for having a home, or low-interest mortgages for working poor; or whether it be a medical clinic offering care to the millions of uninsured working poor in the United States, or a medical practice extending care to the impoverished in developing countries; or whether it be a Church of the Savior in Washington, D.C., that seeks to invest in and offer decent housing for low-income families, the possibilities are endless. We need not fret that we cannot "fix" the world from the top down—our task is to bear witness to and practice the sharing of the kingdom of God, as do a handful of students, some of whom I've had the privilege to teach, who on their own initiative go weekly to prepare a meal for, and then eat and visit with, a group of homeless men and women in Nashville.

The path of discipleship calls us to a life of consistently practicing a giving and sharing that seeks to meet, however we can, the needs of the weak and impoverished, ever remembering that in serving the poor we are serving Christ. Or so Jesus is recounted as having put it, in the parable of the Sheep and Goats in Matthew 25:31–46. As David Lipscomb said in the Reconstruction years of southern poverty, "Let us realize that every helpless, needy one of our brethren is the personification of Christ to us appealing for help. He is our Christ, to be kindly welcomed and generously treated. Shall we cast our Christ from our doors and let him become a beggar from others?"[25]

Jim McClendon notes one striking thing about the Matthew 25 text: that when their deeds of sharing and visitation were recounted at the judgment, the "sheep" did not even recall having done these things, and certainly not having done them to Christ (vv. 37–39). We might put it this way: they were judged worthy not because they set out to show some charity here, and to even give generously there. Instead, their very *character*, their identity, was expressed best in their sharing and giving.[26]

Taking such practices seriously may mean that disciples question their business practices on very different criteria than those commonly employed. Given the immense poverty and need in our world, perhaps it is not sufficient for Christians merely to make a legal profit. Perhaps it will not do to simply get rich honestly. Our discipleship necessitates posing kingdom-related questions about production and selling. The agenda of the kingdom will find plenty at odds with a culture like ours that practices, to use Rodney Clapp's memorable phrase, the "deification of dissatisfaction."[27] That is, why should we use such immense resources in an attempt to make people unhappy, dissatisfied with their present state of existence, so that we can sell them something? And why assume that this is the very meaning of economic existence? Why put resources into frivolities and fads and fashion, when energy, capital, and research can be used to meet basic human needs of the desperately poor? Why pressure people to spend money on things they don't need? Why make the bottom line the bottom line when the profit could be used to offer a "living wage" to those individuals whose labor actually produces the products we sell? Why fall prey to the myth that more is always better, always seeking to capture more of the market share?

We might, for example, take a cue from the eighteenth-century Quaker John Woolman, who gained his livelihood as a shopkeeper and tailor. When his business began to expand and grow, he decided not to pursue wealth, and so intentionally decided to reduce his possibilities for business growth, so as not to be ensnared by the burdens that come with acquiring and holding. Having enough to meet the needs of his family, if more business than he needed came his way, he directed the would-be customers to other shops that could meet their needs, keeping himself free to pursue whatever ministry tasks to which he believed himself called.[28]

Whatever the particulars, we are called to feast at the table of the Lord. Sharing partnership around that table, we find that no one goes away hungry—in more ways than one. We feast in the kingdom of God, receiving God's abundance. Having freely received, we freely give. To do otherwise would make no sense, given the graciousness of our host.

Evangelism
How Disciples "Make a Difference"

The crowning evidence that he lives is not a vacant grave, but a spirit-filled fellowship. Not a rolled-away stone, but a carried-away church.

Clarence Jordan[1]

The world of today needs Christians who remain Christians.

Albert Camus[2]

*T*he gospel proclaims that the coming reign of God has already broken into human history. But why should the world believe this?

The apparent falseness of the claim that Jesus inaugurated the rule of God appears easy enough to establish: merely read history books. Since the time of Jesus, war-making continues, greed consumes, injustice pervades. The kingdom of God has come, you say?—oh, really? Scripture recounts the manner in which believers were warned of the ridicule the scoffers would proffer: "Where is the promise of his coming? For ever since our ancestors died, all things continue as they were from the beginning of creation!" (2 Pet. 3:4). Such criticisms continued into the subsequent centuries of the early church, and the believers' own sacred texts were turned against them. Do not the prophets, asked Trypho, a Jewish critic of the early Christians, declare that with the coming of the Messiah would come a new era in which peace would reign? Do the prophets not envision that with the coming of the Lord's day, the nations would all stream to the house of the Lord, to learn the Lord's ways, and then "beat their swords into plowshares, and their spears into pruning hooks," and putting away the way of the sword, "neither shall they learn war any more" (Isa. 2:2–4; cf. Micah 4:1–3)?

Christians were thus called to account for their faith. Does not the witness of history and prophecy itself deny your claim that Jesus is the Messiah? No, replied the early church father Justin. The fulfillment of God's purposes has already begun, he claimed, and the evidence of this fact lies in the very ethic and lifestyle of the church. Yes, there are portions of the prophetic proclamations yet to be fulfilled, which await the coming advent of Christ. But in the meanwhile, the church lives and exists as a community that bears witness to the reality of the kingdom of God having already invaded human history: "We who were filled with war, and mutual slaughter, and every wickedness, have each through the whole earth changed our warlike weapons, — our swords into ploughshares, and our spears into implements of tillage, — and we cultivate piety, righteousness, philanthropy, faith, and hope, which we have from the Father Himself through Him who was crucified."[3]

Justin's mode of apologetics stands in stark contrast to many contemporary models of apologetics. Books on "Christian Evidences," for example, often proceed upon the assumption that one might appeal to some "objective" court of appeals to demonstrate empirically that Jesus is Lord. But Justin here, at least, employs a different strategy: we claim that Jesus is Lord, and that certain practices accompany that claim, and one may see the truth or falsehood of that claim depending upon the degree to which our lives manifest that claim.

So in his *First Apology*, Justin cites Isaiah 2:3 as evidence for the Messianic status of Jesus. "That it did so come to pass," that the Messianic age began with Jesus, "we can convince you," he boldly asserts: twelve illiterate men went out from Jerusalem, proclaiming by the power of God that they were commissioned to teach the word of God, and "we who formerly used to murder one another do not only now refrain from making war upon our enemies, but also, that we may not lie nor deceive our examiners, willingly die confessing Christ."[4] In other words, Justin asserts that the nonviolent, truth-telling church embodies the new social order foretold by the prophets. You don't believe the new age has come? — asks Justin. Well, just look at the church, and you'll see that all things have begun to be made new.

Justin was not alone among the early church fathers in such a strategy. Irenaeus, also commenting upon Isaiah 2 and Micah 4, claims that the evidence of Jesus as the Messiah lies in the effect of the word of God preached by the Twelve: their message *did* cause "such a change in the state of things" that all the nations of people now constituting the church "did form the swords and war-lances into ploughshares . . . and that they are now unaccustomed to fighting, but when smitten, offer the other cheek."[5] In responding to unbelieving Jews, Tertullian also pointed to the peaceable church: "who else, therefore, are understood but *we*, who, fully taught by the new law, observe these practices . . . ?" The observance of the new has "shone out into the voluntary obediences of peace."[6] Origen makes the very same argument in responding to the pagan Celsus, the one who had insisted that the church "get real," who had asked, "What would happen if everybody did that?" To Celsus, Origen replied, "we no longer take up 'sword against nation,' nor do we 'learn war any more,' having become children of peace, for the sake of Jesus, who is our leader."[7]

This model of evangelism and apologetics ups the ante: if you wish the *world* to believe what you say, you must live as if *you* believe what you say. Our profession and practice will oftentimes require critique of existing structures or practices. Furthermore, Christian theology sometimes requires us, in no uncertain terms, to denounce, to use our voices, to say the things that no one wants said, to say the things that we are afraid to say. As one commentator put it, reflecting upon the manner in which the church was complicit in the Rwandan massacre in 1994, "The greatest complicity was silence masquerading as prudence."[8] But critique and condemnation, if left to themselves, are not the gospel, but only further explication of the problem to which the gospel is the solution. The Good News is neither that the world is going to hell in a handbasket, nor that the world is full of corruption and greed and self-centeredness and animosity and warfare. The gospel, instead, announces the good, abundant, life-giving alternative, calling a community of people to order their lives with all steadfastness according to that alternative. So, Peter Maurin in his pithy way advised: "We should be announcers, not denouncers," and "Be what you want the other fellow to be," and "Don't criticize what is not being done. Find the work you can perform, fit yourself to perform it, and then do it."[9]

Our task is simply to "let the church be the church." Commenting upon the assertion in Ephesians 3 that the church is to declare to the world the manifold wisdom of God, Berkhof notes:

> All resistance and every attack against the gods of this age will be unfruitful, unless the church herself *is* resistance and attack, unless she demonstrates in her life and fellowship how men can live freed from the Powers. We can only preach the manifold

wisdom of God to Mammon if our life displays that we are joyfully freed from his clutches. To reject nationalism we must begin by no longer recognizing in our own bosoms any difference between peoples. We shall only resist social injustice and the disintegration of community if justice and mercy prevail in our own common life and social differences have lost their power to divide. Clairvoyant and warning words and deeds aimed at state or nation are meaningful only in so far as they spring from a church whose inner life is itself her proclamation of God's manifold wisdom to the "Powers in the air."[10]

When in graduate school, I had the great blessing of participating in an accountability and prayer group with several men from our local church, a church for which I also served on the ministerial staff. I shared one evening my deep struggles with my faith — "Sometimes I don't really know if I even 'believe,' " I said. "Sometimes I wonder whether it's all a big game, a farce. I suppose that I continue to struggle with these questions because of my graduate studies, constantly being faced with difficult questions about the nature of faith and doctrine." My good friend Sam, with whom I was on the staff at the church, began laughing: "You're not doubting your faith because you're in graduate school; you're doubting your faith because you work for the church!" Further reflection convinced me Sam was right: in the midst of a setting in which some church members were bickering, acting hatefully, and living spitefully, how could one believe there could be anything to their profession of faith? And there was not only the spitefulness of "those" church members, but at that time in particular, a recurring sin in my own life over which I was experiencing little victory. How can one claim "Jesus is Lord" and live as if he is not, unless Jesus is not really Lord? To reduce the claim that "Jesus is Lord" to arguments over how to "do church" is not sufficient: the church is to offer to the world what God created it to be; the task of the church is to be the church, and if it will not, it is its own worst enemy. The salt that loses its saltiness is perverse, foolish, good for nothing but to be cast out.

In 1948, the world-renowned author and unbeliever Albert Camus addressed the Dominican monastery of Latour-Maubourg. Camus was eminently qualified, as an unbeliever, to address his topic: What does the unbeliever expect of Christians? "For a long time during those frightful years" of World War II, Camus said, "I waited for a great voice to speak up in Rome. I, an unbeliever? Precisely." But it seemed not to come, Camus alleged, as "the executioners multiplied." When told that a voice from Rome did come, in the form of papal encyclicals, he asserted that it could not be understood: "What the world expects of Christians is that Christians should speak out, loud and clear, and that they should voice their condemnation in such a way that never a doubt, never the slightest doubt, could rise in the heart of the simplest man. That they should get away from the abstraction and confront the blood-stained face that history has taken on today. The grouping we need is a grouping of men resolved to speak out clearly and to pay up personally." In other words, said Camus, "the world of today needs Christians who remain Christians."

Why the Gospel Is Not Sectarian

Thanks in no small part to the immense popularity of H. Richard Niebuhr's *Christ and Culture*,[11] it is not uncommon to think of a serious commitment to Christ's way of forgiveness, prayer, reconciliation, sharing, and nonviolence as "sectarian," and thus irrelevant to the workings of human history. Such a way is construed as a "withdrawalist" strategy, concerned with a desire to "keep one's hands clean," desiring to stay unsullied by the "realistic" and "necessary" things that "must be done to get things done." Such Christians are charged with "tribalism," self-righteously concerned with their own little group being more holy than thou, unable to make a difference in the real world.

In response to such critiques, Stanley Hauerwas and William Willimon object: "We reject the charge of tribalism, particularly from those whose theologies serve to buttress the most nefarious brand of tribalism of all — the omnipotent state. The church is the one political entity in our culture that is global, transnational, trans-cultural. Tribalism is not the Church determined to serve God rather than Caesar. Tribalism is the United States of America, which sets up artificial boundaries and defends them with murderous intensity. And the tribalism of nations occurs most viciously in the absence of a church able to say and to show, in its life together, that God, not nations, rules the world."[12]

The gospel is not sectarian, but a call to an indiscriminate, suffering love. The particulars of such love will vary, obviously, with the context, but unlike the principalities and powers, who think it is the power brokers to whom we should cater our concerns, the gospel reminds us that it is particularly "the least" whom we are called to serve, for in the least is embodied the person of Jesus (Matt. 25:31–46). This may mean that the respectable Dallas businessman must learn to go to the trailer park, or that the Christian school must learn to truly honor its immigrant workers with a respectable living wage, or that the old established church must flee the temptation of white flight, or that the physician must challenge the profiteering hospital that turns away the uninsured, or that white southerners should learn Spanish in order to minister to the influx of Hispanics. The possible permutations are innumerable, but they are all part of the fabric of the Good News of the kingdom. The gospel is neither sectarian, nor irrelevant, but the only hope of a world hurtling toward self-destruction; it is the only hope of a world that seems eager to storm the very gates of hell. The gospel is the offer of Good News to a world that, if left to its own devices and methods, would destroy itself. The gospel offers much more realistic responses to the desperate needs of the world. Neighborhood victim-offender reconciliation programs, modeled after Jesus' injunctions to seek reconciliation before going to the judge, offer a long-term, more effective manner to deal with dispute and offense than does a hard-nosed "justice system." The recovery and hope offered in twelve-step groups, modeled after so much of the best of the Christian tradition, provide a response to addictions of whatever stripe that's much more "realistic" than a criminal justice system that responds only with incarceration. Most should be able to see the insanity of the burgeoning super-max prison system in which inmates are caged for twenty-three of every twenty-four hours, especially when the vast majority of those offenders are then released to the larger world, only more hardened and wounded by the "justice" they have received. And where would be the present good of African-Americans in the United States had Martin Luther King Jr., championed the way of the sword rather than the way of suffering love? The same might be asked of the population of India under the British, or South Africa under apartheid, or innumerable others.

If the Good News is the presence of the kingdom of God, then "evangelism" is much more than "saving souls." Evangelism means sharing and showing to the world how to realistically, faithfully, and creatively respond to the real needs of a world laboring under ongoing rebellion. Evangelism means living according to the ways of the kingdom of God and inviting others to join us on the way. Evangelism is not selling Jesus, but showing Jesus; evangelism is not mere telling about Christ, but about being Christ. The prophet Zechariah envisioned the day in which the nations and peoples of the world would hear the news of the reign of God; and they would receive it not because of arm-twisting or guilt-preaching, but because they would recognize it as Good News:

> Thus says the LORD of hosts: Peoples shall yet come, the inhabitants of many cities; the inhabitants of one city shall go to another, saying, "Come, let us go to entreat the favor of the LORD, and to seek the LORD of hosts; I myself am going." Many peoples and strong nations shall come to seek the LORD of hosts in Jerusalem, and to entreat the favor of the LORD. Thus says the LORD of hosts: In those days ten men from nations of every language shall take hold of a Jew, grasping his garment and saying, "Let us go with you, for we have heard that God is with you."
>
> Zechariah 8:20–23

The gospel offers the world a real alternative, the possibility of something truly good, for it is of God. The challenge of evangelism may, however, be first a challenge of discipleship: will we be what we have been called to be? Or will we, all in the name of "relevance," be grasping and grabbing to get our hands on the throttle of the old ways that have been defeated, are on their way out, and are, in the end, irrelevant themselves?

The gospel invites us to forsake the way of playing the world's games, and to follow the good way of Christ. The gospel calls us to the adventure of being mere disciples.

Notes

Acknowledgments

1. Which Yoder used in his undergraduate course at Notre Dame entitled "Christian Attitudes to War, Peace, and Revolution."

2. John Howard Yoder, *The Politics of Jesus: Vicit Agnus Noster*, 2d ed. (Grand Rapids: Eerdmans, 1994).

3. In John Howard Yoder, *The Priestly Kingdom* (Notre Dame, Ind.: University of Notre Dame Press, 1984), 135–50.

4. John Howard Yoder, *Body Politics: Five Practices of the Christian Community Before the Watching World* (Nashville: Discipleship Resources, 1994).

Chapter 1: *"Radical" Discipleship*

1. Leo Tolstoy, *Confession*, trans. David Patterson (New York: W. W. Norton, 1983), 14.

2. Dietrich Bonhoeffer, *The Cost of Discipleship* (New York: Simon and Schuster, 1995), 59.

3. My thanks to my colleague Earl Lavender for drawing my attention to Rwanda as a horrific case that has opened the eyes of missiologists to the failure of traditional, Western Christian evangelism. See the very helpful discussion of Michael L. Budde, "Pledging Allegiance: Reflections on Discipleship and the Church after Rwanda," in *The Church as Counterculture*, ed. Michael L. Budde and Robert W. Brimlow (Albany: State University of New York Press, 2000).

4. And this is, of course, a legitimate line of critique. Why do Western nations who supposedly espouse the just war tradition appear so slow to take up arms in situations of mass killing when no economic interest is at stake? The reigning doctrine of conservative U.S. politics of only using military force when our national interest is at stake betrays the selfish interest pacifists (and the letter of James 4:1–10) always believe to be at work in waging warfare.

5. See also the analysis of Ian Linden, "The Church and Genocide: Lessons from the Rwandan Tragedy," in *The Reconciliation of Peoples: Challenge to the Churches*, ed. Gregory Baum and Harold Wells (Maryknoll, N.Y.: Orbis, 1997), 49ff. esp.

The point here is not to blame the church or Christianity for the genocide, though some have suggested that the ethnic distinctions were made greater and even utilized for purposes of social control with the coming of a "Christian culture." The point here is a more modest one: that the gospel, which proclaims the overcoming of ethnic and racial difference ("neither Greek nor Jew"), failed to be embodied in the widespread nominal Christianity of Rwanda.

6. Cited in Robert E. Hooper, *Crying in the Wilderness: A Biography of David Lipscomb* (Nashville: David Lipscomb College, 1979), 72.

7. David Lipscomb, "Race Prejudice," *Gospel Advocate* (21 February 1878): 121.

8. The school began as the Nashville Bible School and was named Lipscomb College following Lipscomb's death. See the announcement "Bible School" in *Gospel Advocate* (17 June 1891): 377.

9. David Lipscomb, "The Restitution South," *Gospel Advocate* (28 February 1867): 172. See the discussion in Anthony L. Dunnavant, "David Lipscomb on the Church and the Poor," *Restoration Quarterly* 33 (1991): 83.

10. See C. Leonard Allen, *Distant Voices: Discovering a Forgotten Past for a Changing Church* (Abilene, Tex.: Abiline Christian University Press, 1993), 93–94.

11. James H. Cone, *God of the Oppressed*, rev. ed. (Maryknoll, N.Y.: Orbis, 1997), 13. "Black theology" and "Black theologian" are Cone's own self-descriptors.

12. See, e.g., Robert M. Grant, *Augustus to Constantine: The Rise and Triumph of Christianity in the Roman World* (San Francisco: Harper and Row, 1970). His pt. 4, "The Triumph of the Christian Movement," refers to the rise of Constantine following the Diocletian persecution.

13. An extended note of qualification, on several points, is in order here. First, on my use of history: I have not here given sufficient historical evidence to induce a historical type that one might dub "Christendom." Instead, I am more interested in identifying particular ways of thinking that appear with much greater frequency after the so-called "Constantinian shift." My interest in identifying them is because, to my way of understanding the biblical texts, these modes of thinking lead us away from the teaching and intentions of Jesus. These ways of thinking (discussed in chaps. 2 and 3), common in Roman Catholic history, are also common in European Protestant history and American church history. The historical anecdotes I use are just that—anecdotal and illustrative, rather than a careful inductive presentation of historical material in order to develop a historical "type," but I do nonetheless assume that one can induce such a way of thinking, evidenced in my use of the terms "Christendom cataract" and "Constantinian reflexes." But I construe my task here more as a theological one, rather than a historical one—I do believe it fairly evident that one can discern these ways of thinking in the history of "Christendom" as well as in popular American religious culture today, but my primary concern here is to suggest that these ways of thinking distort our reading of biblical texts and our understanding of discipleship. Yoder's article, "The Constantinian Sources of Western Social Ethics," in *The Priestly Kingdom* (Notre Dame, Ind.: University of Notre Dame Press, 1984), 135–50, is one helpful source in this regard. His outline, "The Difference 'Constantine' Made in Moral Reasoning" (unpublished ms.), is another source I've found helpful in conceptualizing these "Constantinian" ways of thinking about Christian ethics. Furthermore, on this historical note, those who criticize

a "Constantinian shift" such as I am assuming here should not depict Constantine as the lone or even primary character in some mythical "fall of the church." The conceptual and ethical categories critiqued here have their roots in earlier Christian fathers, and the full fruit of a fourth-century "shift" developed only after centuries of growth. Nonetheless, the historical events of the fourth century—of "Constantine"—serve as a powerful symbol of what I take to be faulty ways of understanding Jesus' intentions and teaching.

Second, on the distinction between "doctrine" and "ethics." I do not want to suggest by my storytelling that the early church was more primarily concerned with "ethics," and the latter church with "doctrine." Instead, these things always go together. As Yoder's *Politics of Jesus* argues, a refusal to compartmentalize Jesus, and an embrace of, say, Jesus' nonviolence, flows directly from Nicene and Chalcedonian orthodoxy. If we take Jesus as humanly normative, such ethical practices follow as a matter of course.

Third, on whether "Constantine" (taken as a [faulty] theological construct) is the most helpful way to go: I don't know if it is or not. But I find in my teaching that it has the capacity to communicate well something very important. But perhaps there are better ways to go. Gerald Schlabach's very helpful suggestion (in his nicely nuanced critique of Yoder's use of "Constantine") that the concerns of the Deuteronomist are more basic than "Constantine" would be one viable and different way of doing the social critique I want to do here. See his essay in *The Wisdom of the Cross: Essays in Honor of John Howard Yoder*, ed. Stanley Hauerwas et al. (Grand Rapids: Eerdmans, 1999).

Chapter 2: *God's Way of Working*

1. *The So-called Letter to Diognetus*, 7.4, in *Early Christian Fathers*, vol. 1, *The Library of Christian Classics*, trans. and ed. Cyril C. Richardson (Philadelphia: Westminster, 1953), 219.

2. H. R. Loyn and John Percival, eds. and trans., *The Reign of Charlemagne: Documents on Carolingian Government and Administration* (New York: St. Martin's Press, 1975), 52. Or similarly, Charlemagne decreed that "If anyone follows pagan rites . . . let him die," or "if anyone in contempt of the Christian faith should spurn the holy Lenten fast and eat meat, let him die," or "if anyone takes counsel with pagans against Christians, or wishes to persist with them in hostility to Christians, let him die; and anyone who treacherously approves of this against the king or against Christian people, let him die." See the historical background and interpretation by Lawrence G. Duggan, "'For Force Is Not of God'? Compulsion and Conversion from Yahweh to Charlemagne," in *Varieties of Religious Conversion in the Middle Ages*, ed. James Muldoon (Gainesville: University Press of Florida, 1997), 49.

3. *Diognetus*, 5.10ff.; Richardson, *Early Christian Fathers*, 1:217.

4. Augustine, *Letter* 93, excerpted in *From Irenaeus to Grotius: A Sourcebook in Christian Political Thought, 100–1625*, ed. Oliver O'Donovan and Joan Lockwood O'Donovan (Grand Rapids: Eerdmans, 1999), 131. Taken over against other of Augustine's writing, this may be unrepresentative of Augustine's own view of the "new age" following Constantine. Augustine was no Eusebius. But that he said this, and said it in just this way, is of great significance.

5. *Carolingian Chronicles*, trans. Bernhard Scholz with Barbara Rogers (Ann Arbor: University of Michigan Press, 1970), 51.

6. *Carolingian Chronicles*, 166–67.

7. M. K. Gandhi, *Hind Swaraj or Indian Home Rule* (Ahmedabad, India: Navajivan, 1938), 71.

8. *Bede's Ecclesiastical History*, ed. Bertram Colgrave and R. A. B. Mynors (Oxford, U.K.: Clarendon, 1969), 113.

9. Ibid.

10. Ibid.

11. Consider one more, admittedly extreme, example, taken from Edward Gibbon, in *The History of the Decline and Fall of the Roman Empire* (New York: George Macy, 1946), 2:1529–30. In A.D. 602, a centurion named Phocas rose to power as emperor on the tide of public dissatisfaction, usurping the place of the previous emperor Maurice. After being assured of Phocas's Christian orthodoxy, the patriarch of Constantinople consecrated the new emperor at the Church of St. John the Baptist. On the third day of his reign, the new Christian emperor dispatched several of his ministers to Chalcedon, where the just-deposed Maurice and his family had fled. There Phocas's ministers slaughtered, one by one, each of the five sons before their father's eyes, and finally murdered Maurice. Their decapitated bodies thrown into the sea, their heads were put on display in Constantinople. Pope Gregory, rather than calling the tyrant to repentance for his assassinations, instead saluted with "joyful applause," according to the historian Edward Gibbon, the rise of the new emperor. Gregory was "content to celebrate the deliverance of the people and the fall of the oppressor [Maurice]; to rejoice that the piety . . . of Phocas [has] been raised by Providence to the Imperial throne; to pray that his hands may be strengthened against all his enemies; and to express a wish . . . that, after a long and triumphant reign, he may be transferred from a temporal to an everlasting kingdom." Phocas's reign surely *felt* long to his subjects, though it was surely a reign unlike any the Holy Father envisioned. The victims of Phocas's tyranny were often condemned without trial and sentenced to the cruelest of deaths—eyes pierced, tongues ripped out, hands and feet amputated. Some were lashed to death, others burned, and yet others executed with arrows. Heads, limbs, and mangled bodies littered the Roman hippodrome.

12. The Protestant Reformation did not do a great deal to change this basic assumption. As one poignant example, consider the Swiss Reformer Huldrich Zwingli, who ultimately depended upon the magistrate to effect his program of reform and employed the logic of the ends justifying the means in his commonsensical appeal to magistrates to employ the sword for the purposes of God: "Why should the Christian magistrate not destroy statues and abolish the Mass? . . . This does not mean he has to cut the priests' throats if it is possible to avoid such a cruel action. But if not, we would not hesitate to imitate even the harshest examples." Henry Kamen, *The Rise of Toleration* (New York: World University Library, 1967), 46.

13. Letter signed by Hal Hubbell to the *Tennessean*, sometime in fall of 1999. Thanks to Richard Goode for drawing my attention to this letter to the editor.

14. I do not assume that what Jesus meant by "turn the other cheek" is obvious. For example, it could be taken (and has been taken) to mean passive nonresistance, while others (such as Walter Wink) interpret this as a creative, nonviolent response to an oppressive, unjust order.

15. David A. Hoekema, "Aftereffects—The Legacy of Hiroshima and Nagasaki," *The Reformed Journal* 35 (August 1985): 11. Hoekema here decries the complacency of late twentieth-century Christians for not taking seriously the just war tradition; he rightly observes that the just war tradition makes nuclear war immoral. But there is a certain inconsistency

in his observations, given that he rejects using the "tools from the kingdom of hell" to bring about the "kingdom of heaven on earth," given that he accepts the just war tradition, which is itself, I take it, an outgrowth of the logic of the ends justifying the means, at least as an "exception" in difficult circumstances.

16. Will D. Campbell, *Brother to a Dragonfly*, 25th anniversary ed. (New York: Continuum, 2000), 248.

17. This does, however, simply overlook the perception of a large part of the Muslim world, which sees the actions of the United States as the actions of Christians—a presupposition that is not far-fetched, given that then-President Bush, followed by Bill Clinton and George W. Bush, all profess a Christian faith, along with innumerable legislators and judges.

18. Reported by Kim Lawton, "Religious Broadcasters Hear Bush Defend Gulf Action," *Christianity Today*, 11 March 1991, 62. In response to Bush's address, the board of directors of the National Religious Broadcasters unanimously passed two resolutions supporting Bush's prosecution of the war. "We, who nationally and internationally herald the name of the Prince of Peace . . . have resolved . . . to wholeheartedly stand in prayer and in support of our President and the Government of the United States of America *as they do all that is necessary*, though costly, to bring genuine peace in the Middle East" (italics added).

19. From "Punishing Saddam," interview by Leslie Stahl, on CBS's *60 Minutes*, aired 12 May 1996. The text of the interview is available on numerous web sites. See, e.g., www.thestruggle.org/mecc_11/Albrightx.html.

20. "Big Ed" Johnson was the only individual ever to have served three terms as governor of Colorado (1933–1937; 1955–1957) and three terms as senator for Colorado (1937–1955). See www.archives.state.co.us/ govs/johnson.html. The citation is from William H. Chafe, *The Unfinished Journey: America Since World War II*, 4th ed. (New York: Oxford University Press, 1999), 59. My thanks to my colleague Guy Vanderpool for sharing with me this remarkable quote.

21. Quotations from speech by George W. Bush, "War on Terrorism," delivered 8 November 2001, reprinted in *Vital Speeches of the Day*, 1 December 2001, 99. Compare similar rhetoric in "Advancing the Cause of Freedom," delivered 17 April 2002, reprinted in *Vital Speeches of the Day*, 1 May 2002, 420; and "The Coalition Against Terrorism: The United Nations Place in the Fight," delivered 10 November 2001, reprinted in *Vital Speeches of the Day*, 1 December 2001, 102, in which Bush asserts that "Civilization, itself, the civilization we share, is threatened."

22. Tom Tripp, "Christ's Love," *Leadership* 15, no. 1 (winter 1994): 47.

23. From *Against Faustus*, 22.76, in O'Donovan and O'Donovan, *From Irenaeus to Grotius*, 118.

24. See the summary of Justo L. González, *Faith and Wealth: A History of Early Christian Ideas on the Origin, Significance, and Use of Money* (San Francisco: Harper and Row, 1990), chap. 13. Also see chap. 10 of this book for more discussion of this topic.

25. As recounted by Marius Reiser, "Love of Enemies in the Context of Antiquity," *New Testament Studies* 47 (October 2001): 425–26.

26. Celsus cited by Origen, *Against Celsus*, 8.68, in *Ante-Nicene Fathers* (hereafter ANF), vol. 4, ed. Alexander Roberts and James Donaldson (1885; repr. Peabody, Mass.: Hendrickson Publishers, 1999), 665.

27. Origen, *Against Celsus*, 8.68; ANF 4:666.

28. Origen, *Against Celsus*, 8.70; ANF 4:666.

29. Cited in Donald Durnbaugh, *The Believers' Church: The History and Character of Radical Protestantism* (Scottdale, Pa.: Herald, 1985), 257.

Chapter 3: *Pledging Allegiance to the Kingdom of God*

1. Cicero, *On the Laws*, 2.19, cited in Eberhard Arnold, *The Early Christians: In Their Own Words*, 4th ed. (Farmington, Pa.: Plough, 1997), 61.

2. Robert S. Alley, *So Help Me God: Religion and the Presidency, Wilson to Nixon* (Richmond, Va.: John Knox, 1972), 79.

3. This latter rewording of the mission statement was subsequently reversed. This story is reported by Ken Sehested, "Loyalty Test," *Christian Century*, 2 March 1994, 212–14. See also the follow-up report in "Air Force Chaplain Loses Case," *Christian Century*, 7 December 1994, 1153–54.

4. Some, of course, will object that my way of putting it here is insufficient by saying that the apparent tension can be resolved by a notion of dual citizenship in both the kingdom of God and in the nation-state of which we happen to be a part. But this is only a more complicated way of still effectively setting aside the lordship of Jesus, assuming his way has nothing to do with those issues with which the nation-states are concerned, issues like violence and warfare, injustice and oppression, or scarcity and wealth.

5. Bill Tibert, unpublished sermon preached at Covenant Presbyterian Church, Colorado Springs, Col., 23 May 1993. Cited in Richard Hays, *The Moral Vision of the New Testament: Community, Cross, New Creation* (San Francisco: HarperSanFrancisco, 1996), 458.

6. "The United States Military Academy is the guardian of values that have shaped the soldiers who have shaped the history of the world," George W. Bush proclaimed at the 2002 commencement of West Point. Reported by the *New York Times*, 2 June 2002, at http://www.nytimes.com/2002/06/02/international/02PREX.html?ex=1024022162&ei=1&en=1cb0bf0bc0aa3142.

7. Eusebius, *Life of Constantine*, trans. Averil Cameron and Stuart G. Hall (Clarendon Ancient History Series; Oxford, U.K.: Clarendon Press, 1999), 2.55.1, 113. So Constantine prayed, for example, that he might be used to bring about healing and comfort for the Christians who had been persecuted in the eastern part of the empire, that he might be allowed to offer "healing through me your servant." After all, continued his prayer, "by your guidance I have undertaken deeds of salvation and achieved them [and] . . . led a conquering army. Whatever the public need may anywhere require, following the same tokens of your merit I advance against the enemy."

8. Ibid., 1.5.1–2, 69.

9. Cited by Eldon J. Eisenach, *The Next Religious Establishment: National Identity and Political Theology in Post-Protestant America* (New York: Rowman and Littlefield, 2000), 32.

10. Ezra Stiles, "The United States elevated to Glory and Honor. A Sermon preached before His Excellency Jonathan Trumbull, Esq L.L.D. Governor and Commander in Chief, and the Honorable The General Assembly of the State of Connecticut, Convened at Hartford, at the Anniversary Election, May 8, 1783," in *The Pulpit of the American Revolution*, ed. John Wingate Thornton (1860; repr. New York: Capo, 1970), 403.

11. Ibid., 407. Stiles proceeded to describe what he believed to be the future "political welfare of God's American Israel." Given his assumption that both America and Israel were the people of God, Stiles used the history of Israel as "allusively prophetic of the

future prosperity and splendor of the United States" (ibid., 403; cf. 440). Already has the United States seen the work of God in its midst: the American Israel "has already risen to an acknowledged sovereignty among the republics and kingdoms of this world. And we have reason to hope, and, I believe, to expect, that God has still greater blessings in store for this vine which his own right hand hath planted, to make us high among the nations in praise, and in name, and in honor." One significant piece of evidence Stiles argued was the leadership of George Washington in the Revolutionary War: "Congress put at the head of this spirited army the only man on whom the eyes of all Israel were placed. . . . [T]his American Joshua was raised up by God, and divinely formed, by a peculiar influence of the Sovereign of the universe, for the great work of leading the armies" (ibid., 439, 443).

12. Ibid., 442–43, 446.

13. See James Davison Hunter, *Culture Wars: The Struggle to Define America* (New York: BasicBooks, 1991): 109–10.

14. Chafe, *Unfinished Journey*, 58.

15. Bush, "Advancing the Cause of Freedom," 420.

16. Cited in Abraham Heschel, *The Prophets* (New York: Perennial Classics, 2001), 212.

17. Leo Tolstoy, "Church and State," in *Tolstoy's Writings On Civil Disobedience and Non-Violence*, trans. Aylmer Maude (orig., n.d.; repr. New York: Bergman, 1967), 278.

18. Cited by Origen, *Against Celsus*, 4.23.

19. Ibid., 8.75.

Chapter 4: *The Gospel: Repent, for the Kingdom Is at Hand*

1. Clarence Jordan, *The Substance of Faith and Other Cotton Patch Sermons by Clarence Jordan*, ed. Dallas Lee (New York: Association, 1972), 24.

2. Karl Barth, *Prayer: According to the Cathechisms of the Reformation*, trans. Sara F. Terrien (Philadelphia: Westminster, 1952), 51.

3. As Stanley Hauerwas puts it. See the very helpful essay, "Jesus and the Social Embodiment of the Peaceable Kingdom," in *The Hauerwas Reader*, ed. John Berkman and Michael Cartwright (Durham, N.C.: Duke University Press, 2001), 116–41. On the holy war idea, see 133.

4. One very helpful work that does a storytelling of the biblical account being mindful of the sensitivities of the "postmodern" world is the very fine book by J. Richard Middleton and Brian J. Walsh, *Truth Is Stranger Than It Used to Be: Biblical Faith in a Postmodern Age* (Downers Grove, Ill.: InterVarsity Press, 1995). My account here is very similar to their storytelling, though they do so at much greater length and detail than the brief following discussion.

5. Heschel, *Prophets*, 222–23.

6. Cf. John Howard Yoder's "The Original Revolution," in *For the Nations: Essays Public and Evangelical* (Grand Rapids: Eerdmans, 1997), 165.

7. Barth, *Prayer*, 46–47.

8. See H. Sasse, *aion* in *Theological Dictionary of the New Testament* 1:197ff., ed. Gerhard Kittel, trans. Geoffrey Bromiley (Grand Rapids: Eerdmans, 1964), which discusses the often parallel and/or synonymous use of *kairos*, such as *ho kairos houtos* (Mark 10:30; Luke 18:30); *ho nun kairos* (Rom. 3:26; 8:18; 11:5; 2 Cor. 8:14); and *ho kosmos houtos* (1 Cor. 3:19; 5:10; 7:31; Eph. 2:2). Johannine writings usually use the latter (John 8:23; 9:39; 11:9;

12:25, 31; 13:1; 16:11; 18:36; 1 John 4:17). The uses are not always synonymous, however; see Oscar Cullmann, *Christ and Time: The Primitive Christian Conception of Time and History*, rev. ed., trans. Floyd V. Filson (Philadelphia: Westminster Press, 1964), chap. 1. Of course context must always determine the meaning of a word, rather than imposing upon any particular text some predetermined content of a word.

I depend upon a great deal of Cullmann's work in this chapter, though he visually graphs the eschatology of the New Testament quite differently than I do here. If my memory serves me correctly, I believe Leonard Allen at Abilene Christian University once graphed the New Testament eschatology in the manner represented here.

9. I do not mean to suggest by my use of Scripture here that there is always a simple, flatly developed eschatology equally found in all the New Testament writings. Taking the later two citations, for example, Colossians focuses more upon the realized nature of the kingdom and purposes of God in history, while in 1 Corinthians, Paul had to deal with opponents who had an "overrealized" eschatology. Nonetheless, this tension between the now and the not-yet does appear to undergird the entire New Testament canon.

10. Cullmann, *Christ and Time*, 84.

Chapter 5: *The Savior: The Slaughtered Lamb*

1. John Howard Yoder, *The Politics of Jesus: Vicit Agnus Noster*, 2d ed. (Grand Rapids: Eerdmans, 1994), 39.

2. Soren Kierkegaard, *Provocations: Spiritual Writings of Kierkegaard*, ed. Charles E. Moore (Farmington, Pa.: Plough, 1999), 236.

3. Yoder, *Politics of Jesus*, 96.

4. Jordan, *Substance*, 42.

5. Ibid., 46.

6. Thieleman J. van Braght, *The Martyr's Mirror: The Story of Seventeen Centuries of Christian Martyrdom, from the Time of Christ to* A.D. *1660* (orig. Dutch ed., 1660; 14th Eng. ed., Scottdale, Pa.: Herald, 1985), 741–42.

7. There has been a great deal written on this, both in the field of New Testament studies and in terms of social analysis and ethics. In the former, see, e.g., G. B. Caird, *Principalities and Powers: A Study in Pauline Theology* (Oxford, U.K.: Clarendon, 1956); and Hendrikus Berkhof, *Christ and the Powers*, trans. John H. Yoder (orig. Dutch, 1953; trans. Scottdale, Pa.: Herald, 1977). In the latter see Walter Wink's trilogy, *Naming the Powers: The Language of Power in the New Testament* (Philadelphia: Fortress, 1984); *Unmasking the Powers: The Invisible Forces That Determine Human Existence* (Philadelphia: Fortress, 1986); and *Engaging the Powers: Discernment and Resistance in a World of Domination* (Minneapolis: Fortress, 1992); Jacques Ellul, *The Presence of the Kingdom*, trans. Olive Wyon (Philadelphia: Westminster, 1951); and Yoder, *Politics of Jesus*, chap. 8. Yoder relies mostly upon the work of Berkhof.

8. See Caird, *Principalities and Powers*, viii.

9. To use Yoder's examples in *Politics*, 138.

10. Yoder, *Politics*, 142–43.

11. See Yoder, *Politics*, 142–43; and Wink, all three volumes of his trilogy cited in ch. 5 n. 7 above, for which this is a summary of his basic thesis.

12. Wink, *Engaging*, chap. 2.

13. G. Contenau, *Everyday Life in Babylon and Assyria* (London: E. Arnold, 1954), 148.

14. Wink, *Engaging*, 139–40.

15. Much of the following discussion follows Richard Bauckham, *The Theology of the Book of Revelation* (New York: Cambridge University Press, 1993), 66–108.

16. Rev. 22:16; cf. allusions to Ps. 2 in 2:18, 26–28; 11:15, 18; 12:5, 10; 14:1; 19:15.

17. Bauckham, *Theology*, 91.

18. Cf. Yoder, *Politics*, 24; Jordan, *Substance*, 56; N. T. Wright, *Jesus and the Victory of God*, 457–58; and Howard Thurman, *Jesus and the Disinherited* (Boston: Beacon, 1996).

19. Yoder, *Politics*, 39.

20. Kierkegaard, *Provocations*, 236–37.

Chapter 6: *The Church: The Body of Christ*

1. Dietrich Bonhoeffer, *The Cost of Discipleship* (New York: Simon and Schuster, 1995), 91.

2. As quoted in James Wm. McClendon, Jr., *Biography as Theology: How Life Stories Can Remake Today's Theology* (Nashville: Abingdon, 1974), 103.

3. Ibid., 91. My recounting here is dependent on McClendon, 89–113.

4. Ibid., 91.

5. Ibid., 96.

6. Ibid., 103.

7. Kierkegaard, *Provocations*, 227.

8. Ibid., 232.

9. As John Ortberg suggests in *The Life You've Always Wanted* (Grand Rapids: Zondervan, 1997), 78.

10. Hays, *Moral Vision*, 24.

11. Martin Luther King, Jr., "Letter from Birmingham Jail," in *A Testament of Hope: The Essential Writings and Speeches of Martin Luther King, Jr.*, ed. James M. Washington (San Francisco: HarperSanFrancisco, 1986), 300.

12. When Jordan's Koinonia Farm came increasingly under threat from outside forces, sentries were assigned to stand watch as part of the community's nonviolent response. Dorothy Day, on a visit to the farm, volunteered to stand guard, positioned by the gate in a station wagon. During her watch, a car sped by, and a shotgun blast sent pellets into the car, with Day scarcely avoiding death or serious injury. See the account in Lee Griffith, *The War on Terrorism and the Terror of God* (Grand Rapids: Eerdmans, 2002), 260.

13. Much of this synopsis follows the helpful introduction to Dorothy Day's work by Robert Ellsberg in *Dorothy Day: Selected Writings*, ed. Robert Ellsberg (Maryknoll, N.Y.: Orbis, 1992), xv–xli.

14. Ibid., xvi.

15. Cited in Griffith, *War*, 259.

16. Bonhoeffer, *The Cost of Discipleship*, 91.

17. C. Leonard Allen, *The Cruciform Church: Becoming a Cross Shaped People in a Secular World* (Abilene, Tex.: Abilene Christian University Press, 1990).

18. Paul Minear provides a very helpful guide through the many things this claim might mean in the context of the apostle's letter to the Galatians. I generally follow his lead in the

remainder of this discussion. See *To Die and to Live: Christ's Resurrection and Christian Vocation* (New York: Seabury, 1977), chap. 3.

19. I do not mean to suggest that a flabby ecumenism is what Paul is here advocating; I am suggesting, however, that to estrange and separate ourselves from others who profess the name of Christ is, from the very start, a failure.

20. Minear, *To Die*, 73.

Chapter 7: *Worship: Why Disciples Love Their Enemies*

1. This is one of the undergirding theses of Yoder's *For the Nations: Essays Public and Evangelical* (Grand Rapids: Eerdmans, 1997). See also Duane K. Friesen, *Artists, Citizens, Philosophers: Seeking the Peace of the City* (Scottdale, Pa.: Herald, 2000).

2. This claim, if expanded, would need to be carefully nuanced, for the similarities in the examples given here are by way of analogy, rather than by way of one-to-one correspondence. The meaning of "separation of church and state," for example, differs according to the angle of approach: if one seeks to "separate church and state" as did the sixteenth-century Anabaptists, then one is concerned with "the right way to be church." If, on the other hand, one seeks to separate church and state as did the early liberal political philosophers, then one is concerned with "the right way to be state." And there are obviously profound differences between the two.

3. George F. Will, "Conduct, Coercion, Belief," *Washington Post*, 22 April 1990, B7. My attention was first drawn to this article by Michael Baxter, C.S.C., discussed in his article cowritten with Stanley Hauerwas, "The Kingship of Christ: Why Freedom of 'Belief' Is Not Enough," in Hauerwas, *In Good Company: The Church as Polis* (Notre Dame, Ind.: University of Notre Dame Press, 1995). Some of my comments here are indebted to their article.

4. There are numerous places where this is documented. See, e.g., John Driver, *How Christians Made Peace with War: Early Christian Understandings of War* (Scottdale, Pa.: Herald, 1988); and the older classic work on Christians and warfare by Roland Bainton, *Christian Attitudes Toward War and Peace: A Historical Survey and Critical Re-evaluation* (New York: Abingdon, 1960). There are increasing numbers of Christians serving in the Roman military from A.D. 170 on, but this practice remained in tension with the teaching of the church. Obviously there is much more to be said, with greater nuance, than what I say here.

5. All cited in Bainton, *Christian Atttitudes*, 77.

6. Seen especially in his discussion of the ethics of war-making and the ethics of receiving the "crown" from Caesar, *The Chaplet*, chaps. 11–12; ANF 3:99–101.

7. *The Chaplet*, chap. 11; ANF 3:100.

8. Yoder, *Politics*, 51.

9. Heschel, *Prophets*, 204.

10. This is most certainly the case near the end of my writing this book, as George W. Bush is vigorously pursuing war against Iraq, when both the Vatican, the National Council of Churches, and other church bodies have insisted that preemptive war violates the just war tradition. Nonetheless, there is very little move by Christians in the military to disobey the commands of the commander-in-chief. While the Vatican is making serious efforts to communicate its disapproval to the White House, it appears, from my vantage point, to

be doing little to encourage Catholic military personnel to refuse to participate in these unjustified war preparations.

11. See Yoder's treatment of this problem in his discussion of the just war tradition, *When War Is Unjust: Being Honest in Just War Thinking* (Minneapolis: Augsburg, 1984).

12. Heschel, *Prophets*, 237; cf. 231. In addition to Isa. 19:23–25, see this vision of the nations coming together to worship in Isa. 45:20; 56:1–7; 60:6–7; 66:18; Jer. 3:17; 4:2; 12:16; 16:19–21; Zeph. 3:9; Zech. 2:11; 8:20–23; 14:16–21; Mal. 1:11.

13. Campbell, *Brother*, 221.

14. Cited in Griffith, *War*, 263.

Chapter 8: *Baptism: Why Disciples Don't Make Good Americans (or Germans, or Frenchmen)*

1. Cited in Durnbaugh, *Believers' Church*, 179.

2. There is no good term to use here. "Anabaptist" was originally a term of derision, meaning "rebaptizer." But of course the "Anabaptists" did not believe they were "rebaptizing," but simply recovering the New Testament practice of baptism. "Radical reformer" is another common label; but "radical" too often carries with it the notion of "off the wall," "far out," or "idealistic." Again, these reformers saw themselves as simply seeking to put into practice Christian discipleship which was "far out" over against the claims of established Christianity, but not "far out" over against the claims of the New Testament.

3. All the quotes from the Schleitheim Confession in this and following paragraphs are taken from *The Legacy of Michael Sattler*, ed. and trans. John Howard Yoder (Classics of the Radical Reformation; Scottdale, Pa.: Herald, 1973), 36–43.

4. Ibid., 40.

5. *Concerning Rebaptism* (1528) in *Martin Luther's Basic Theological Writings*, ed. Timothy F. Lull (Minneapolis: Fortress, 1989), 345; cf. 368–69.

6. Among other charges. In Yoder, *Michael Sattler*, 70–71.

7. Ibid., 75.

8. The classic text recording the deaths of the Anabaptists is Thieleman J. van Braght's *Martyr's Mirror*, cited in chap. 5 n. 6 above.

9. Cited by Hays, *Moral Vision*, 33.

10. Carl Spain, "Modern Challenges to Christian Morals," in *Christian Faith in the Modern World: The Abilene Christian College Annual Bible Lectures 1960* (Abilene, Tex.: Abilene Christian College Students Exchange, 1960), 216–17, taken from http://www.mun.ca/rels/restmov/texts/race/haymes15.html.

11. See Jordan, *Substance*, 71.

12. Leo Tolstoy, "Patriotism, or Peace?" in *Tolstoy's Writings on Civil Disobedience and Non-Violence* (New York: Bergman, 1967), 141.

13. From a sermon by Stuart Briscoe, "Christmas 365 Days a Year." Confirmed by personal correspondence with Briscoe, 4 February 2003.

Chapter 9: *Prayer: Why Disciples Trust God rather than Their Own Calculations*

1. Walter Wink, "History Belongs to the Intercessors," *Sojourners*, October 1990, 11–12.

2. Barth, *Prayer*, 23.

3. I do not mean to simply discount the debates between the Deontologists and the Utilitarians (though I think the debate often asked the wrong sets of questions), nor do I mean to use "utilitarian" in a technical sense as referring to any one system of the varied thinkers who are labeled as "Utilitarians." Throughout, I mean it as the move to trump the call to faithfulness to the way or teaching of Christ because of the supposed "consequences" of acting otherwise. Considering the consequences of one's action is not "unfaithful," and is very often necessary *and* an act of faithfulness; but to set aside obedience to Christ in the name of the calculable results, especially when the calculations do not take into account the power of a God who raises the dead, I take as unfaithfulness.

4. Of course, in the Genesis account, Abraham does on several occasions try to "make things turn out right," and it is precisely those moments when he either causes trouble for others, or is told to wait upon God's timing (see Gen. 12:10–20; 16:1–16; 17:15–22).

5. But do not such war heroes celebrated in Hebrews 11 actually provide counterevidence to the claim that disciples ought to walk in the way of the nonviolent Jesus? No, for the Hebrews writer is instead making this point: that the people of God are called first and foremost to faithfulness, and they then trust that God will provide as is necessary. Gideon, Samson, and Jericho are all classic examples of instances in which the people of God—without mighty armories or military might or extensive weapons of war—did the unthinkable. They were victorious over their enemies by trusting that God was faithful. Now, in Christ, we are called to the same thing: to trust that as we walk in the way of the cross, in the way of unjust suffering, God will provide and will vindicate the righteous.

6. Scott Harrison, "Prayer," *Leadership* 16, no. 2 (Spring 1995): 49.

7. To use the example suggested by Thomas Keating, *Open Mind, Open Heart: The Contemplative Dimension of the Gospel* (New York: Continuum, 1992), 94.

8. Keating, *Open Mind*, 71. Keating makes this claim in the more particular context of contemplative prayer but it is just as helpful direction within the context of discipleship considered more comprehensively. This is an excellent book for understanding contemplative prayer and providing helpful, methodical practices to make contemplative prayer a transforming part of one's life.

9. As Wink suggests in "History Belongs to the Intercessors," 14.

10. Barth, *Prayer*, 57–58.

11. Thomas R. Kelly, *A Testament of Devotion*, intro. by Richard Foster (San Francisco: HarperSanFrancisco, 1992), 33.

12. Ibid., 34.

13. Jean-Jacques Antier, *Charles de Foucauld* (San Francisco: Ignatius, 1999), 340.

14. Thomas Merton, *Contemplation in the World of Action* (Garden City, N.Y.: Doubleday, 1971), cited by Charles McCarthy, "Prayer and Revolution," *Catholic Peace Fellowship Bulletin*, December 1978, 1–4.

Chapter 10: *Communion: Why Disciples Share Their Wealth*

1. Winthrop Hudson, *The Great Tradition of the American Churches* (Gloucester, Mass.: Peter Smith, 1970), 184.

2. Ibid., 180–82.

3. Cited by Hudson, *Great Tradition*, 185.

4. Ibid., 184. Italics mine.

5. Stiles, "The United States elevated to Glory and Honor," 519–20.

6. Richard Foster, *Money, Sex, and Power: The Challenge of the Disciplined Life* (San Francisco: Harper and Row, 1985), 23.

7. Ibid., 65.

8. Ibid., 19.

9. Much of this section is indebted to John Mark Hicks, *Come to the Table: Revisioning the Lord's Supper* (Orange, Calif.: New Leaf Books, 2002); and Yoder's *Body Politics*, chap. 2.

10. The narrative does not explicitly mention "table" or eating and drinking, but the hospitality extended Jesus by Zacchaeus would appear to assume this.

11. The imperfect tense of "sell" in Acts 2:45 indicates ongoing action, so the NASB translates the verse this way: "and they began selling their property and possessions, and were sharing them with all, as anyone might have need."

12. *Didache*, 4.8; ANF 7:378. For much of this section, I am indebted to the work of González, *Faith and Wealth*; see especially p. 92 for his discussion of the *Didache*.

13. *Didache*, 5.2; ANF 7:379.

14. *Epistle to Diognetus*, 5.7; ANF 1:27.

15. *Epistle to Diognetus*, 10.4–6; ANF 1:29.

16. González, *Faith and Wealth*, 228.

17. Ibid., 228. He concludes his survey of the early church fathers by summarizing their viewpoint this way: "To accumulate wealth is to pervert it, not only because real wealth must always be moving and active, but also because the purpose of wealth is to meet human need. . . . This line of argument repeatedly leads the authors to conclude that the intended use of wealth is the common good. Private property is justifiable only to the extent it is used for sharing, to promote the equality that the present order does not foster," 229.

18. *The Sermon on the Mount*, excerpted in O'Donovan and O'Donovan, *From Irenaeus to Grotius*, 599.

19. Ibid., 600–1.

20. Cited in Paul Althaus, *The Ethics of Martin Luther*, trans. Robert C. Schultz (Philadelphia: Fortress, 1972), 47. Althaus provides a very helpful discussion of Luther's "two kingdoms," which is obviously more complicated than presented here—nonetheless, the critique stands. Luther systematically sets aside the teaching of Jesus as lacking concrete relevance in social and political realms, accepting the standing order of the use of the sword as legitimate practice for Christians.

21. I do not mean to suggest that all who appropriate the label "business ethics" would suggest this. I have two colleagues in the College of Business at Lipscomb, for example, who insist that the approach to "business ethics" described here is *not* a sufficient Christian account of participation in the business world.

22. While socialist orders presumably have a concern for the common good, twentieth-century socialist orders, on the other hand, viciously employed the same strategy as capitalist orders, employing coercion and militarism as the means to bring about their alleged common good. As a consequence, the possession of capital becomes the sole right of the state, so that socialism merely changes the actor in the sin of capitalism: no longer is it the individual who is free to control and manipulate and dispose of wealth as he or she sees fit, without concern for God or neighbor; instead, the unredeemed, self-seeking state controls and manipulates and disposes of wealth as it sees fit, viciously defending its own self-interest in the name of the good of humanity or history.

23. Adam Smith had his own moral philosophy, which he trusted would guide individuals participating in that economic system. But as numerous theologians and philosophers have suggested, liberalism is ultimately parasitic off of inherited moral traditions, incapable of sustaining substantive moral commitments itself. But then again, that need to be parasitic can be taken as an opening for communicating the Good News—that the church can bear witness to the goodness of sharing wealth, meeting needs, and serving the community.

24. Peter Maurin, *Easy Essays* (Chicago: Franciscan Herald, 1984), 116–17.

25. David Lipscomb, "Aid to Christians in Need—How Shall it be Administered?" *Gospel Advocate* 12 (17 March 1870): 253. See discussion in Dunnavant, "David Lipscomb on the Church and the Poor," 78.

26. James Wm. McClendon, Jr., *Ethics* (Nashville: Abingdon, 1986), 59.

27. Rodney Clapp, "Why the Devil Takes VISA," *Christianity Today*, 7 October 1996, 19–33.

28. See *The Journal and Major Essays of John Woolman*, ed. Phillips P. Moulton (New York: Oxford University Press, 1971), 52; and Paul Rosenblatt, *John Woolman* (New York: Twayne, 1969), 71.

Chapter 11: *Evangelism: How Disciples "Make a Difference"*

1. Jordan, *Substance*, 29.

2. Albert Camus, *Resistance, Rebellion, and Death*, trans. Justin O'Brien (New York: Knopf, 1961), 70.

3. Justin, *Dialogue with Trypho*, chap. 100; ANF 1:254.

4. Justin, *First Apology*, chap. 39; ANF 1:175–76.

5. Irenaeus, *Against Heresies*, 4.34.4; ANF 1:512.

6. Tertullian, *An Answer to the Jews*, chap. 3; ANF 1:154.

7. Origen, *Against Celsus*, 5.33; ANF 4:558.

8. Ian Linden, "Church and Genocide," 54.

9. All cited in Griffith, *War*, 260.

10. Berkhof, *Christ*, 51.

11. H. Richard Niebuhr, *Christ and Culture* (New York: Harper and Row, 1951).

12. Stanley Hauerwas and William H. Willimon, *Resident Aliens* (Nashville: Abingdon, 1989), 42–43. The authors continue: "We must never forget that it was modern, liberal democracy, in fighting to preserve itself, that resorted to the bomb in Hiroshima and the firebombing in Dresden, not to mention Vietnam. This is the political system that must be preserved in order for Christians to be politically responsible?"